Studies in Development Economics and Policy
General Editor: **Anthony Shorrocks**

UNU WORLD INSTITUTE FOR DEVELOPMENT ECONOMICS RESEARCH (UNU-WIDER) was established by the United Nations University as its first research and training centre and started work in Helsinki, Finland, in 1985. The purpose of the Institute is to undertake applied research and policy analysis on structural changes affecting the developing and transitional economies, to provide a forum for the advocacy of policies leading to robust, equitable and environmentally sustainable growth, and to promote capacity strengthening and training in the field of economic and social policy-making. Its work is carried out by staff researchers and visiting scholars in Helsinki and through networks of collaborating scholars and institutions around the world.

UNU World Institute for Development Economics Research (UNU-WIDER)
Katajanokanlaituri 6B, FIN-00160 Helsinki, Finland

Titles include:

Tony Addison, Henrik Hansen and Finn Tarp *(editors)*
DEBT RELIEF FOR POOR COUNTRIES

Tony Addison and George Mavrotas *(editors)*
DEVELOPMENT FINANCE IN THE GLOBAL ECONOMY
The Road Ahead

Tony Addison and Alan Roe *(editors)*
FISCAL POLICY FOR DEVELOPMENT
Poverty, Reconstruction and Growth

George G. Borjas and Jeff Crisp *(editors)*
POVERTY, INTERNATIONAL MIGRATION AND ASYLUM

Ricardo Ffrench-Davis and Stephany Griffith-Jones *(editors)*
FROM CAPITAL SURGES TO DROUGHT
Seeking Stability for Emerging Economies

David Fielding *(editor)*
MACROECONOMIC POLICY IN THE FRANC ZONE

Basudeb Guha-Khasnobis *(editor)*
THE WTO, DEVELOPING COUNTRIES AND THE DOHA DEVELOPMENT AGENDA
Prospects and Challenges for Trade-led Growth

Basudeb Guha-Khasnobis, Shabd S. Acharya and Benjamin Davis *(editors)*
FOOD INSECURITY, VULNERABILITY AND HUMAN RIGHTS FAILURE

Basudeb Guha-Khasnobis and Ravi Kanbur *(editors)*
INFORMAL LABOUR MARKETS AND DEVELOPMENT

Basudeb Guha-Khasnobis and George Mavrotas *(editors)*
FINANCIAL DEVELOPMENT, INSTITUTIONS, GROWTH AND POVERTY REDUCTION

Aiguo Lu and Manuel F. Montes *(editors)*
POVERTY, INCOME DISTRIBUTION AND WELL-BEING IN ASIA DURING THE TRANSITION

George Mavrotas *(editor)*
DOMESTIC RESOURCE MOBILIZATION AND FINANCIAL DEVELOPMENT

George Mavrotas and Anthony Shorrocks *(editors)*
ADVANCING DEVELOPMENT
Core Themes in Global Economics

Mark McGillivray *(editor)*
HUMAN WELL-BEING
Concept and Measurement

Mark McGillivray *(editor)*
INEQUALITY, POVERTY AND WELL-BEING

Robert J. McIntyre and Bruno Dallago *(editors)*
SMALL AND MEDIUM ENTERPRISES IN TRANSITIONAL ECONOMIES

Vladimir Mikhalev *(editor)*
INEQUALITY AND SOCIAL STRUCTURE DURING THE TRANSITION

E. Wayne Nafziger and Raimo Väyrynen *(editors)*
THE PREVENTION OF HUMANITARIAN EMERGENCIES

Machiko Nissanke and Erik Thorbecke *(editors)*
GLOBALIZATION AND THE POOR IN ASIA
Can Shared Growth be Sustained?

Machiko Nissanke and Erik Thorbecke *(editors)*
THE IMPACT OF GLOBALIZATION ON THE WORLD'S POOR
Transmission Mechanisms

Matthew Odedokun *(editor)*
EXTERNAL FINANCE FOR PRIVATE SECTOR DEVELOPMENT
Appraisals and Issues

Laixiang Sun *(editor)*
OWNERSHIP AND GOVERNANCE OF ENTERPRISES
Recent Innovative Developments

Guanghua Wan *(editor)*
UNDERSTANDING INEQUALITY AND POVERTY IN CHINA
Methods and Applications

UNU-WIDER *(editors)*
WIDER PERSPECTIVES ON GLOBAL DEVELOPMENT

**Studies in Development Economics and Policy Series Standing Order
ISBN 978–0–333–96424–8 hardback; 978–0–230–20041–8 paperback**
(outside North America only)

You can receive future titles in this series as they are published by placing a standing order. Please contact your bookseller or, in case of difficulty, write to us at the address below with your name and address, the title of the series and one of the ISBNs quoted above.

Customer Services Department, Macmillan Distribution Ltd, Houndmills, Basingstoke, Hampshire RG21 6XS, England

---

Domestic Resource Mobilization and Financial Development

Edited by

George Mavrotas

palgrave
macmillan

in association with the United Nations
University – World Institute for Development
Economics Research

First published 2008 by
PALGRAVE MACMILLAN
Houndmills, Basingstoke, Hampshire RG21 6XS and
175 Fifth Avenue, New York, N.Y. 10010
Companies and representatives throughout the world

PALGRAVE MACMILLAN is the global academic imprint of the Palgrave Macmillan division of St. Martin's Press, LLC and of Palgrave Macmillan Ltd. Macmillan® is a registered trademark in the United States, United Kingdom and other countries. Palgrave is a registered trademark in the European Union and other countries.

ISBN-13: 978–0–230–20176–7
ISBN-10: 0–230–20176–8

This book is printed on paper suitable for recycling and made from fully managed and sustained forest sources. Logging, pulping and manufacturing processes are expected to conform to the environmental regulations of the country of origin.

A catalogue record for this book is available from the British Library.

A catalog record for this book is available from the Library of Congress.

10 9 8 7 6 5 4 3 2 1
17 16 15 14 13 12 11 10 09 08

Printed and bound in Great Britain by
CPI Antony Rowe, Chippenham and Eastbourne

To the memory of my father,
Gerasimos Mavrotas

Contents

List of Figures

List of Tables

Acknowledgements

This study has been prepared within UNU-WIDER's research on Globalization, Finance and Growth, linked to the project on Financial Sector Development for Growth and Poverty Reduction. I would like to thank the three anonymous referees for their constructive comments and insightful suggestions, which have been of great benefit to the volume. Thanks also to Adam Swallow, UNU-WIDER's Publications Assistant, for outstanding editorial advice, and to Barbara Fagerman, Senior Programme Assistant at UNU-WIDER, for superb administrative support and advice. I would like also to take this opportunity to express my gratitude to Tony Shorrocks, Director of UNU-WIDER, for his strong support and encouragement during the life of this project.

UNU-WIDER gratefully acknowledges the financial contributions to the research programme by the governments of Denmark (Royal Ministry of Foreign Affairs), Finland (Ministry for Foreign Affairs), Norway (Royal Ministry of Foreign Affairs), Sweden (Swedish International Development Cooperation Agency – Sida) and the United Kingdom (Department for International Development).

Notes on the Contributors

Ernest Aryeetey is Professor of Economics and Director of the Institute of Statistical, Social and Economic Research (ISSER) of the University of Ghana, Legon. He studied Economics at the University of Ghana and gained his PhD at the University of Dortmund, Germany. His research work focuses on the economics of development, with a particular emphasis on institutions and their role in development, regional integration, economic reforms, financial systems in support of development and small-enterprise development. He has published widely on these subjects.

Mina Baliamoune-Lutz is Associate Professor of Economics at the University of North Florida. Her recent publications include articles in *Empirica*, *African Development Review*, *Business Economics*, *Information Technology for Development*, *Savings & Development*, *Journal of Policy Modeling*, and the *Journal of African Economies*, in addition to several book chapters and discussion and policy papers at UNU-WIDER, ICER (Italy) and Boston University. Her research focuses on human well-being, and on the effects of institutions and trade on African development. She holds a PhD in Economics from Northeastern University.

Salvatore Capasso is Associate Professor of Economics at the University of Naples, 'Parthenope'. He gained his PhD from the University of Manchester, UK, where he has also been a research fellow. He is currently also affiliated to the Centre for Studies in Economics and Finance at the University of Salerno, Italy, and to the Center for Research on International Economics at the University of Wisconsin, Milwaukee, USA.

Panicos O. Demetriades is Professor of Financial Economics in the Department of Economics at the University of Leicester. He has published widely in the area of finance and development, focusing on causality issues using time-series methods, and policy questions such as financial liberalization and government ownership of banks. He has acted as consultant to the World Bank, the African Development Bank and the OECD. He is currently directing a large research project under the ESRC's World Economy and Finance Research Programme. He holds a PhD in Economics from the University of Cambridge, and BA and MA degrees from the University of Essex, UK.

Bassam A. Fattouh is Reader in Finance and Management at the School of Oriental and African Studies, University of London, and Senior Research Fellow at the Oxford Institute for Energy Studies, UK. His research interests focus on the relationship between finance and growth, capital structure, and oil prices and markets.

Alemayehu Geda has a PhD and is currently Associate Professor at the Department of Economics, Addis Ababa University, and a researcher at the African Economic Research Consortium, Economic Commission for Africa, and the University of London, SOAS. His research and research interests are in areas of macroeconomics and macroeconometric modelling, and international trade and development finance in Africa.

Iftekhar Hasan is the Cary L. Wellington Professor of Finance at the Rensselaer Polytechnic Institute, Troy, USA. He also serves as the Scientific Adviser at the Central Bank of Finland; a visiting scholar at the Federal Reserve Bank of Atlanta, USA; and a research fellow at the Berkeley Center of Entrepreneurial Studies at the Stern School of Business at New York University, USA. He has published over 160 articles in reputed academic journals, as book chapters and proceedings. He is the editor of the *Journal of Financial Stability* and associate editor of, among others, the *Journal of Money, Credit and Banking*, the *Journal of Banking and Finance*, and the *Journal of International Money and Finance*.

Robert Lensink is Professor of Finance and Financial Markets at the University of Groningen, the Netherlands. His main research interests include finance and development, corporate investments, and international finance. He has published several books, and more than sixty papers in international journals, such as the *Economic Journal*, *World Development*, *Journal of Development Studies*, *Journal of Public Economics*, *Journal of Money, Credit, and Banking* and the *Journal of Banking and Finance*.

Samuel Munzele Maimbo is a Senior Financial Sector Specialist in the World Bank's Africa Finance and Private Sector Unit. A Rhodes Scholar, he has a PhD in Public Administration from the University of Manchester, UK; an MBA degree from the University of Nottingham, UK, and a Bachelor of Accountancy Degree from the Copperbelt University, Zambia.

He is a Fellow of the Association of Chartered Certified Accountants, and the Zambia Institute of Certified Accountants.

George Mavrotas is the Chief Economist of the Global Development Network (GDN), formerly a research fellow and project director at UNU-WIDER, and prior to that was on the Economics faculties of the Universities of Oxford and Manchester, UK. He is the author and co-author of more than 100 publications, including papers in leading peer-reviewed journals, chapters in edited volumes and books on a wide range of development issues. His publications include *Advancing Development: Core Themes in Global Economics* (Palgrave Macmillan); *Commodity Supply Management by Producing Countries* (Oxford University Press); *Financial Development, Institutions, Growth and Poverty Reduction* (Palgrave Macmillan); and *Development Finance in the Global Economy: The Road Ahead* (Palgrave Macmillan). He holds a D.Phil in Economics from Oxford University.

Machiko Nissanke is Professor of Economics at the School of Oriental and African Studies (SOAS), University of London. She previously worked at Birkbeck College, University College London (UCL), and the University of Oxford. She was also Research Fellow of Nuffield College, Oxford and the Overseas Development Institute, London. She has published numerous books and journal articles in the fields of finance, trade and development, and has served many international organizations as adviser and co-ordinator of research programmes, including the UNU-WIDER project, 'The Impact of Globalization on the World's Poor'.

Sang-Ik Son is Deputy Director of the Statistical Research Institute, Korea National Statistical Office, Daejeon, South Korea. He holds an MSc degree in Economics from the University of Warwick, UK, and a PhD in Economics from the University of Manchester, UK. His research interests are in econometrics (panel data analysis), CGE models and macroeconomics.

Pham Thi Thu Trà is a lecturer at Cantho University, Vietnam. She gained her PhD in Economics from the University of Groningen, the Netherlands in September 2006. Her research interests cover the economics of information, the theory of financial intermediation, and development economics, and her publications include papers in *Economics of Transition, Topics in Theoretical Economics* and *Applied Financial Economics Letters*. She is actively involved in policy-relevant research for Vietnam.

Mingming Zhou is Assistant Professor of Finance at the University of Alaska–Fairbanks, USA having gained her PhD in Finance from Rensselaer Polytechnic Institute, Troy, USA, in 2007. Her major area of interest is in corporate finance, financial intermediation and capital markets. She has presented her research at several international conferences, has published in the working paper series of various central banks (including the Federal Reserve Board in Washington, DC, and the Bank of Finland, Helsinki) and in reputed finance journals including the *Journal of Banking and Finance.*

List of Abbreviations

ACB	Asia Commercial Bank, Vietnam
ADB	African Development Bank
AIB	Agricultural and Industrial Bank, Ethiopia (renamed DBE)
AMIZ	Association of Micro-finance Institutions in Zambia
BCM	Banque Commerciale du Maroc
BFSA	Banking and Financial Services Act, Zambia, 1994
BIDV	Bank for Investment and Development of Vietnam
BMCE	Banque Marocaine du Commerce Exterieur, Morocco
BMCI	Banque Marocaine du Commerce et d'Industrie, Morocco
BoZ	Bank of Zambia
CBB	Construction and Business Bank, Ethiopia
CBE	Commercial Bank of Ethiopia
CPI	consumer price indices
CRDB	Co-operative and Rural Development Bank, Tanzania
CSRC	China Securities Regulatory Committee
CSV	costly state verification
DBE	Development Bank of Ethiopia
DFID	Department for International Development, UK
DFIs	development finance institutions
EIC	Ethiopian Insurance Corporation
EU	European Union
FBS	Finance Building Society, Zambia
FDI	foreign direct investment
GDP	gross domestic product
GDS	gross domestic savings
GNDI	gross national disposable income
GNS	gross national savings
GRZ	Government of the Republic of Zambia
HSB	Housing and Saving Bank, Ethiopia (renamed CBB)
IBMM	interbank money market
ICB	Industry and Commerce Bank of Vietnam (Incomebank)
IFS	*International Financial Statistics*, IMF
IMF	International Monetary Fund
IPOs	initial public offerings
JSBs	joint stock banks
JVBs	joint venture banks

LC	Letter of Credit
MBT	Micro Banks Trust, Zambia
MEDaC	Ministry of Economic Development and External Co-operation, Ethiopia
MFIs	micro finance institutions
NBC	National Bank for Commerce, Tanzania
NBE	National Bank of Ethiopia
NBFIs	non-bank financial institutions
NGOs	non-governmental organizations
NSCB	National Savings and Credit Bank, Zambia
OECD	Organisation for Economic Co-operation and Development
OLS	ordinary least squares
PABS	Pan African Building Society
PSSA	Pension and Social Security Authority, Ethiopia
RMB	*renminbi*, people's currency, China
ROSCAs	rotating saving and credit associations
SAPs	structural adjustment programmes
SBV	State Bank of Vietnam
SCAs	savings and credit associations
SCS	savings and credit societies
SHSE	Shanghai Stock Exchange
SMEs	small and medium-sized enterprises
SOCBs	state-owned commercial banks
SOE	state-owned enterprise
SSA	Sub-Saharan Africa
SZSE	Shenzhen Stock Exchange
UNCDF	United Nations Capital Development Fund
UN-DESA	UN Department of Economic and Social Affairs
UNU-WIDER	World Institute for Development Economics Research of the United Nations University
USD/US$	United States dollar (currency)
VAR	vector autoregressive
VBARD	Vietnam Bank for Agriculture and Rural Development
VCB	Foreign Trade Bank of Vietnam (Vietcombank)
VECM	vector error-correction model
VND	Vietnam dong (currency)
WDI	*World Development Indicators*, World Bank
WTO	World Trade Organization
ZNBS	Zambia National Building Society
ZNCB	Zambia National Commercial Bank
ZNPF	Zambia National Provident Fund

1
Domestic Resource Mobilization and Financial Development: Introduction

George Mavrotas

Recent years have witnessed a new interest in the relationship between finance and growth, at both micro and macro levels, and empirical research has blossomed,[1] but the relationship between domestic resource mobilization and financial development has not been properly explored.[2] However, issues related to domestic resource mobilization and financial development are central to the overall development process and recently they have been raised in connection with the attainment of the Millennium Development Goals (MDGs). Financial development, broadly defined to include not just financial sector deepening but also improvements in the efficiency of the financial sector and the banking institutions in developing countries and emerging economies, can enhance domestic resource mobilization, which is vital for pro-poor growth.[3]

The policy agenda has recently moved in new and interesting directions, partly because of the relevance as well as the importance of domestic resource mobilization for accelerating progress in achieving the MDGs, and partly through the emergence of new initiatives, such as the United Nations International Year of Microcredit (2005) and the 'blue book for policy-makers', *Building Inclusive Financial Sectors for Development*, published in 2006 by the United Nations Capital Development Fund (UNCDF) and the UN Department of Economic and Social Affairs (UN-DESA), and which emphasized in particular the issue of 'financial access' and the centrality of 'inclusive financial sectors' (UNCDF and UN-DESA 2006; see also Cheru and Bradford 2005; Claessens 2005).

It is broadly recognized that developing economies often lack an appropriate financial sector, one that provides incentives for individuals to save and acts as an efficient intermediary to convert these savings into

1

credit for borrowers. The financial liberalization experience of many low-income countries in recent years, although in the right direction in certain cases, seems to suggest that transforming the financial structure of an economy is a complex process that assumes a deep understanding of the entire set of interactions between financial sector reforms and the economy. At the same time, the experience of the Asian financial crisis clearly suggests that, while financial liberalization may be desirable, the process must be regulated correctly, and this requires the building of institutional capacity – a costly, though important, process (Brownbridge and Kirkpatrick 1999; Stiglitz 1999, 2002).[4]

It is equally fair to argue that, until very recently, building the domestic financial system towards domestic resource mobilization has been neglected as a potential source of development financing in connection with the MDGs. However, there is substantial potential there which, if realized, can help to accelerate progress significantly with the MDGs. It also needs to be stressed that the above important route has the additional advantage of engaging local communities directly in the overall development financing process. Further to building the financial system as whole, it is also vital to provide micro-credit and to create insurance mechanisms for the poor (Dercon 2004).

The above discussion clearly suggests that, while substantial progress has been made in recent years on the research and policy front in this important area, a number of issues remain unresolved and require further attention. In this regard, this volume brings together a collection of essays by leading experts in the field, who discuss various aspects of the financial development–domestic resource mobilization nexus in an effort to delve more deeply into this important relationship. The volume also provides a good balance of recent theoretical developments in this area; the application of recent innovations in econometric methodology; important case studies that discuss country experiences with financial sectors reforms – in both Africa and Asia (including China); and useful policy lessons.

An important issue in the overall finance–growth literature is related to the role of stock market development in the growth process. Salvatore Capasso argues in Chapter 2 that since the 1990s economists have devoted considerable attention to the study of the relationship between financial market development and economic growth. In particular, the emergence of stock markets with economic development is an intriguing and interesting aspect of such a relationship, and as yet has been relatively unexplored. The chapter examines the most recent findings in the theoretical and empirical literature in an attempt to determine the rationale behind the development of stock markets along the path of growth, and the nature of the interrelationship between real and financial variables.

The bulk of the literature on financial development is associated with empirical work on the overall relationship between financial–sector development and economic growth. George Mavrotas and Sang-Ik Son, in Chapter 3, explore the relationship between financial–sector development (broadly defined as going beyond financial depth) and economic growth using a database covering 65 countries (both industrial and developing) over the period 1960–99, and by employing various indicators of financial development in the empirical analysis. Empirical results obtained from the estimation of a series of panel data models seem to suggest that financial development does contribute to economic growth, although the magnitude of the impact varies depending on the type of financial indicator employed, the level of development (that is, industrial *vis-à-vis* developing countries) as well as the impact of other non-financial variables in the process. The authors also find evidence that seems to suggest that financial development can accelerate growth by improving the allocation of capital.

A substantial part of the financial development literature deals with financial crises, particularly after the emergence of the Asian crisis in 1997. Chapter 4, by Panicos Demetriades and Bassam Fattouh, provides a novel empirical analysis of the South Korean credit market and reveals large volumes of excess credit since the late 1970s, indicating that a sizeable proportion of total credit was being used to refinance unprofitable projects. The authors argue that their findings are consistent with theoretical literature suggesting that soft budget constraints and over-borrowing were significant factors behind the Korean financial crisis of 1997–8.

Iftekhar Hasan and Mingming Zhou, in Chapter 5, document the financial and institutional developments of China since the 1980s, as China was transforming successfully from a rigid, centrally-planned economy to a dynamic market economy. The authors examine empirically the relationship between financial development and economic growth in China by employing a panel sample covering 31 Chinese provinces during the important transition period of 1986–2002. The evidence reported by the authors suggests that the development of financial markets, institutions and instruments have been associated robustly with economic growth in China.

Chapter 6, by Machiko Nissanke and Ernest Aryeetey, examines the source of financial market fragmentation in Sub-Saharan Africa within the framework of institutional economics. By using fieldwork data from Ghana, Malawi, Nigeria and Tanzania, the authors analyse financial risk management, the transaction costs for loan screening and monitoring, and contract enforcement. They show how, faced with various institutional constraints, the range of clientele selected by both formal and informal lenders becomes both narrow and at the extreme ends of the market. The chapter also evaluates the prevailing state of managing risks for market structure, and binding institutional constraints for market transformation and deepening in Sub-Saharan Africa.

Using a vector error-correction model, Chapter 7, by Mina Baliamoune-Lutz, explores the short-run dynamics and long-run linkages between financial reform and the mobilization of domestic saving in Morocco. In the short run, financial depth (defined as the volume of intermediation) is shown to have a positive influence on private saving, while increases in real interest rates have a negative impact. The author argues that the effectiveness of financial intermediation does not seem to have a *direct* effect on saving, but has a significant influence on the volume of intermediation. In the long run, savings have a stable relationship with financial reform but the influence of interest rates remains negative, implying that the income effect dominates in the long run as well.

The focus of Chapter 8 by Alemayehu Geda is on the structure and performance of Ethiopia's financial sector in the pre- and post-reform periods. Geda notes that, since 1992, Ethiopia has been engaged in liberalizing its financial sector: the hallmark of the strategy being gradualism. The approach is not without problems, according to the author, especially from Bretton Woods institutions that saw the reform as a sluggish process. The chapter examines this liberalization programme by analysing the performance of the sector both before and after the reform. The author notes that, given the nascent development of the financial sector in the country, the relatively good shape in which the existing financial institutions find themselves, and given that supervision and the regulatory capacity of the regulating agency is weak, the government's strategy of gradualism and its overall reform direction is encouraging. However, the chapter also argues for charting out a clearly defined time-frame for liberalization, and exploring the possibility of engaging with foreign banks to acquire new technology to enhance the efficiency of the financial sector in general, and the banking sector in particular.

Chapter 9, by Samuel Maimbo and George Mavrotas, explores the relationship between financial-sector reforms and savings mobilization in Zambia. The authors argue that, while an extensive literature exists on financial-sector development and savings levels in developing countries, there does not seem to be any satisfactory work on the above nexus for Sub-Saharan African countries, particularly Zambia. Along these lines, the chapter examines the linkages between the financial reforms of the early 1990s and savings mobilization. It considers the characteristics of banks and non-bank financial institutions (in particular microfinance institutions) and savings levels, and identifies problems associated with the relatively poor performance of savings in recent years. It concludes with a set of policy guidelines for strengthening savings mobilization, highlighting the expected effect on poverty-reducing growth.

The final chapter in this volume, by Pham Thi Thu Trà and Robert Lensink, deals with the determinants of loan contracts to business firms from a private bank in Vietnam. The authors focus on the main loan contract features the bank uses in lending to business firms; namely, loan maturity, collateral and loan interest rate. Based on the simultaneous equation model of Dennis *et al.* (2000) and the bank's loan contracting policies, they examine the possible interdependency of the three different loan contract terms. They try also to determine which firm characteristics and exogenous factors are relevant for loan contracts. They find strong interdependencies between these contract terms with significant bi-directional relationships between collateral and loan maturity, loan rate and loan maturity, and a uni-directional relationship between loan rate and collateral. The authors argue that the conflicting signs within the collateral–loan maturity relationship and the loan interest rate–loan maturity relationship can be explained by their hypothesis that the choice for a certain loan maturity is determined primarily by borrowers' behaviour, whereas the loan rate and the collateral requirements are determined primarily by banks' policies. In addition, their results support the relevance of firm quality, agency costs of debt, and relationship lending in loan contract design.

A central message that emanates clearly from the volume is that policies enhancing domestic resource mobilization – for example, by mobilizing domestic savings, expanding the tax base in developing countries (particularly in Sub-Saharan Africa), increasing access to financial services, and deepening financial sector development – have a prominent role to play in the challenging effort to use all available sources, both domestic and external, to accelerate progress with the MDGs. In particular:

• *Deepening financial sector development* is becoming a key priority in lowincome countries, along with the challenge to move beyond financial deepening towards *improving substantially the efficiency of the financial sector.*

- Policies that attempt to build better financial institutions (thereby increasing the confidence of savers), encourage competition and provide a broader variety of instruments for saving can further strengthen *the overall savings mobilization process* in low-income countries with substantial gains in the area of poverty-reducing growth and MDG achievement.
- Most individuals, and small and medium-sized enterprises continue to depend on informal and non-financial assets for their savings facilities and arrangements. Policy-makers need to encourage *the role played by microfinance institutions*, which, with a relatively smaller cost base, is a more viable option in the effective delivery of financial savings facilities to low-income individuals, and small and medium-scale enterprises, especially in rural areas.
- On the other hand, *the challenge for microfinance institutions* is to create structures that facilitate successful clients of microfinance-institutions to access larger, more diverse and longer-term sources of finance.
- Efforts to improve domestic resource mobilization should be made within the overall context of *improving the state of the economy*. Investment in domestic financial assets will only be successful if the domestic currency is stable, interest rates are positive, and local banks and non-banking financial institutions are managed prudently and safely.
- Last, but not least, *improving access to savings institutions* is of crucial importance for domestic resource mobilization. Rural savings mobilization, in particular, requires an institutional network providing easy access to potential savers. The absence of savings institutions collecting deposits from the rural sector, especially in remote areas, may simply discourage saving or encourage consumption, and perhaps wasteful expenditure, or it may lead to saving in a non-monetized form.

It is hoped that this volume will contribute in a fruitful and forward-looking way to the ongoing debate in the international development community regarding the mobilization of domestic resources in developing countries, and the crucial role that financial development can and should play in this regard.

Notes

1 Arestis and Demetriades (1997), Levine (1997), Caprio *et al.* (2001), Demirgüç-Kunt and Levine (2001), World Bank (2001), Green and Kirkpatrick (2002), Goodhart (2004), Wachtel (2004), Abiat and Mody (2005), Detragiache *et al.*

(2005), Green *et al.* (2005) and Rousseau and Wachtel (2005); more recently, another strand of literature has worked to shed light on issues related to the important link between financial-sector development and poverty reduction – see Beck *et al.* (2004), Honohan (2004), Green *et al.* (2005), Claessens and Feijen (2006) and Guha-Khasnobis and Mavrotas (2008).

2 Among the few exceptions are the study by Bandiera *et al.* (2000), which, by using data on a selected group developing countries, has concluded that financial-sector development does not necessarily raise private savings; Loayza *et al.* (2000), who focus on the factors affecting savings disparities across the world; Kelly and Mavrotas (2003), who show a rather strong positive impact of a financial-sector development index on private savings in Sri Lanka over the period 1970–97; and more recently, Kelly and Mavrotas (2008), who estimate the impact of various measures of financial development on savings for a heterogeneous panel of seventeen African countries; Mavrotas (2005) provides a detailed discussion.

3 The need to strengthen the domestic financial sectors in low-income countries stems also from the fact that the current international finance architecture has not been able to address the various credit constraints that developing countries face, partly a result of the numerous problems associated with external finance (for example, foreign aid, but also private capital flows); see Akyüz and Cornford (2002) for a comprehensive discussion in connection with the overall globalization process, and Addison (2007) for an authoritative assessment of development finance issues.

4 At the same time, it should be borne in mind that the quality of financial institutions in low-income countries may crucially affect the overall relation-ship between finance and growth, as recent work seems to suggest – see Demetriades and Andrianova (2008), among others, for a detailed discussion.

References

Abiat, A. and Mody, A. (2005) 'Financial Reform: What Shakes It? What Shapes It?', *American Economic Review*, 95(1): 66–88.

Addison, T. (2007) 'International Finance and the Developing World: the Next Twenty Years', in G. Mavrotas and A. Shorrocks (eds), *Advancing Development: Core Themes in Global Economics* (Basingstoke: Palgrave Macmillan for UNU-WIDER).

Akyüz, Y. and Cornford, A. (2002) 'Capital Flows to Developing Countries and the Reform of the International Financial System', in D. Nayyar (ed.), *Governing Globalization: Issues and Institutions* (Oxford: Oxford University Press for UNU-WIDER).

Arestis, P. and Demetriades, P. (1997) 'Financial Development and Economic Growth: Assessing the Evidence', *Economic Journal*, 107(May): 783–99.

Bandiera, O., Caprio, G., Honohan, P. and Schiantarelli, F. (2000) 'Does Financial Reform Raise or Reduce Saving?', *Review of Economics and Statistics*, 82(2): 239–63.

Beck, T., Demirgüç-Kunt, A. and Levine, R. (2004) 'Finance, Inequality and Poverty: Cross-country Evidence', Policy Research Working Paper 3338, World Bank, Washington, DC.

Brownbridge, M. and Kirkpatrick, C. (1999) 'Financial Sector Regulation: Lessons of the Asia Crisis', *Development Policy Review*, 17(3): 243–66.

Caprio, G., Honohan, P. and Stiglitz, J. (eds) (2001) *Financial Liberalization: How Far, How Fast?* (Cambridge: Cambridge University Press).

Cheru, F. and Bradford, C. (eds) (2005) *The Millennium Development Goals: Raising the Resources to Tackle World Poverty* (London/New York: ZED Books; in association with the Helsinki Process on Globalization and Democracy).

Claessens, S. (2005) 'Access to Financial Services: A Review of the Issues and Public Policy Objectives', Policy Research Working Paper 3589, World Bank, Washington DC.

Claessens, S. and Feijen, E. (2006) *Financial Sector Development and the Millennium Development Goals* (Washington, DC: World Bank).

Demetriades, P. and Andrianova, S. (2008) 'Sources and Effectiveness of Financial Development: What We Know and What We Need to Know', in B. Guha-Khasnobis and G. Mavrotas (eds), *Financial Development, Institutions, Growth and Poverty Reduction* (Basingstoke: Palgrave Macmillan for UNU-WIDER).

Demirgüç-Kunt, A. and Levine, R. (eds) (2001) *Financial Structure and Economic Growth* (Cambridge, Mass: MIT Press).

Dennis, S., Nandy, D. and Sharpe, G. (2000) 'The Determinants of Contract Terms in Bank Revolving Credit Agreements', *Journal of Financial and Quantitative Analysis*, 35: 87–110.

Dercon, S. (ed.) (2004) *Insurance Against Poverty* (Oxford: Oxford University Press for UNU-WIDER).

Detragiache, E., Gupta, P. and Tressel, T. (2005) 'Finance in Low-Income Countries: An Empirical Exploration', Working Paper 05/167, IMF, Washington DC.

Goodhart, C. (ed.) (2004) *Financial Development and Economic Growth: Exploring the Links* (Basingstoke: Palgrave Macmillan).

Green, C. J. and Kirkpatrick, C. (2002) 'Finance and Development: An Overview of the Issues', *Journal of International Development*, 14(2): 207–10.

Green, C. J., Kirkpatrick, C. and Murinde, V. (2005) 'How Does Finance Contribute to the Development Process and Poverty Reduction?', in C. J. Green, C. Kirkpatrick and V. Murinde (eds), *Finance and Development: Surveys of Theory, Evidence and Policy* (Cheltenham: Edward Elgar).

Guha-Khasnobis, B. and Mavrotas, G. (eds) (2008) *Financial Development, Institutions, Growth and Poverty Reduction* (Basingstoke: Palgrave Macmillan for UNU-WIDER).

Honohan, P. (2004) 'Financial Development, Growth and Poverty: How Close Are the Links?', in C. Goodhart (ed.), *Financial Development and Economic Growth: Exploring the Links* (Basingstoke: Palgrave Macmillan).

Kelly, R. and Mavrotas, G. (2003) 'Financial Sector Development – Futile or Fruitful?', WIDER Discussion Paper 2003/14, UNU-WIDER, Helsinki.

Kelly, R. and Mavrotas, G. (2008) 'Savings and Financial Sector Development: Panel Cointegration Evidence from Africa', *European Journal of Finance* (forthcoming).

Levine, R. (1997) 'Financial Development and Economic Growth: Views and Agenda', *Journal of Economic Literature*, 35: 688–726.

Loayza, N., Schmidt-Hebbel, K. and Serven, L. (2000) 'What Drives Private Saving Across the World?', *Review of Economics and Statistics*, 82(2): 165–81.

Mavrotas, G. (2005) 'Savings and Financial Sector Development: An Assessment', in C. J. Green, C. Kirkpatrick and V. Murinde (eds), *Finance and Development: Surveys of Theory, Evidence and Policy* (Cheltenham: Edward Elgar).

Rousseau, P. and Wachtel, P. (2005) 'Economic Growth and Financial Depth: Is the Relationship Extinct Already?', WIDER Discussion Paper 2005/10, UNU-WIDER, Helsinki.

Stiglitz, J. (1999) 'Responding to Economic Crises: Policy Alternatives for Equitable Recovery and Development', *The Manchester School*, 67(5): 409–27.

Stiglitz, J. (2002) *Globalization and Its Discontents* (London: Penguin).

UNCDF and UN-DESA (2006) *Building Inclusive Financial Sectors for Development* (New York: United Nations).

Wachtel, P. (2004) 'How Much Do We Really Know about Growth and Finance?', *Research in Banking and Finance*, 4: 91–113.

World Bank (2001) *Finance for Growth: Policy Choices in a Volatile World* (New York: Oxford University Press).

2
Stock Market Development and Economic Growth

Salvatore Capasso

Introduction

In the wake of substantial empirical evidence, recent decades have seen economists devoting considerable attention to the study of the inter-relationship between financial variables and the processes of real resource allocation. These studies have directed their efforts towards challenging the idea of an existing dichotomy between the real and financial worlds, which has long been assumed by a large part of the literature, and has found strong theoretical support in the Modigliani and Miller (1958) theorem.

Indeed, the real world seems to depict a quite different state of affairs. As the data show, the structure of financial markets, far from being stable and static, moves along with economic growth and capital accumulation in many economies. Furthermore, the co-movements of financial markets and economic systems appear to display significant regularities. At low stages of economic development, when economies are relatively poor, financial systems are somewhat rudimentary: financial intermediation is scarce and financial instruments are simple and basic. In these stages, stock markets are completely absent. As economies develop, financial intermediation grows, more complex and articulated financial instruments appear in the market, and stock markets emerge. These represent very general regularities and describe in broad terms the development of financial markets and the inter-relationship of financial development and capital accumulation. However, the data also provide other, more specific, features of the co-movements between financial and real variables. These features might differ from country to country, and from period to period, but they still say a lot about the relevance of financial variables in the process of real resource allocation.

Until now, the literature has focused mainly on the role of financial intermediation in the process of economic growth and capital accumulation. Indeed, many studies have analysed the channels through which banks and other financial intermediaries may help to increase, for example, the savings rate or the average productivity of capital and, in turn, growth. Recently, however, a new wave of interest in a specific aspect of financial market development has occupied economists' investigative activity. This is the role played by stock market development in the process of economic development.

The renewed interest, which is predominantly theoretical, stems from the fact that, despite the large body of empirical evidence, many questions remain unanswered. Why do stock markets develop relatively late in the process of economic development? Why do firms change corporate financing decisions, preferring debt over equity in richer countries? Is it economic development that engineers transformations in financial systems and determines the emergence of stock markets, or, on the contrary, is it stock market development that spurs economic growth? These, together with other questions, have been analysed extensively by a large number of recent theoretical and empirical studies.

Significantly, the evolution of financial markets does not appear to be a straightforward and linear phenomenon. A complex bundle of connections between the relevant variables makes it difficult to uncover (and replicate through modelling) the real dynamics of the economic systems. Among these empirical facts, one surfaces as particularly interesting. The emergence and expansion of stock markets does not usually give rise to the simple substitution of financial intermediation with equity financing in the economy. Rather, the expansion of stock markets always appears to be followed by an initial expansion of debt and bank financing, to such an extent that the equity/debt ratio in the economy first decreases, and only increases with further economic development. Figure 2.1 provides a description of the evolution of financial markets in a sample of countries including advanced OECD economies and some major emerging markets.

In order to explain the emergence and evolution of stock markets, and to take into account the impact of such modifications in financial markets on economic development, the literature has followed different routes. Despite the differences, however, these studies can be clustered into two major groups. The first group deals with the emergence of stock markets as a pure macroeconomic phenomenon: for these studies, the modifications in financial systems are the result of changing costs

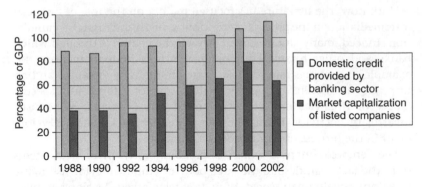

Figure 2.1   Domestic credit provided by bank sector and stock market capitalization
Note: The data are annual averages of the values in the following sample countries:
Australia, Belgium, Canada, France, Germany, Greece, Rep. of Ireland, Italy, Japan, Norway,
Portugal, Spain, United Kingdom, United States, Rep. of Korea, China, Malaysia, India,
Argentina, Brazil, Mexico, South Africa, Turkey, Russian Federation.
Source: World Bank (2004).

associated with different financial institutions. The second group is
more interested in analysing the corporate financing decisions of
individual firms: these studies try to verify how firms' financing choices
change with capital accumulation. I shall refer to the approach followed
by the first group as the 'institutional approach', and to the second as the
'instrumental approach'.

My main objective is to examine critically the current state of the
theoretical literature which, although substantial, has left space for
further investigation. The aim is to organize and manage the main
results of these studies in order to shed light on the issue of stock market
development and economic growth, and to open new avenues for a
different approach to the empirical evidence. And it is necessary to start
from the empirical evidence in order to understand the evolution of the
theoretical literature.

Empirical evidence

A large body of empirical studies clearly shows that the development of
stock markets is strongly and positively correlated with the level of economic development and capital accumulation. This is a solid and
uncontroversial result, and it appears to be true across time and for many
countries. Indeed, the data confirm that, as economies develop, equity
markets tend to expand both in terms of the number of listed companies

and in terms of market capitalization (Atje and Jovanovich 1993; Demirgüç-Kunt and Levine 1996a, 1996b; Demirgüç-Kunt and Maksimovic 1996; Korajczyk 1996; Levine and Zervos 1996, 1998). This result, however, does not suggest a direct and monotonic expansion of the share of equity markets in the financial system. In reality, the expansion of equity markets always appears to be preceded and accompanied by the general expansion of the overall financial system. And, to a careful observer, far from being a simple and straightforward fact, the co-evolution of real and financial variables is a complex and multi-faceted phenomenon. Indeed, the expansion of stock markets generally follows the development of commercial banks and other financial inter-mediaries which, in many cases, continues as equity markets expand. This process produces an apparently puzzling situation: an expanding equity market together with a financial system dominated persistently by banks and their financial products. Even if the evidence often appears to be bewildering, and in many circumstances difficult to interpret, some simple, general, stylized facts about the relationship between financial development and economic growth can be drawn from the empirical literature (King and Levine 1993a, 1993b; De Gregorio and Guidotti 1995; Beck *et al.* 2000, 2001; Green *et al.* 2005). These facts are summarized in the following points:

- In the early stages of economic development, financial markets are very thin and very rudimentary. During these stages, financial markets are dominated by banks, or similar types of financial intermediaries. Stock markets are completely absent or, if they exist in any form, their size is negligible.
- As capital accumulates, financial intermediaries develop, the number of financial instruments increases, as does the level of sophistication and complexity of financial contracts, and the flow of resources and funds accruing to the financial market increases its size. Stock markets start developing both in terms of the number of listed firms and market capitalization.
- As the economy continues to grow, equity markets develop further, as do banks and other financial intermediaries.
- Stock markets appear to develop in a non-monotonic ways. In economies where stock markets are relatively small, capital accumu-lation seems to be followed by a relative increase in the banks' share in the financial system; while in economies where the stock market has already reached a reasonable size, further development of the market causes an increase in the equity markets' share. In other words,

evidence shows that the equity/debt ratio first decreases, and only with further development of the stock market does it increase.

The co-evolution of equity markets and capital accumulation is only one aspect of the more general inter-relationship between economic growth and the expansion of the financial system. Since the seminal contributions of Goldsmith (1969) and McKinnon (1973), economists have devoted considerable attention to the role played by financial intermediation in the process of real resource allocation and capital accumulation. Only very recently have economists focused their attention specifically on the role of stock markets in the process of economic development. Interestingly, these recent studies have not only revealed novel theoretical and empirical aspects of the channels of interaction between real and financial variables, but they have also been able to shed light on individual firms' optimal financial choices in connection with economic development.

Before turning to a synthetic description of these studies, it is necessary to agree, at the outset, on a definition of equity markets' development, and to specify a measure of such development. In doing so, it is useful to observe that the development of a stock market can be identified by means of quantitative or qualitative measurements, or by a combination of the two. Different routes can be pursued. The primary route to follow in order to assess the expansion of a stock market is to look at changes in its dimension. A simple measure of a stock market's size is the total value of all the shares in the market at each point in time (market capitalization), or the average of this value over a period. Market size is important because the level of savings mobilization and risk diversification depend strongly on this indicator. Of course, a measure of a stock market's size needs to take into account the dimension of the economic system overall. For this reason, the typical measurement employed in empirical analyses is the ratio of market capitalization to gross domestic product (GDP) (market capitalization/GDP). Stock market size can also be measured by the number of listed companies in the stock exchange in each period. Although market size is an important indicator of stock market development, this measurement by itself does not capture all the relevant features of a financial market's development. Indeed, a developed market is also an efficient and liquid market in which financial funds can be mobilized at low cost and can move easily from one investment to the other. These qualitative features of market development can be captured by indicators such as the volume of shares traded in each period and the degree of concentration. While the first of these indices measures the level of liquidity in the market, the second takes into account the level of risk diversification. Finally, in order to capture the main features of financial market development, one must not forget to take into account the institutional and regulatory framework that represents the basic organization of the market. It is useful to provide a brief and schematic description of such indicators:

- *Market capitalization ratio*: this is calculated by dividing the value of listed companies (market capitalization) by the GDP. It gives a measure of the size of the stock market relative to the size of the economy. It is a good measure of the relative size of the stock market in the economy.
- *Number of listed companies*: this specifies the number of all companies listed in the country's stock exchange at any given time. This indicator is also a measure of stock market size.
- *Total value traded*: this gives the total value of shares traded during the period. Total value traded divided by GDP gives a measure of the liquidity in the market. Market liquidity measures how easily securities can be bought and sold. This indicator complements the market capitalization ratio and signals whether market size is matched by trading activity.
- *Turnover ratio*: the total value of shares traded during the period divided by the average market capitalization for the period. Average market capitalization is calculated as the average of the end-of-period values for the current period and the previous period.
- *Institutional and regulatory framework*: the degree of development of a market is strongly influenced by the regulatory system. Differences in regulatory systems, for example, are often used to explain the great differences in equity market development between countries such as the UK, the USA and Canada on the one hand, and Japan, Germany, France and Italy on the other, despite their similar levels of economic development.
- *Concentration*: the degree of market concentration is important to show how well a market really works. A very high degree of concentration signals a heavy and illiquid market. In such circumstances, the benefits of risk diversification in markets are very low. A measure of concentration could be provided, for example, by the average size of firms listed in the stock market (see Figure 2.2).

Tables 2.1(a) and (b) describe some of these indicators of stock market development for two groups of countries: a sample of advanced OECD

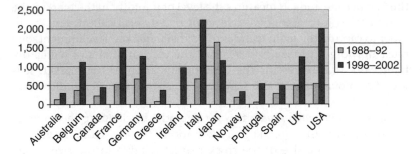

Figure 2.2   Average firm size listed on the stock market (US $m)
Note: The average firm size in the reference period is calculated on the basis of the average market capitalization and the average number of listed firms over the same period.
Source: World Bank (2004).

countries and some major emerging economies. Significantly, for almost all of these countries, the market capitalization ratio and the number of listed firms show that the size of stock markets has increased over time. Furthermore, as witnessed by the total stock traded over GDP indicator, stock markets have been increasingly active, showing an increase in the level of liquidity in recent decades. Through these and other indicators, empirical studies have provided hard evidence of the co-evolution of stock market development and economic growth, and highlighted the most relevant features of this inter-relationship.

By studying a relatively large set of forty countries in the period 1979–88, and focusing on the dynamics of market size, Atje and Jovanovic (1993) have found a strong positive correlation between the level of financial development and stock market development and economic growth. In a more recent study, Levine and Zervos (1998) obtain similar results on a larger set of observations. They sampled forty-seven countries from 1976 to 1993, and found that stock market liquidity measured as the value of stock traded relative to the size of the market and the size of the economy was strongly and positively correlated to the rate of economic growth. They also observe that the level of banking development, measured as the ratio of bank loans to the private sector to GDP, is positively correlated with the level of economic growth. The significance of stock market development in the process of economic growth is also confirmed by Beck and Levine (2001) who, by applying novel econometric procedures, tested for the independent impact of banks and stock markets on growth. Again, Beck and Levine found that the expansion of both banks and stock markets significantly affected growth.

Table 2.1 Stock market development indicators
(a) Sample of advanced OECD countries

	Market capitalization of listed companies (% of GDP)			Number of listed domestic companies			Total value of stocks traded (% of GDP)		
	1988–92	1993–7	1998–2002	1988–92	1993–7	1998–2002	1988–92	1993–7	1998–2002
Australia	44.99	68.59	96.90	1,143	1,157	1,280	14.13	30.50	57.36
Belgium	36.40	42.05	75.34	181	149	163	4.03	7.59	18.84
Canada	46.52	69.89	102.66	1,128	1,226	1,862	14.07	35.42	64.34
France	28.51	37.75	87.51	646	550	810	9.12	21.27	64.99
Germany	21.48	27.38	55.85	549	580	880	29.55	23.69	54.02
Greece	11.60	18.04	91.98	128	205	307	2.06	7.44	66.16
Rep. of Ireland		49.32	71.54		80	74		16.15	33.20
Italy	14.63	20.17	53.88	220	233	277	3.31	10.27	50.76
Japan	105.39	66.39	67.68	2,056	2,269	2,595	55.78	24.78	41.02
Norway	18.99	32.28	37.31	118	151	193	9.46	16.64	31.03
Portugal	13.49	21.62	49.63	181	171	106	3.02	8.29	34.07
Spain	24.39	36.00	76.17	410	372	1,333	7.80	30.74	143.43
UK	91.74	131.27	164.21	1,853	2,024	1,912	40.39	48.90	121.74
USA	62.70	98.07	146.77	6,689	7,988	7,133	34.31	77.43	242.59

(Continued)

Table 2.1   Continued
(b) Sample of major emerging countries

	Market capitalization of listed companies (% of GDP)			Number of listed domestic companies			Total value of stocks traded (% of GDP)		
	1988–92	1993–7	1998–2002	1988–92	1993–7	1998–2002	1988–92	1993–7	1998–2002
Rep. of Korea	43.62	32.30	55.90	667	730	1,228	37.71	48.07	162.31
China	2.46	12.06	38.54	33	416	1,056	2.11	21.53	39.88
Malaysia	111.42	248.99	143.10	292	549	791	21.66	162.22	44.06
India	14.83	34.87	29.56	3,204	4,983	5,821	6.85	17.24	50.06
Argentina	5.46	16.85	55.11	178	154	116	2.59	5.92	2.60
Brazil	9.00	27.57	33.00	579	545	458	3.76	16.79	15.08
Mexico	19.92	36.76	22.37	202	194	179	6.58	14.65	6.84
South Africa	123.16	161.71	148.44	721	639	584	6.54	16.35	59.30
Turkey	7.39	19.74	32.93	98	204	295	3.12	22.00	52.12
Russian Fed.	0.05	9.03	23.96	20	115	225		1.24	6.19

Note: The data are the author's calculation of averages over five-year periods.
Source: World Bank (2004).

As already outlined, beyond this apparently clear and general result, the dynamic interaction between financial and real variables is an articulated and multi-faceted phenomenon that can differ greatly from country to country. In order to get an idea of these differences in the evolution of the financial systems, it is useful to mention the contraposition between the so-called bank-based financial system predominant in continental Europe and Japan, and the so-called market-based system predominant in the Anglo-Saxon countries. In the former countries, in which the banking sector strongly dominates the financial sector, economic growth and capital accumulation have involved a significantly less perceptible development of equity markets despite these countries displaying similar levels of capital accumulation to Anglo-Saxon countries.

Although the dynamic patterns of financial systems can differ greatly from country to country, some general stylized facts about the development of equity markets can be drawn from the literature. As outlined by Demirgüç-Kunt and Maksimovic (1996), stock markets do not develop in a monotonic way, and neither does (as one might wrongly deduce) the development of equity markets directly crowd out the banking sector and other financial intermediaries. Rather, the dynamics of equity markets seem to depend on the level of economic development and on the level of the stock market development itself. In specific terms, when economies have thin and underdeveloped stock markets, capital accumulation leads to an increase in the share in the economy of debt and bank financing. As economies grow and stock markets develop, further expansion of stock markets leads to a relative increase of equity financing in the economy. In other words, given that stock market development depends on growth, the bank debt–equity ratio in the economy tends to increase at low levels of capital accumulation, and to decrease only when stock markets have reached a reasonable size.

Demirgüç-Kunt and Maksimovic (1996) provide an explanation for this finding based on the effect of equity market development on the cost of access to credit. The idea is that, in the initial stages of economic development, the expansion of stock markets increases both the opportunity for risk sharing and the flow of information in the market. These, in turn, allow firms to access bank loans more easily and cheaply, and to increase the level of leverage. However, as stock markets develop further, issuing equity becomes more convenient because of the falling costs of going public, and firms substitute equity for debt. In line with these ideas, Pagano (1993) shows more formally that, because of trading externalities in the market and the strategic behaviour of listing companies, the size of the stock market is crucial in explaining its own development. Indeed, a firm that goes public increases the risk-sharing opportunities for investors through portfolio diversification.

The idea is simple. Assume a situation where borrowing constraints and lack of liquidity force entrepreneurs to go public. The price they get from flotation depends on the behaviour of other entrepreneurs and on the size of stock market. Indeed, if few entrepreneurs decide to list their companies, the gains from portfolio diversification are low and few investors will demand shares in the market. As a consequence, the share price will be kept low, and so will the return on flotation. Therefore, the return on flotation for each entrepreneur depends strategically on what all other entrepreneurs do. If many entrepreneurs decide to go public, the return on flotation will be higher, and equity issue will be relatively more convenient. A thicker equity market makes equity issue less costly. Extending this idea into a dynamic framework, one could infer that strategic complementarities in the stock market could well explain the non-monotonic behaviour of the debt–equity ratio along the path of capital accumulation.

Volatility of stock prices is another empirical aspect of stock market development that has received considerable attention in the literature. By itself, volatility of stock returns is not an indicator of stock market development. However, high levels of volatility, by affecting average portfolio risk, can have a significant effect on the return on investment and growth. There are a variety of channels through which high volatility can have a negative impact on investment and growth:

- It may cause great instability in the financial system as a whole.
- It can decrease the supply of financial funds, and raise the cost of access to capital by discouraging saving by risk-averse individuals.
- To the extent that equity markets help to channel resources towards the most profitable investment through price signalling, highly volatile stock prices cause misallocation of resources because prices do not indicate return on investments correctly.

These arguments would suggest that high volatility should have a negative effect on growth and capital accumulation. Along this line of reasoning, Singh (1997) sustains that, because of high volatility, the large expansion of stock markets in developing countries, far from helping industrialization and fostering capital accumulation, can hamper economic growth. Indeed, according to Singh, the expansion of stock markets in developing countries since the beginning of the 1980s has not been caused by the endogenous evolution of financial systems – as described above – but rather by means of ad hoc governmental programmes of privatization and financial liberalization. This financial 'de-repression', as denoted by Singh, however, has occurred without a change in the regulatory system or infrastructure, which remain inadequate to support well-functioning equity markets. The result is very volatile stock markets that are unable to carry out the roles they play in advanced economies, such as monitoring, screening, and information gathering – which is how they enhance growth.

Although the arguments on the potential negative impact of volatility on growth appear to be very convincing, Levine and Zervos (1998) did not find any significant relationship between volatility and growth in the sample countries over the period considered. They measure volatility as a twelve-month rolling standard deviation estimate on stock returns, regress this estimate on the rate of growth and obtain no significant results.

Open economies with deeply integrated financial markets can benefit from cross-border capital flows and from larger flows of financial resources pouring into the market. As theory suggests, international financial integration, by bringing about a greater degree of portfolio and risk diversification, may boost the propensity to save and invest and, through this channel, can foster growth (Devereux and Smith 1994; Obstfeld 1994). In other words, internationally integrated financial markets can be associated potentially with higher rates of growth and capital accumulation. There is no doubt that financial globalization can benefit stock markets more than other financial institutions, because the former can mobilize financial resources at low cost. One can therefore argue that while financial globalization is not a direct indicator of stock market development, the international integration of financial markets would increasingly be expected to be accompanied by expanding stock markets and higher rates of economic growth. Following these theoretical suppositions, Korajczyk (1996) investigated whether internationally integrated stock markets are positively correlated with capital accumulation and economic growth. In order to measure international market integration, Korajczyk adopted an International Arbitrage Pricing Model for twenty-four national markets. This gives a benchmark equilibrium model which gives stock returns in hypothetical fully integrated markets. The deviation of effective stock returns from these benchmark values gives a measure of the distance of these economies from full integration. In line with the theory, Korajczyk found that market segmentation was higher for developing than for developed countries. Moreover, market integration tends to increase as capital accumulates, showing a positive correlation between stock market integration and economic growth.

Theoretical issues

Despite this overwhelming empirical evidence, a number of questions remain unanswered. Why do stock markets develop later than other financial institutions in the process of capital accumulation? How can the apparent complementarity between the equity market and the banking sector be explained? Why do some countries have stock markets that are overdeveloped while others are very thin (notwithstanding their level of economic development)? Finally, is it the development of stock markets that spurs economic growth, or is it the process of capital accumulation and growth that transforms the financial system and causes the development of stock markets?

These are among the questions that a growing body of theoretical studies have tried to answer recently. It is clear that, in order to address these issues, it is necessary first to understand the exact role of the stock market in the process of real resource allocation, and how the financing decisions of firms affect investments. Second, it is necessary to determine the possible channels of interaction between real and financial variables.

The literature on this issue can be categorized as having followed two main routes: the institutional approach and the instrumental approach. The institutional approach focuses on the macroeconomic role of stock markets. By identifying and understanding the working of stock markets, and the main differences between the functioning of financial intermediaries, it is possible to understand why equity markets emerge at an advanced stage of economic development, and the correlation of stock market development with the evolution of the banking system. The instrumental approach focuses, instead, on the microeconomic aspect of the optimal financial choices of the firms. It typically studies the differences between equity financing and debt financing, and how corporate finance affects the investment decisions of firms. The objective of these studies is to understand why, depending on the level of capital accumulation in the economy, firms change their preferred source of external funds and switch from debt financing to equity issue. These analyses, in turn, also need to explain the reverse causal relationship and to establish how the above changes in the financial system affect the process of economic growth.

Institutional approach

Modern financial systems depend on two main financial institutions: one is commercial banks; the other, stock markets. Although these institutions have the same ultimate aim, to convey financial funds from lenders to final borrowers, they do so through very different channels, and play very different roles. Understanding these different roles can help us to shed light on the mechanisms through which financial variables can influence resource allocation and, in turn, economic growth. Indeed, as the theory has established exhaustively, the functioning of financial markets can determine the flow of resources channelled to investment as well as the optimal choice of the types of investments and projects to be financed.

In order to understand the process through which financial intermediation emerges and changes along the path of capital accumulation, and, most importantly for our purposes, in order to understand why, as capital accumulates, banks and financial intermediaries are replaced by stock markets, it is necessary to focus on the specific functioning of these institutions and to look for the main differences that might influence the process of economic growth.

For a long time, the literature has reflected deep study of the functional activities of financial intermediaries. Despite this, it is only recently that economists have focused specifically on the role of financial intermediation in the process of economic development.[1] The results of these studies are quite clear. Banks and other financial intermediaries can influence the process of resource allocation and investments through the following channels:

- Financial intermediaries free resources in the economy by reducing transaction costs through the economies of scale involved in their activities. Moreover, they supply specific services, such as brokerage, which reduce friction and let financial flows move more easily and at a lower cost through the system.
- Banks and financial intermediaries bring about significant improvements in risk diversification by supplying a wide array of financial assets with very specific features. This should increase the propensity of risk-averse agents to save and invest.
- One of the main functions of financial intermediaries is the maturity transformation of financial assets. The consequent increase in the

array of financial assets stimulates the supply of financial funds, and of savings and investments.

- Banks collect and produce a large amount of information. This reduces the intensity of information asymmetry between lenders and borrowers, and improves the allocation of resources.
- Banks facilitate long-term relationships and commitments. Long-term relationships are very important, particularly when firms have no established long-term track records and reputation problems are, therefore, severe. Under these circumstances, long-term relationships may decrease the amount of credit rationing, which otherwise would be very high, given the reputation problems.

While progress in the literature on financial intermediation and economic growth has been quite substantial, the literature on the specific role of stock markets in the process of economic development is still comparatively slight, and many aspects remain to be explored. Despite this, a number of interesting features of the inter-relationship between equity market development and growth have been already disclosed. Stock markets can support resource allocation and spur growth through very different channels. Below I attempt to summarize the results:

- *Reduction in transaction costs and liquidity costs.* By reducing transaction costs and liquidity costs, stock markets can have a positive effect on the average productivity of capital (Levine 1991; Bencivenga *et al.* 1996).
- *Resource pooling and saving mobilization.* By pooling resources on larger projects that would otherwise have difficulty in accessing finance, stock markets can mobilize savings and spur the rate of investment (Greenwood and Smith 1997).
- *Acquisition of information about firms.* By promoting the acquisition of information about firms, stock markets may promote and improve resource allocation and the average productivity of capital (Grossman and Stiglitz 1980; Kyle 1984; Allen 1993; Holmstrom and Tirole 1993).
- *Corporate control.* By exerting a continuous and strict control over the management of firms, stock markets have a positive effect on firms' investment decisions and the average return on investments (Diamond and Verrecchia 1982; Laffont and Tirole 1988; Scharfstein 1988; Jensen and Murphy 1990).
- *Risk diversification.* By improving risk diversification through internationally integrated stock markets and increasing the array of

possible investments, stock markets can augment both the rate of saving and the rate of investment (Saint-Paul 1992; Devereux and Smith 1994; Obstfeld 1994).

The duration of investment projects – in conjunction with the expected rate of return and the relevant risk – is a very important variable for investors. Investors, who strictly prefer shorter-term assets, might find investments with particularly long maturities unattractive. Moreover, disrupting an investment project before it has reached maturity can be very costly in terms of missed profit and lower rates of return. Following this line of argument, Levine (1991) built a theoretical model showing that, by reducing these liquidation costs, and increasing the average productivity of capital and the rate of saving, stock markets can foster capital accumulation and growth. In fact, by their nature, equity markets make it possible to transfer the ownership of investment projects that have not yet ended without disrupting physical production. This feature of stock markets has two effects: (i) it attracts more resources into long-term investments from investors who would not have committed their finances for long periods of time; and (ii) it reduces the loss of resources that would have occurred with the disruption of physical production. Both of these effects will spur growth. The first does this by increasing the saving rate; and the second by reducing actual resources lost by the premature liquidation of investments.

Following Levine, Bencivenga *et al.* (1996) maintain that equity markets can increase the average productivity of capital and, in turn, affect growth positively by decreasing liquidity costs. The idea is that projects that require longer periods of time to complete are usually also investments with a higher expected return. These projects, however, will not be adopted by investors who do not want to tie up their financial resources for a long time. Therefore, assets with long maturities will never be in demand, unless these can be liquidated easily and at low cost. Again, equity markets make these projects attractive to investors by allowing the trading of all or part of a project's ownership at any time. The channels of interaction between stock markets and capital accumulation and growth are quite clear. As equity markets develop, longer-maturity projects with higher rates of return become more attractive, the average productivity of capital increases, and so does the rate of growth.

In a framework where agents face liquidity and productivity shocks, financial markets can help to reallocate resources towards the most productive investments by reducing idiosyncratic risks. Indeed, by considering an economy in which both banks and stock markets coexist, Greenwood and Smith (1997) show that financial markets, by decreasing liquidity risk, increase savings and pool resources towards larger, more productive projects. The average productivity of investment increases, and so does the rate of growth. However, while equity markets always increase the growth rate relative to the case of autarky, equity markets increase the growth rate relative to banks only if agents are relatively risk averse.

For Allen (1993), the emergence of equities depends primarily on the degree of complexity of the production structure, and on information-gathering costs. One of the advantages of stock markets is that they allow for efficient risk sharing by providing incentives for investors to search for information. The basic idea is well known in the literature. Grossman (1976, 1978), Grossman and Stiglitz (1980) and Diamond and Verrecchia (1982) build theoretical models in which stock markets cluster together efficiently very different investors' information. Stock prices therefore tend, in efficient markets, to reflect the true valuation of underlying investment projects and constitute a clear signal for the actual rates of return on capital. As a consequence, stock prices are an efficient instrument for correct resource allocation, and because of this they can boost economic development and growth. It is clear that where the production system is more complex, as Allen (1993) outlines, the process of information acquisition is more difficult and the working of equity markets in the process of capital accumulation will be more effective. Although, at first sight, this explanation appears to be satisfactory, two questions remain. What is the difference between equity markets and banks, given that banks also help in providing information through monitoring and screening? And why do stock markets appear only at an advanced stage of economic development, and in some countries but not in others?

The answers to these two questions are to be found in the processes of information transfer between firms' managements and the market, and in the possibility of identifying optimal investment strategies. In the presence of very simple productive systems, when optimal investment opportunities and management policies can be identified easily – for example, because these policies are limited in number, or because the feasible options do not change very rapidly over time – the banking system can gather enough information for optimal resource allocation. A typical example of a productive system in which simple pro-duction processes prevail is one dominated by the agriculture sector. Determination of optimal investment opportunities and control of management strategies are not difficult to carry out in such a framework.

However, as the number of firms' investment opportunities increases, and the production processes become increasingly difficult to control (not only by external observers, but also by firms' management teams), continuous monitoring becomes essential for the efficient allocation of resources. Stock markets, under such circumstances, become the best instrument for optimal investment control and risk diversification. Stock markets are more costly for the system overall than banks. However, they become more convenient when the production system becomes more complex. Banks and financial intermediaries in general do not allow for continuous monitoring. This explains why banks prevail in economies with simpler production structures – for example, economies dominated by the agricultural sector, and stock markets become increasingly important as economies grow and display more articulated and complex productive systems.

One final observation on the market structure is necessary. The hypothesis of complete and efficient markets throws up some theoretical puzzles over the existence of incentives for information production. As pointed out by Grossman and Stiglitz (1980), if markets are complete and perfect, then prices will reflect all available information in the market. Therefore, given that collecting information is costly, no one will have any incentive to collect information and monitor firms. This paradox is solved by Grossman and Stiglitz by assuming incomplete markets, and by assuming variables that are unobservable by participants.

Another channel through which stock markets can have a positive effect on growth is the continuous monitoring of firms' managements, which greatly improves resource allocation. Indeed, continuous monitoring and control can provide the most effective incentives for managers to choose investment projects that maximize firms' market value, and therefore increase the average return on capital and investment. The interests of the managers of firms' do not coincide with the interest of the firms' shareholders and owners and, as a consequence, managers' decisions might be in conflict with the firms' aims and profitability. Such a potential conflict of interest generates a typical agency problem, which can be solved by means of credible threats and incentive-compatible contracts. Incentives for managers to act in the best interests of firms come from two main sources: one is the threat of a possible takeover; the other the introduction of effective incentive-compatible payment schemes.

Quotation on the stock market might potentially force managers to try to maximize the value of the firm, since publicly quoted firms that perform poorly might become the target of possible takeovers, which usually entail the removal of the management team. This threat may be sufficient to encourage managers to act in the interests of the firm (Laffont and Tirole 1988; Sharfestein 1988; Stein 1988). From a different perspective, but with similar effects, the continuous monitoring of firms' performance following quotation on the stock market makes it possible to build optimal compensation schemes that may force managers to put in high levels of effort and take the best resource allocation decisions (Diamond and Verrecchia 1982; Jensen and Murphy 1990).

Despite the success of the above arguments in highlighting clearly the benefits of stock markets and providing a satisfactory description of the channels through which quotation on stock markets can affect investment decisions and the growth rate of the economy, some interesting questions remain unanswered. If the continuous monitoring from stock markets is so valuable, why do not all firms decide that being publicly quoted is best? The answer to this question is essentially that monitoring is costly for firms (Holmstrom and Tirole 1993). As Holmstrom and Tirole argue, monitoring is valuable because it gives speculators information advantages that can be turned into profits. The higher the value of the information, the higher the value of monitoring will be. However, information advantages are strictly linked to the share price. Only if the actual share price is far from the fair value, and someone knows it, is there the possibility of a profit. Information and monitoring costs result in a lower share price and a loss for the owner.

Finally, another channel through which stock markets may have a positive effect on capital accumulation and economic growth is the improvement of risk diversification through international, financially integrated markets. Indeed, as shown by Obstfeld (1994), an increase in the degree of international integration of stock markets reduces the level of average investment risk through diversification and leads to a shift in the global portfolio from safe, low-yield projects to riskier, high-yielding ones. This shift induces an increase in capital productivity and in the savings rate, both of which should boost growth. However, it is also necessary to recognize that portfolio diversification, depending on the agents' degree of risk aversion, can decrease the level of savings and have a negative effect on growth (Devereux and Smith 1994).

Instrumental approach

The most recent literature on stock market development and economic growth has shifted the focus from the role of markets and institutions to the nature of the underlying financial contracts. The objective of this literature is to explain the emergence and evolution of stock markets by analysing how capital accumulation affects firms' optimal financing choice and, in turn, how firms' corporate financing decisions affect investments and capital accumulation. Evidently, this kind of analysis needs to investigate in detail the main features of the optimal financial contracts available to firms: costs, benefits and possible impacts on the production process. Although intuitively straightforward and apparently simple, this type of investigation faces theoretical obstacles. In a standard Arrow–Debreu framework, in which markets are perfect, agents are fully informed and there are no transaction costs, the Modigliani–Miller theorem holds and the value of a firm is unaffected by how that firm is financed. In this framework, whether the firm issues equity or takes on debt in order to raise money is completely irrelevant to the firm's investment decisions as well as to its market valuation. Under these conditions, a firm's financial capital structure is completely irrelevant for real resource allocation. As a consequence, the frictionless Arrow–Debreu setup needs to be modified in order to develop a theory that can explain the connections between financial and real variables. Economists have modified this framework in different ways; for example, by introducing different kinds of market frictions, such as liquidity costs and transaction costs, or by assuming imperfect information between borrowers and lenders. Thus, the arguments are that financial markets can affect growth through the reduction of liquidity risks, or because they can increase the flow of savings and channel such resources towards more productive alternatives (Greenwood and Jovanovich 1990; Bencivenga and Smith 1991; Levine 1991; Saint-Paul 1992; Blackburn and Hung 1998, among others).[2]

Similar arguments have been put forward to explain the dynamic role of stock markets in the process of real resource allocation. However, only recent developments in the literature on optimal financial contracts under information asymmetry have provided significant insights for new avenues of investigation on the co-evolution of equity market development and economic growth. These recent studies on stock market development integrate microeconomic models of optimal financial contracts under information asymmetry into dynamic general equilibrium models.

In the presence of information asymmetries between lenders (typically households) and borrowers (typically firms), different informational problems might arise and the exchange of resources can become costly, sometimes to such an extent as to prevent capital markets from functioning at all. For example, problems of adverse selection might arise when firms have the possibility of hiding their expected profits or their level of efficiency. Problems of moral hazard might arise because of the incentive for firms to misreport the actual return on their investments. These informational problems generate agency costs, and the financial contract is the result of agents' attempts to reduce these costs. The financial contract, as well as the financial market, is therefore endogenously determined. The link between growth and finance arises because growth can affect the level of agency costs and hence financial arrangements, while the structure of the credit market affects growth because it determines the amount of resources invested and the allocation of capital.

The optimal financial contract, depending on the nature of information asymmetries and on agents' endowments, might display very different features. Typically, financial contracts take only two forms: one is equity; the other, debt. The differences between the two are quite sharp. Equity entails a repayment that depends on firm's profits (or losses) and, in specific terms, it entails a repayment that is directly proportional to a firm's investment returns. Debt, on the other hand, involves a fixed, predetermined repayment that does not depend on a firm's profits, up to the point that profit is enough to repay the lender the amount has been promised contractually. Therefore, while debt involves bankruptcy, equity does not. Despite these clear differences, the literature on corporate finance has found it difficult to justify the issue of equity, even in a framework with information asymmetries. In fact, debt always dominates equity repayment. Intuitively, if the firm-borrower has private information of very high rates of return on the project in need of external finance, it is not going to choose a repayment that involves proportional sharing of the return on those projects with others (equity repayment). If debt is available, the firm is always going to choose this form of repayment even in the presence of very high bankruptcy costs. Indeed, the issue of equity very often involves sending negative signals to the market (Leland and Pyle 1977; Myers and Majluf 1984) and results in a negative appraisal of the firm. Equity is treated as a residual alternative and a suboptimal choice compared to debt.

The most recent studies have moved towards a different approach that hinges essentially on a very simple consideration. Equity and debt involve very different financial costs and the issue of only equity, or only debt, or a combination of the two, is simply the result of a firm's optimal investment decision, taken in order to minimize those financial costs.

As can easily be understood, these studies on a firm's optimal financial structure are strictly related to the literature on Initial Public Offerings (IPOs). The decision to go public and to issue shares is a complex one, depending on institutional factors as well as on the economic environment. In practice, the decision to enter the stock market involves the comparison of a wide array of costs and benefits. Pagano *et al.* (1998) provide a detailed empirical analysis of the major determinants of IPOs. Using a large database of Italian firms, they find that ultimately three major factors determine the decision of a firm to go public: (i) the stock market valuation of other firms in the same industry; (ii) the company's size; and (iii) the destination of the raised funds; that is, how firms employ these resources.

Very simple and intuitive reasons lie behind these results. The higher the valuation of firms in a given sector, the more probable it is that a firm operating in the same sector will go public. This finding confirms the arguments of Pagano (1993) that the issue of new equity is essentially a matter of strategic complementarities in the market, and the optimal solution to problems of information asymmetries. The probability of going public is also positively affected by a company's size. The larger the firm, the more convenient will be quotation on the stock market. This evidence seems to confirm the existence of fixed costs of listing, and of economies of scale. Finally, the results of this study suggest that firms do not usually issue equity to finance expansionary investments, but rather to repay outstanding debt or to reduce negative financial positions. Interestingly, Pagano *et al.* (1998) also find support for the existence of a kind of complementarity between equity and debt. Indeed, they find that going public enables companies to borrow more cheaply; equity reduces the cost of debt. Although Pagano *et al.* do not consider explicitly the impact of IPOs on capital accumulation, their results provide very interesting insights into the issue.

Recent studies explain the emergence of equity markets by analysing the optimal financial contract under information asymmetry, and by investigating the changes involved as a result of capital accumulation.

Information asymmetries can strongly modify agents' incentives, and therefore also contractual agreements between borrowers and lenders. A typical incentive problem, for example, arises when lenders are unable to observe directly the outcomes of the projects to be financed, and therefore face moral hazard problems. The implication of such problems is that lenders must monitor, or verify, the claims of borrowers about the returns of projects. However, since verification is costly, lenders find it optimal to verify only in a limited set of possible contingent states. Typically, the optimal solution to a standard costly state verification (CSV) problem, under the assumption that agents are risk neutral and monitoring costs do not depend on project returns, is always a debt contract. In other words, the loan repayment is predetermined and independent of the actual outcome of the investment (Townsend 1979; Diamond 1984; Gale and Hellwig 1985; Williamson 1986, 1987a, 1987b). The reason is that debt, which involves a fixed repayment, does not require costly monitoring provided that the contractual repayment is honoured. This would not be feasible if the loan repayment were a function of the project's return – for example, equity – and monitoring would be required in all states.

Boyd and Smith (1996, 1998) modify the standard CSV framework in order to provide an account of why equity might dominate debt, at least in some circumstances. In Boyd and Smith, borrowers have access to two alternative projects for producing capital. The first project has a higher expected return, which is known to the lender. The actual return on the project, however, is unobservable to outsiders. If the lender wants to verify the result of production, they must incur a cost that is decreasing in the price of capital (the interest rate). The second project has a lower expected return, but the actual return on this project is costlessly observable to the lender. Interestingly, Boyd and Smith show that the ways in which the lender optimally finances the two projects are different. In specific terms, while the unobservable project is financed optimally via a debt contract, the observable project is financed through an equity issue. The dependence of the equity–debt choice on growth is easily explained. For a low level of capital accumulation, when the interest rate is high, monitoring costs are relatively low. As a consequence, agents tend to use the unobservable technology. This, in turn, implies that debt finance is more widespread than equity finance. As capital accumulates, and the price of capital decreases, monitoring costs increase, and the unobservable technology becomes less and less profitable. As a result, equity finance will make up a larger share of the economy. This process explains the emergence of stock markets at later stages of economic development.

Although the positive correlation between stock market development and economic growth has been established empirically, the causal relationship between these variables is still an obscure point. Is it stock market development that spurs economic growth, or capital accumulation that drives the emergence and development of equity markets? Blackburn *et al.* (2005) provide an account of the possible two-way linkages between stock market development and economic growth, and an alternative interpretation of the development of equity markets. To these authors, the emergence of equity contracts is the result of lenders' attempts to solve multiple enforcement problems when a firm's choice of investment project and level of effort devoted to that project are private information. Capital accumulation can influence the development of equity markets because it can affect the degree of control that the lender has over these choices. The analysis is based on a principal–agent framework in which the borrower-firm (the agent) has access to an array of different projects, each with an expected return that depends on the risk of the project itself and on the amount of effort the borrower exerts. The lender (principal), who has the task of designing the optimal financial contract, cannot control the firm's effort directly, but has the option either to impose its own choice of project at a cost, or to leave this choice up to the borrower. The optimal financial contracts under these two alternative scenarios are not the same. When the lender chooses the project, the optimal financial contract is typically a debt contract. When the firm chooses the project, the contract is a mixture of debt and equity. The reason for this is that, when the choice of project is imposed by the lender, a fixed repayment (debt contract) is sufficient to induce the optimal level of effort by the firm. In contrast, when the choice of project is made by the borrower, a fixed repayment is not enough to induce the best level of effort, nor the best choice of project; in this case, part of the payment must be a function of the actual return (equity payment) in order to induce the borrower to exert the optimal effort.

The optimal choice of contract depends essentially on the cost to the lender of taking charge of project selection. In Blackburn *et al.* (2005) this cost is represented by the wage that the lender is forgoing by not supplying his/her labour in the market, and instead spending their time selecting and imposing the project choice on the borrower. At low levels of capital accumulation, when the return to labour is relatively low, and the wage rate is also low, this cost is low and the debt contract dominates. As the economy develops, and the wage rate prevailing in the market goes up, the cost of imposing the project choice increases until it eventually becomes optimal for the lender not to interfere directly in this choice – then the financial contract will involve both debt and equity. When equity markets appear, the economy jumps from a low capital accumulation path to a high capital accumulation path, so that growth is stimulated temporarily. The reason is that fewer resources are wasted in the economy for project selection. This could explain the positive impact of stock market development on growth.

The role of information asymmetries in financial contract design is extremely important, not only in qualitative but also in quantitative terms. Recently, Bolton and Freixas (2000) have argued that, when firms have superior information about the returns on their investments, the costs associated with the optimal security used to finance those investments depend on the degree of informational asymmetry. This is simply because lenders, who cannot a priori observe project returns, take an average of all possible outcomes. As in a typical 'lemons market', owners of projects with high returns will be penalized, since their projects will be valued at a lower average price. This is referred to as the dilution cost of asymmetric information. Under such circumstances, Bolton and Freixas (2000) show that firms' optimal capital structure consists of two main forms of securities: equity and/or debt. The type of security issued depends on the level of dilution costs, together with the level of bankruptcy costs associated with the loss of future income following the borrower's inability to repay the debt.

In a dynamic context, the level of information asymmetry is not fixed, but changes over time. It is commonly argued, for example, that in many countries the level of information available in the market increases considerably with the introduction of new communication technologies and the diffusion of many sources of information. It is therefore possible, in the wake of Bolton and Freixas' arguments, to imagine that economic growth and capital accumulation, by bringing about an improvement in the level of information diffusion, engender a modification in the costs of financial securities and spur the development of equity financing. Following this line of argument, the emergence and growth of stock markets can be seen as the result of a reduction in the severity of information problems.

This idea can be modelled in a simple way (see Capasso 2008). Assume that different types of firms have access to different sets of projects with different expected returns. Assume also that the return on all (or some) of these projects depends on specific market conditions. The market value of a project reflects the level of information available in the market. Under the assumption that the same project yields different returns to different firms (because some firms are more efficient than others, for example), the value attached by the market to a project will depend on which types of firms find it optimal to carry out that project. If a project is run only by high-productivity firms, then the market value will be high. On the other hand, if the project is run by less efficient firms, then its value will be lower, or 'diluted'. This dilution cost is one of the factors that can determine the optimal choice of one form of security over another. If lenders know which firms prefer to operate which project, then the set of projects undertaken will signal precisely the nature and type of firms in the market. If, on the other hand, some firms have access to common projects, then the types of firms in the market can be inferred only probabilistically, by observing the projects. The higher the number of firms accessing the same sets of projects, the lower the probability will be of correctly inferring a firm's type. Now, if the set of 'common projects' undertaken becomes smaller for some reason (for example, because some of these projects become economically inefficient), then the signal from the market becomes stronger and the possibility of inferring a firm's type becomes higher. The link with growth arises from the fact that capital accumulation reduces the incentive of some low productivity firms to operate projects that are typical of more efficient firms. Thus capital accumulation leads to an improvement in the 'visibility' of more efficient firms, it decreases the cost of equity issue and causes an expansion of stock markets.

Conclusions

The positive correlation between stock market development and economic growth is a well-known empirical fact. Stock markets appear to emerge and develop only when economies reach a reasonable size, and the level of capital accumulation is high. Notwithstanding such uncontroversial empirical evidence, the causal relationship remains a debated issue in the literature. Is it stock markets that boost growth (for example, by reducing liquidity and monitoring costs), or is it capital accumulation that induces a modification in the financial system, which causes the emergence of equity financing – for example, by engendering modifications in the optimal financial contract? In recent years, a growing body of theoretical literature has attempted to provide satisfactory answers to this question. These efforts have given rise to distinct methodological approaches that have highlighted both the macroeconomic and institutional aspects of the phenomenon, and its microeconomic roots.

On the one hand, this large body of investigation has disclosed many interesting features of financial market development and provided new insights on the effects of financial variables on economic growth, while on the other hand it has raised further questions, opening new avenues for further research. In particular, recent work, by focusing on individual firms' optimal financing choice and on the optimal financial contract, has transferred issues of corporate finance from a purely microeconomic level of discussion to a macroeconomic one, and have raised innovative and exciting questions that deserve to be dealt with. One of these is the role played by information dynamics and information technology diffusion on firms' financing choice and, in turn, on financial market development and economic growth.

Notes

1 Battacharia and Thakor (1993) develop a broad survey on the most relevant studies on financial intermediation. Levine (1997) presents a large survey on the latest literature on financial intermediation and economic growth.
2 Levine (1997) and Becsi and Wang (1997) provide a very broad review of this literature.

References

Allen, F. (1993) 'Stock Markets and Resource Allocation', in C. Mayer and X. Vives (eds), *Capital Markets and Financial Intermediation* (Cambridge: Cambridge University Press), 81–108.

Atje, R. and Jovanovic, B. (1993) 'Stock Markets and Development', *European Economic Review*, 37: 632–40.

Battacharya, S. and Thakor, A. V. (1993) 'Contemporary Banking Theory', *Journal of Financial Intermediation*, 3: 2–50.

Beck, T. and Levine, R. (2001) 'Stock Markets, Banks, and Growth: Correlation or Causality?', Policy Research Working Paper 2670, World Bank, Washington, DC.

Beck, T., Levine, R. and Loayza, N. (2000) 'Finance and the Sources of Growth', *Journal of Financial Economics*, 58(1–2): 261–300.

Beck, T., Demirgüç-Kunt, A., Levine, R. and Maksimovic, V. (2001) 'Financial Structure and Economic Development: Firm, Industry and Country Evidence', in A. Demirgüç-Kunt and R. Levine (eds), *Financial Structure and Economic Growth: A Cross-Country Comparison of Banks, Markets, and Development* (Cambridge, Mass.: MIT Press).

Becsi, Z. and Wang, P. (1997) 'Financial Development and Growth', *Economic Review*, Federal Reserve Bank of Atlanta, 46–62.

Bencivenga, V. R. and Smith, B. D. (1991) 'Financial Intermediation and Endogenous Growth', *Review of Economics Studies*, 58(2): 195–209.

Bencivenga, V., Smith, B. and Starr, R. M. (1996) 'Equity Markets, Transactions Costs, and Capital Accumulation: An Illustration', *The World Bank Economic Review*, 10(2): 241–65.

Blackburn, K. and Hung, V. (1998) 'A Theory of Growth, Financial Development and Trade', *Economica*, 65: 107–24.

Blackburn, K., Bose, N. and Capasso, S. (2005) 'Financial Development, Financing Choice and Economic Growth', *Review of Development Economics*, 9(2): 135–49.

Bolton, P. and Freixas, X. (2000) 'Equity, Bonds and Bank Debt: Capital Structure and Financial Market Equilibrium under Asymmetric Information', *Journal of Political Economy*, 2(208): 324–51.

Boyd, J. and Smith, B. (1996) 'The Coevolution of Real and Financial Sectors in the Growth Process', *The World Bank Economic Review*, 10(2): 371–96.

Boyd, J. and Smith, B. (1998) 'The Evolution of Debt and Equity Markets in Economic Development', *Economic Theory*, 12: 519–60.

Capasso, S. (2008) 'Endogenous Information Frictions, Stock Market Development and Economic Growth', *The Manchester School*, 76(2): 204–22.

De Gregorio, J. and Guidotti, P. E. (1995) 'Financial Development and Economic Growth', *World Development*, 23: 433–48.

Demirgüç-Kunt, A. and Levine, R. (1996a) 'Stock Market Development and Financial Intermediaries: Stylized Facts', *The World Bank Economic Review*, 10(2): 291–321.

Demirgüç-Kunt, A. and Levine, R. (1996b) 'Stock Markets, Corporate Finance and Economic Growth: An Overview', *The World Bank Economic Review*, 10: 223–39.

Demirgüç-Kunt, A. and Maksimovic, V. (1996) 'Stock Market Development and Financing Choices of Firms', *The World Bank Economic Review*, 10: 341–69.

Devereux, M. B. and Smith, G. W. (1994) 'International Risk Sharing and Economic Growth', *International Economic Review*, 35(4): 535–50.

Diamond, D. (1984) 'Financial intermediation and Delegated Monitoring', *Review of Economic Studies*, 51: 393–414.

Diamond, D. and Verrecchia, R. E. (1982) 'Optimal Managerial Contracts and Equilibrium Security Prices', *Journal of Finance*, 37: 275–87.

Gale, D. and Hellwig, M. (1985) 'Incentive-compatible Debt Contracts: The One-period Problem', *Review of Economic Studies*, 52: 647–63.

Goldsmith, R. Y. (1969) *Financial Structure and Development* (New Haven/London: Yale University Press).

Green, C. J., Kirkpatrick, C. and Murinde, V. (2005) *Finance and Development: Surveys of Theory, Evidence and Policy* (Cheltenham: Edward Elgar).

Greenwood, J. and Jovanovic, B. (1990) 'Financial Development, Growth, and the Distribution of Income', *Journal of Political Economy*, 98: 1076–107.

Greenwood, J. and Smith, B. (1997) 'Financial Markets in Development, and the Development of Financial Markets', *Journal of Economic Dynamics and Control*, 21: 141–81.

Grossman, S. (1976) 'On the Efficiency of Competitive Stock Markets Where Traders Have Diverse Information', *Journal of Finance*, 31: 573–85.

Grossman, S. (1978) 'Further Results on the Informational Efficiency of Competitive Stock Markets', *Journal of Economic Theory*, 18: 81–101.

Grossman, S. and Stiglitz, J. E. (1980) 'On the Impossibility of Informationally Efficient Markets', *American Economic Review*, 70: 393–408.

Holmstrom, B. and Tirole, J. (1993) 'Market Liquidity and Performance Monitoring', *Journal of Political Economy*, 101(4): 678–709.

Jensen, M. C. and Murphy, K. J. (1990) 'Performance Pay and Top-management Incentives', *Journal of Political Economy*, 98: 225–64.

King, R. G. and Levine, R. (1993a) 'Finance and growth: Schumpeter Might be Right', *Quarterly Journal of Economics*, 108: 717–37.

King, R. G. and Levine, R. (1993b) 'Finance Entrepreneurship, and Growth: Theory and Evidence', *Journal of Monetary Economics*, 32: 513–42.

Korajczyk, R. (1996) 'A Measure of Stock Market Integration for Developed and Emerging Markets', *The World Bank Economic Review*, 10(2): 267–89.

Kyle, A. S. (1984) 'Market Structure, Information, Futures Markets, and Price Formation', in G. Storey, A. Schmitz and A. H. Sarris (eds), *International Agricultural Trade: Advanced Readings in Price Formation, Market Structure, and Price Instability* (Boulder, Col.: Westview Press).

Laffont, J. and Tirole, J. (1988) 'Repeated Auctions of Incentive Contracts, Investment, and Bidding Parity with an Application to Takeovers', *Rand Journal of Economics*, 19: 516–37.

Leland, H. and Pyle, D. (1977) 'Informational Asymmetries, Financial Structure and Financial Intermediation', *Journal of Finance* (Papers and Proceedings), May.

Levine, R. (1991) 'Stock Markets, Growth and Tax Policy', *The Journal of Finance*, 46: 1445–65.

Levine, R. (1997) 'Financial Development and Economic Growth: Views and Agenda', *Journal of Economic Literature*, xxxv: 688–726.

Levine, R. and Zervos, S. (1996) 'Stock Market Development and Long-run Growth', *The World Bank Economic Review*, 10(2): 223–39.

Levine, R. and Zervos, S. (1998) 'Stock Markets, Banks and Economic Growth', *American Economic Review*, 88: 537–57.

McKinnon, R. I. (1973) *Money and Capital in Economic Development* (Washington, DC: Brookings Institution).

Miller, M. and Modigliani, F. (1958) 'The Cost of Capital, Corporation Finance and the Theory of Investment', *American Economic Review*, 48: 251–97.

Myers, S. C. and Majluf, N. S. (1984) 'Corporate Financing and Investment Decisions When Firms Have Information That Investors Do Not Have', *Journal of Financial Economics*, 13: 187–221.

Obstfeld, M. (1994) 'Risk-Taking, Global Diversification, and Growth', *American Economic Review*, 85(5): 1310–29.

Pagano, M. (1993) 'The Flotation of Companies on the Stock Market: A Coordination Failure Model', *European Economic Review*, 37: 1101–25.

Pagano, M., Panetta, F. and Zingales, L. (1998) 'Why Do Companies Go Public? An Empirical Analysis', *Journal of Finance*, 53: 27–61.

Saint-Paul, G. (1992) 'Technological Choice, Financial Markets and Economic Development', *European Economic Review*, 36: 763–81.

Scharfstein, D. (1988) 'The Disciplinary Role of Takeovers', *Review of Economic Studies*, 55: 185–99.

Singh, A. (1997) 'Financial Liberalisation, Stock Markets and Economic Development', *Economic Journal*, 107: 771–82.

Stein, J. C. (1988) 'Takeovers Threats and Managerial Myopia', *Journal of Political Economy*, 96: 61–80.

Townsend, R. (1979) 'Optimal Contracts and Competitive Markets with Costly State Verification', *Journal of Economic Theory*, 21(2): 265–93.

Williamson, S. D. (1986) 'Costly Monitoring, Financial Intermediation and Equilibrium Credit Contracting', *Journal of Monetary Economics*, 18: 159–79.

Williamson, S. D. (1987a) 'Costly Monitoring, Loan Contracts, and Equilibrium Credit Rationing', *Quarterly Journal of Economics*, 102: 135–45.

Williamson, S. D. (1987b) 'Financial Intermediation, Business Failures, and Real Business Cycles', *Journal of Political Economy*, 95: 1196–216.

World Bank (2004) *World Development Indicators* (Washington, DC: World Bank).

3
Financial Development and Economic Growth: Further Evidence from Panel Data Models

George Mavrotas and Sang-Ik Son

Introduction

Issues related to the overall relationship between financial development and economic growth have received considerable attention in recent years, and numerous studies have been published on this important topic. Although the issue is far from new,[1] in the 1990s empirical studies using large cross-section datasets emerged, with a particular focus on the empirics of the finance–growth relationship – see Fry (1988), Wachtel and Rousseau (1995), Hermes and Lensink (1996), Arestis and Demetriades (1997), Levine (1997), Demirgüç-Kunt and Levine (2001), World Bank (2001), Green and Kirkpatrick (2002), Wachtel (2004) and Green *et al.* (2005) among others, for comprehensive reviews of this literature.

A central issue is the measurement of financial development. As argued quite rightly by Bandiera *et al.* (2000), measuring financial-sector development is not an easy procedure, since there is no concrete definition of financial development. In this regard, an ideal index of financial development should attempt to measure both the various aspects of the deregulatory *and* the institution-building processes in financial-sector development. However, measuring these aspects is a difficult, if not impossible, task. Common measures of financial development used in the empirical literature have been financial depth or selected financial indicators. Financial depth in particular has been used extensively – in much of the earlier as well as recent literature – as a measure of financial-sector development. However, it could well be argued that, when one considers the likely channels through which a more developed financial system helps to promote growth, it becomes rather evident that, though quite useful and readily available, banking depth (usually measured as M2/GDP or M3/GDP) is unlikely to be a wholly reliable indicator of financial-sector development.[2]

In this chapter, we use a panel data set composed of 2,535 observations from the adjusted data for 65 countries (both industrial and developing) spanning the period 1960–99. The database, constructed on the basis of the World Bank database (described in detail in Beck *et al.* 1999), is an attempt to extend and develop the database on financial development and structure. We also employ various measures of financial development rather than using only the standard (though problematic) financial depth indicator; in doing so, we construct a financial development index, using the method of principal components, which was used subsequently in the econometric analysis. On the empirical front, we employed three main empirical panel data models: namely, the pooled model; the fixed effects model; and the random effects model, and carried out sensitivity analysis to examine the robustness of the empirical results obtained. Finally, this chapter also explores the linkages between finance and input factors of capital accumulation and productivity growth in the growth equation.

Data and measurement issues: financial and other variables

Constructing indicators of financial development

To measure the size of financial intermediaries we use, in line with Beck *et al.* (1999), the ratio of deposit money bank domestic assets to deposit money bank domestic assets plus central bank domestic assets (hereafter, commercial-central bank, or *CMB*). This indicator measures the relative importance of deposit money banks relative to central banks. The indicator is persuasive inasmuch as central banks lose relative importance as one moves from low- to high-income countries, and the other financial intermediaries gain relative importance. Thus a measure of the relative size of financial intermediaries is a useful indicator of development.

As another measure of the size of financial intermediaries, Beck *et al.* (1999) proposed the ratio of liquid liabilities to GDP. In this chapter, liquid liabilities (hereafter *LQ*) equals currency plus demand and interest-bearing liabilities of banks and other financial intermediaries divided by GDP. Liquid liabilities has been a typical measure of financial depth, the broadest available indicator of financial intermediation, including all financial sectors of central bank assets, deposit money banks assets, and other financial institutions assets.

To measure the activity of financial intermediaries, following Beck *et al.* (1999), we employ the ratio of private credit by deposit money banks and other financial institutions to GDP (hereafter, private credit or *PCR*). This indicator isolates credit issued to the private sector compared to credit issued to governments and public enterprises; thus it measures the mobilized savings that are channelled to private firms.

The above indicators can capture different aspects of the financial development process compared to a simple financial depth indicator; thus they seem to be more appropriate in examining the finance–growth relationship. However, we still need an 'eclectic' indicator to capture in a comprehensive way all kinds of changes in the financial sector in terms of activity, structure and size, rather than separate variables dealing with single aspects, respectively. In view of this, we construct, using principal component analysis, a Financial Sector Development Index (hereafter *FSDI*), which is the linear combination of the financial indicators *PCR*, *CMB* and *LQ*:

$$Z1_{it} = a_{1i}PCR_{it} + a_{2i}CMB_{it} + a_{3i}LQ_{it}$$

$$= FSDI_{it} \qquad (3.1)$$

where $Z1_{it}$ is the first principal component and coefficient vector (a_{1i}, a_{2i}, a_{3i}) calculated from the time-series data for each country. The method of principal components involves transforming the sub-variables into a new set of variables that will be uncorrelated pairwise, and of which the first will have the maximum possible variance, the second the maximum possible variance among those uncorrelated with the first, and so on. This approach has also been used by Demetriades and Luintel (1996), Bandiera *et al.* (2000) and Kelly and Mavrotas (2003) although not in the context of panel data analysis.

All raw data for the variables used in the empirical analysis have been obtained from the electronic version (2001) of the IMF's *International Financial Statistics* (IFS) and the electronic version (2001) of World Bank's *World Development Indicators* (WDI), apart from Ethiopia's GDP data, which was obtained from the UN's *Yearbook of National Accounts*. The raw dataset covers 65 countries over the period 1960–99 (forty years), but the time-span of data employed after adjustment is 1961–99 (thirty-nine years) for 65 countries.[3] The raw data can be split into two main groups: stock variables and flow variables. Whereas stock variables are measured at the end of a period, flow variables are defined relative to a period. This presents problems in measuring both in terms of correct timing and of deflating correctly. To address these problems, a data adjustment process is required.

For data adjustment we used the method proposed by Beck, Demirgüç-Kunt and Levine (1999) and Beck, Levine and Loayza (1999). More precisely, we deflated the end-of-year financial balance sheet items (f) by the end-of-year consumer price indices (CPI), and deflated the GDP series by the annual CPI. Then we computed the average of the real financial balance sheet item in year t and $t-1$, and divided the average by real GDP measured in year t. Accordingly, private credit (*PCR*) is calculated using IFS data and the following formula:

$$PCR_{it} = \frac{(0.5)\ [f_{it}/CPI(e)_{it} + f_{i,t-1}/CPI(e)_{i,t-1}]}{GDP_{it}/CPI(a)_{it}} \qquad (3.2)$$

where f stands for credit by deposit money banks and other financial institutions to the private sector (IFS lines 22d + 42d); *GDP* is from IFS (line 99b); *CPI(e)* is end-of-period CPI (IFS line 64); and *CPI(a)* is the average annual CPI. The f and end-of-period CPI are either the value for December or, where not available, the value for the last quarter. Where the end-of-period CPI in 1960 and 1961 is not available, the average annual CPI has been used. In addition, some data on CPI were estimated using the average annual increase rate of the following three years,[4] where CPI data in the early 1960s are missing or not available.

Commercial–central bank (*CMB*), which is the ratio of commercial bank domestic assets divided by commercial bank plus central bank domestic assets, is calculated using IFS data and the following formula:

$$CMB_{it} = \frac{DB_{it}}{DB_{it} + CB_{it}} \qquad (3.3)$$

where *DB* is assets of deposit money banks (IFS lines 22a–d), and *CB* is central bank assets (IFS lines 12a–d).

The data on liquid liabilities (*LQ*) is obtained from 'liquid liabilities (M3) as per cent of GDP' in the WDI 2001 of the World Bank. If the data from the World Bank were not fully available for the period of 1961–99 we used money and quasi-money (M2), calculated using IFS data and the following formula:

$$LQ_{it} = \frac{(0.5)\ [m_{it}/CPI(e)_{it} + m_{i,t-1}/CPI(e)_{i,t-1}]}{GDP_{it}/CPI(a)_{it}} \qquad (3.4)$$

where m is money (IFS line 34) plus quasi-money (IFS line 35); *GDP* (IFS line 99b); *CPI(e)* is end-of-period CPI (IFS line 64); and *CPI(a)* is the average annual CPI.

Our Financial Sector Development Index (*FSDI*) is calculated as the linear combination of the financial indicators *PCR*, *CMB* and *LQ*, using principal component analysis. Under the assumption of heterogeneity across countries we estimated coefficients of the principal components for each country in our sample.

Financial development and sources of growth

In line with the endogenous growth model, we also tried to examine the relationship between financial development and sources of growth. King and Levine (1993) have argued that financial services can accelerate growth by: (i) improving the allocation of capital; and (ii) enhancing the productivity of firms. In this case, the dependent variables are physical-capital accumulation (K) and productivity growth (φ); ln K denotes the natural-log level of real gross fixed capital formation. These data also come from the WDI of the World Bank. If they are not available from WDI, the data on K are calculated using the raw data obtained from IFS (IFS line 93e, Gross Fixed Capital Formation).

To measure productivity growth, φ, we use Lucas's (1993) endogenous growth theoretical framework:

$$y(t) = AK(t)^{\alpha}[u\,H(t)]^{(1-\alpha)} \tag{3.5}$$

where u is the fraction of time people spend producing goods; H is human capital; and $\beta - 1 - \alpha$. In this model, the growth of human capital input depends on the savings rate s:

$$\frac{dK(t)}{dt} = sy(t) \tag{3.6}$$

while the growth of human capital depends on the amount of quality-adjusted time devoted to its production:

$$\frac{dH(t)}{dt} = \delta(1 - u)H(t) \tag{3.7}$$

where $\delta(\geq 0)$ is the depreciation rate.

We can specify the effective labour force, $E = uH(t) = uH(0)e^{\delta(1-u)t}$. Thus

$$y(t) = AK(t)^{\alpha}\,E(t)^{(1-\alpha)} \tag{3.8}$$

Accordingly, the effective labour force allocates its time fraction (u) to work and the remaining time fraction ($1 - u$) to human capital accumulation; that is, education and human capital evolves at the growth rate $H/H = \delta(1 - u)$. As an actual measure of productivity, we define the variable effective labour force (E) as a labour force (L) multiplied by human capital *(Sch)*; that is, $E = L \times Sch$. The data on labour force are obtained from 'Labour force, total' in the World Development Indicators, while Human Capital *(Sch)* is from 'School enrolment, tertiary' in the World Development Indicators 2001. After taking natural logarithms on both sides and time derivatives to get the growth rate of aggregate output, the above equation is rewritten as

$$\frac{y}{y} = \frac{A}{A} + \alpha \frac{K}{K} + (1 - \alpha) \frac{E}{E} \qquad (3.9)$$

Thus the measure of total factor productivity is given by

$$\varphi = \frac{A}{A} = \frac{y}{y} - \alpha \frac{K}{K} - (1 - \alpha) \frac{E}{E} \qquad (3.10)$$

In other words, we can measure productivity growth by subtracting the increase rate of gross fixed capital formation and the growth rate of human capital augmented labour force from the GDP growth rate.

Other variables

In order to explore the linkages between financial-sector development and the growth variables we also use a conditioning information set containing the other explanatory variables in the growth model. Under the open economy assumption, the conditioning information set includes the basic input variables, control and policy variables as well as open economy variables.

Basic input variables

The basic input variables include the variables of scale effects and human capital. A scale effect means that an expansion of the aggregate labour force, L, raises the per capita growth rate for the economy in the endogenous growth model. In particular, under the assumptions of learning-by-doing and knowledge spillovers, the per capita growth rates would increase over time as the labour force grew over time. We consider a simple neoclassical production function with labour-augmenting technology for firm i: $Y_i = F(K_i, A_i L_i)$, where A_i is the index of knowledge available to the firm. Under the assumptions of learning-by-doing and knowledge spillovers,[5] the change in each firm's technology term, A_i, corresponds to the economy's overall learning and is proportional to the change in the aggregate capital stock, K. Thus we can replace A_i by K in the above equation, and if the production function takes the Cobb–Douglas form, then, output for firm i is given by

$$Y_i = A \cdot (K_i)^\alpha \cdot (KL_i)^{1-\alpha} \qquad (3.11)$$

The private marginal product of capital can be obtained by differentiating with respect to K_i, and assuming $k_i = k$:

$$\frac{\partial Y_i}{\partial K_i} = A\alpha L^{1-\alpha} \tag{3.12}$$

A firm's profit can be written as

$$L_i \cdot [f(k_i, K) - (r + \delta) \cdot k_i - w] \tag{3.13}$$

where $f(\cdot)$ is the intensive form of the production function in Equation (3.11), δ is the depreciation rate, $r + \delta$ is the rental price of capital, and w is the wage rate. Profit maximization and zero-profit condition imply

$$\frac{\partial y_i}{\partial k_i} = f(k, K) = r + \delta, \quad \text{or} \quad r = \frac{\partial y_i}{\partial K_i} - \delta$$

$$\frac{\partial Y_i}{\partial L_i} = f(k, K) - k \cdot f(k, K) = w \tag{3.14}$$

If we substitute Equation (3.14) into the condition for optimization, $\gamma_c = (1/\theta) \cdot (r - \rho)$, from the Keynes–Ramsey rule, then

$$\gamma_c = \left(\frac{1}{\theta}\right) \cdot (A\alpha L^{1-\alpha} - \delta - \rho) \tag{3.15}$$

where γ_c equals growth rate, θ is the elasticity of marginal utility, and ρ is the ▓▓▓▓▓▓me preference. Therefore, this result reflects the positive effect of L on the private marginal product of capital by satisfying the condition of $f'(L) > 0$, and an expansion of labour force raises the per capita growth rate (Barro and Sala-i-Martin 1995). Data on the variable representing scale effects are obtained from 'Labour force, total' in WDI 2001.

The variable human capital (*Sch*) is used to obtain the data on the effective labour force (*E*) to calibrate the values of parameters of labour and capital, and measure productivity growth (φ). We use 'percentage of tertiary school enrolment to total population' as a proxy for the human capital stock in the economy. The data on human capital are obtained from 'School enrolment, tertiary' in the WDI 2001, as described above.

Control and open economy variables

The control variables used in the empirical analysis are the two policy variables – that is, the inflation rate (*INFL*) and the ratio of government expenditure to GDP (*GEXP*), as indicators of macroeconomic stability in the growth equation. The data source for both variables is the WDI. Under the assumption of an open economy, our conditioning information set includes two open economy variables: openness to trade (*OTR*) and foreign direct investment (*FDI*). The variable *OTR* is the sum of exports and imports as a share of GDP. Data on trade openness are obtained from IFS (IFS lines 90c + 98c).

The theoretical foundation regarding the effects of FDI on growth derives from either neo-classical models or endogenous growth models. In neoclassical models of growth, FDI increases the volume of investment and its efficiency, and leads to long-term level effects and medium-term transitional increases in growth. Endogenous growth models, on the other hand, consider long-run growth as a function of technological progress, and provide a framework in which FDI can permanently increase the rate of growth in the host economy through technology transfer, diffusion and spillover effects. The data on *FDI* are obtained from 'Foreign direct investment, net inflows (% of GDP)' in WDI 2001. The variables used in this chapter and their relevant data sources are reported in Table 3.1.

Table 3.1   Variables and data sources used

Variables	Notation	Unit	Data sources
1. Dependent variables			
Per capita GDP growth	Y	$\ln(Y)$	WDI, IFS
Capital growth	K	$\ln(K)$	WDI, IFS
Productivity growth	φ	1 + increase rate	rate of tu
2. Financial variables			
Financial Sector Development Index	*FSDI*	Principal component of *PCR, CMB, LQ*	
Private credit	*PCR*	f/Y	IFS
Liquid liabilities	*LQ*	m/Y	WDI, IFS
Commercial–central bank	*CMB*	*Com.B./Cen.B.*	IFS
3. Conditioning information set			
(i) Basic input variables			
Scale effects	*SE*	$\ln(SE)$	WDI
Human capital	*Sch*	%, tertiary education	WDI
(ii) Control and policy variables			
Government expenditure	*GEXP*	*G-exp./Y*	IFS
Inflation rate	*INFL*	1 + increase rate	WDI
(iii) Open economy variables			
Openness to trade	*OTR*	$(ex+im)/Y$	IFS, WDI
Foreign direct investment	*FDI*	%, net inflows to GDP	WDI

Notes and Sources:
IFS – *International Financial Statistics*, IMF.
WDI – *World Development Indicators*, World Bank.

Empirical results

Specification and estimation of the empirical model

We employ a one-way error component model that only has individual effects. The error component model is probably the most commonly used approach for modelling economic relationships using panel data.[6]

The functional form to be tested empirically regarding the finance–growth relationship is as follows:

$$Y_{it} = \beta_1 FSDI_{it} + X_{it}\beta'_{ik} + \epsilon_{it} \tag{3.16}$$

$$k = 2,\ldots, K; \; i = 1,\ldots,N; \; t = 1,\ldots,T$$

where Y denotes per capita real GDP growth; $FSDI$ is the financial variable that is the first principal component obtained from PCR, CMB, LQ; and X is a $(K-1) \times 1$ row vector of the conditioning information set that controls for other independent variables associated with economic growth; β is the $K \times 1$ column vector of slope parameters; and ϵ is the white noise error term. This equation will be estimated using three different panel specifications: the *pooled model*; the *fixed effects model*; and the *random effects model*.

We use a one-way error component model for the disturbances, with

$$\epsilon_{it} = \mu_i + v_{it} \tag{3.17}$$

where μ_i denotes the individual specific effect and v_{it} denotes the remainder disturbance. In the case of the random effects model we further assume that

$$E[v_{it}] = E[\mu_i] = 0 \tag{3.18}$$

$$E[\mu\mu'] = \sigma_\mu^2 I_N, \qquad E[vv'] = \sigma_v^2 I_{NT}$$

$$E[v_{it}\mu_j] = 0 \quad \text{for all } i, t \text{ and } j$$

$$E[v_{it}v_{js}] = 0 \quad \text{if } t \neq s \text{ or } i \neq j$$

$$E[\mu_i\mu_j] = 0 \quad \text{if } i \neq j$$

Table 3.2 reports the results of the panel regressions, with adjusted data of 2,535 observations from the sample of 65 countries over the period 1960–99. Overall, the estimation results seem to suggest a statistically significant and positive relationship between financial-sector

Table 3.2   Estimation results from panel data models: full sample, 65 countries, 1960–99

Dependent variable: Y_{it}	Pooled model (*OLS estimator*)	Fixed effects model (*WG estimator*)	Random effects model (*GLS estimator*)
Constant	9.179351	–	7.220740
	(0.0000)		(0.0000)
FSDI	0.258960	0.505274	0.505676
	(0.0142)	(0.0000)	(0.0000)
lnSE	−0.003476	0.294496	0.292341
	(0.9296)	(0.0000)	(0.0000)
GEXP	7.888969	0.662648	0.666403
	(0.0000)	(0.0000)	(0.0000)
INFL	0.004546	−0.00029	−0.00028
	(0.0166)	(0.0676)	(0.0700)
OTR	−0.092896	0.304499	0.305842
	(0.2712)	(0.0000)	(0.0000)
FDI	−0.092896	0.013785	0.013810
	(0.0024)	(0.0000)	(0.0000)
No. of observations	2535	2535	2535
DF	2528	2464	2528
R_2	0.0410	0.9941	–
F_1 test	18.03	5934.35	–
	(0.0000)	(0.0000)	
F_2 test	–	6222.73	–
		(0.0000)	
LR test	–	12906.88	–
		(0.0000)	
LM test	–	–	45265.15
			(0.0000)
Hausman test	–	–	10.75
			(0.0963)

Note: Parentheses reports *P*-value of *t*-statistic.

development and economic growth. The second column in the table reports OLS estimation results related to the pooled model, the third column reports results related to the within-group estimation of the fixed effects model, and the fourth column shows GLS estimation coefficients in the random effects model.

In the case of the pooled model, the coefficient of *FSDI* is positive, in line with findings of much of the literature on the subject, but the other coefficients are rather inconsistent with their respective hypotheses. From the values of the estimated *t*-statistics it can be seen that the coefficients of *SE* and *OTR* are not statistically significant at any level, while *FSDI* and *INFL* are significant at the 5 per cent level and *FDI* at the 1 per cent significance level. Testing the overall significance of the regression using F_1 value of 18.03 with $K(6)$ df in the numerator and $NT - K - 1(2528)$ df in the denominator rejects the null hypothesis H_0: $\beta_1 = \beta_2 = \ldots = \beta_K = 0$ at the 1 per cent level of significance.

When we include the fixed effects in the specification, all the estimated coefficients are statistically significant at the 1 per cent level apart from *INFL* (significant at the 10 per cent level), as we can see from Table 3.2 (column 3). The R^2 value of 0.9941 in the fixed effects model is extremely high compared to the very low explanatory power of the pooled model. The estimator of standard deviation in the pooled model is 2.1543 while that in the fixed effects model is 0.1997. This suggests that adding the fixed effects to the model reduces the amount of residual variation substantially.[7]

When we consider the random effects model, the GLS estimator is

$$\hat{\beta}_{GLS} = (X'W_nX + \theta X'B_nX)^{-1}(X'W_nX + \theta X'B_n y) \qquad (3.19)$$

where

$$\theta = \frac{\sigma_\nu^2}{\sigma_\nu^2 + T\sigma_\mu^2} = \frac{0.0398839}{(0.0398839 + 39 \times 6.26411)} = 0.00016323$$

The value of θ is negligibly trivial. This means that the GLS estimator in the random effects model tends towards to the within-group estimator rather than the between-group estimator. In addition, the P-values of t-statistics indicate that all the estimated coefficients of the independent variables are statistically significant at the 1 per cent level, apart from *INFL*, which is significant at the 10 per cent level.

Testing for fixed effects and random effects

In testing the significance of the fixed effects, the F_2 test and likelihood ratio (*LR*) test perform well for the one-way error component model. The F_2 test can test the joint significance of the dummies; that is, H_0: $\mu = \mu_i \forall i$. This is a simple Chow test with the restricted residual sums of squares (*RRSS*) being that of OLS on the pooled model and the unrestricted residual sum of squares (*URSS*) being that of the within-group estimation on the fixed effects model. Thus

$$F_2 = \frac{(RRSS - URSS)/(N-1)}{URSS/(NT - K - N)} = \frac{(R_U^2 - R_R^2)/(N-1)}{(1 - R_U^2)/(NT - K - N)} \sim F_{n-1,\,n(t-1)-k}$$

$$= \frac{(0.9941 - 0.041)/64}{(1 - 0.9941)/2464} = 6222.731 \tag{3.20}$$

This value of the F_2 statistic with 64 df of numerator and 2464 df of denominator is highly significant at the 1 per cent level. The one-sided *LR* test for testing the significance of the fixed effects has the following form:

$$LR = -2 \log \frac{l(res)}{l(unres)} \quad asy \sim \chi^2(J)$$

$$= -2(1 - 5930.831 - 522.60) = 12906.886 \tag{3.21}$$

where $l(res)$ denotes the restricted maximum likelihood value being that of OLS on the pooled model, while $l(unres)$ denotes the unrestricted maximum likelihood value being that of within-group estimation on the fixed effects model. This is distributed as the chi-square distribution with 64 df equal to the number of restrictions imposed (J). The *P*-value of obtaining a chi-square value of 12906.886 is about 0.0000. Hence one could reject the null hypothesis that it has no fixed effect; that is, $H_0: \mu = \mu_i \,\forall i$.

As a mis-specification test for the random effects model, the Lagrange-multiplier (LM) and Hausman tests are widely used. For the random one-way error component model, the LM test to test $H_0: \sigma_\mu^2 = 0$ has a test statistic:

$$LM = \frac{NT}{2(T-1)} \left[\frac{\hat{\epsilon}'(I_N \otimes J_T)\hat{\epsilon}}{\hat{\epsilon}'\hat{\epsilon}} \right]^2 \quad asy \sim \chi^2(1)$$

$$= 45265.15 \tag{3.22}$$

where $\hat{\epsilon}$ is the OLS residual vector (Breusch and Pagan 1980). Under the null hypothesis, LM is asymptotically distributed as chi-squared with one degree of freedom. The 1 per cent critical value from the chi-squared distribution with one degree of freedom is 6.6349, so the value of the LM statistic is highly significant. Thus the evidence in favour of the error components model is robust.

In the case of panel data models, a Hausman test can also be performed (see Baltagi 1995). The null hypothesis is H_0: $E(\epsilon_{it}/X_{it}) = 0$, which is a critical assumption in the error component regression. If the disturbances contain individual invariant effects (the μ_i) which are unobserved and correlated with the X_{it}, then, $E(\epsilon_{it}/X_{it}) \neq 0$, and the *GLS* estimator $\hat{\beta}_{GLS}$ becomes biased and inconsistent for β. However, the transformation within wipes out these μ_i and leaves the within-group estimator $\hat{\beta}_{WG}$ unbiased and consistent for β. The test compares $\hat{\beta}_{GLS}$ and $\hat{\beta}_{WG}$, both of which are consistent under the null hypothesis H_0: $E(\epsilon_{it}/X_{it}) = 0$, but which will have different probability limits if H_0 is not true. In fact, $\hat{\beta}_{WG}$ is consistent whether H_0 is true or not, while $\hat{\beta}_{WG}$ is consistent and asymptotically efficient under H_0, but is inconsistent when H_0 is false. The essential ingredient for the test is based on $\hat{q} = (\hat{\beta}_{GLS} - \hat{\beta}_{WG})$. The variance of $\hat{q}$ is

$$\text{var}\,\hat{q} = \text{var}(\hat{\beta}_{GLS}) + \text{var}(\hat{\beta}_{WG}) - \text{cov}(\hat{\beta}_{GLS}, \hat{\beta}_{WG}) - \text{cov}(\hat{\beta}_{GLS}, \hat{\beta}_{WG})' \qquad (3.23)$$

Under H_0, plim $\hat{q} = 0$, and $\text{cov}(\hat{q}, \hat{\beta}_{GLS}) = 0$. Using the fact that $\hat{\beta}_{GLS} - \beta = (X'\Omega^{-1}X)^{-1}X'\Omega^{-1}\epsilon$, and $\hat{\beta}_{WG} - \beta = (X'WX)^{-1}X'W\epsilon$, we finally get

$$\text{cov}(\hat{\beta}_{GLS}, \hat{q}) = \text{var}(\hat{\beta}_{GLS}) - \text{cov}(\hat{\beta}_{GLS}, \hat{\beta}_{WG})$$

$$= (X'\Omega^{-1}X)^{-1} - (X'\Omega^{-1}X')^{-1}X'\Omega^{-1}E(\epsilon\epsilon')WX(X'WX)^{-1}$$

$$= (X'\Omega^{-1}X)^{-1} - (X'\Omega^{-1}X')^{-1} = 0 \qquad (3.24)$$

or

$$\text{cov}(\hat{\beta}_{GLS}, \hat{\beta}_{WG}) = \text{var}(\hat{\beta}_{GLS})$$

Inserting this into Equation (3.23) produces the required covariance matrix for the test:

$$\text{var}\,\hat{q} = \text{var}(\hat{\beta}_{WG} - \hat{\beta}_{GLS}) = \text{var}(\hat{\beta}_{WG}) - \text{var}(\hat{\beta}_{GLS})$$

$$= \sigma_v^2(X'WX)^{-1} - (X'\Omega^{-1}X)^{-1} \qquad (3.25)$$

Hence, the Hausman test statistic is given by

$$H = (\hat{\beta}_{WG} - \hat{\beta}_{GLS})[\text{var}(\hat{q})]^{-1}(\hat{\beta}_{WG} - \hat{\beta}_{GLS}) \qquad asy \sim \chi^2(K) \qquad (3.26)$$

and under H_0 of no correlation is asymptotically distributed as $\chi^2(K)$, where K denotes the dimension of slope vector β. In our case, the value of the Hausman test statistic is $H = 10.75$ (P-value $= 0.0963$). Hence, the null hypothesis is not rejected at the 1 per cent level of significance, and even at the 5 per cent level, because the 5 per cent critical values from the χ^2 distribution with 6 df are 12.59. In other words, the hypothesis that the individual effects are uncorrelated with the other regressors in the model cannot be rejected. The result of the test clearly favours the GLS estimator over the random effects model. Therefore, based on the LM test, which is decisive regarding the presence of individual effects, and the Hausman test, which suggests that these effects are uncorrelated with the other variables in the model, we can conclude that, from the two alternatives we have considered, the random effects model seems to be the preferred choice.

Decomposing the total effect of *FSDI* on economic growth

Our financial sector development indicator has a positive sign, in line with much of the empirical literature of the impact of financial-sector development on growth. It is important to remember, however, that the financial-sector development indicator employed in the empirical analysis, namely *FSDI*, is a representative financial variable, which is a linear combination of the three financial indicators, namely private credit (*PCR*), commercial–central bank (*CMB*) and liquid liabilities (*LQ*). In view of this, we can derive the individual effects of the three variables – namely, *PCR*, *CMB* and *LQ* – on economic growth by decomposing the coefficient of *FSDI*. Following Kendall's method (for an illustration, see Johnston 1991), in order to obtain estimates of the coefficients of *PCR*, *CMB* and *LQ* we need to regress Y on the retained principal components and transform back from the regression coefficients on the principal components. Suppose, for example, that there are three X variables and we retain only the first principal component:

$$z_1 = a_{11}X_1 + a_{21}X_2 + a_{31}X_3 \tag{3.27}$$

The regression of Y on z_1 is then

$$y = b_1 z_1 + e \tag{3.28}$$

Using Equations (3.27) and (3.28) we can compute the effects of each of the Xs on y as follows:

$$y = b_1 a_{11}X_1 + b_1 a_{21}X_2 + b_1 a_{31}X_3 \tag{3.29}$$

And finally we can obtain the following result:

$$Y = 0.24703 \, PCR + 0.19613 \, CMB + 0.23155 \, LQ \qquad (3.30)$$

This result shows that the three financial variables have a positive effect on economic growth. The coefficient estimates of *PCR, CMB* and *LQ* are 0.247, 0.1961 and 0.2315, respectively. Thus, in view of the magnitude of estimates, it can be concluded that *PCR* is the most effective indicator on real per capita GDP growth compared to the other two indicators. *LQ* seems to have an impact similar to *PCR*, while *CMB* has a relatively small effect on economic growth. From these results we can conclude that all the financial variables of private credit, liquid liabilities and commercial–central bank are not only positively related to real per capita GDP but they also have significant impacts on economic growth.

Industrial *vis-à-vis* developing countries

It makes sense to assume rather different effects of financial-sector development on growth between industrial and developing countries. To test this hypothesis we divided the sample into two subgroups of 24 industrial countries and 41 developing countries, and obtained the regression results reported in Table 3.3. When we look at the results of the industrial country group, the results of the mis-specification tests seem to favour the fixed effects model over both the random effects model and the pooled model. In the fixed effects model, *FSDI* enters significantly at the 1 per cent level with a coefficient estimate of 0.2370, and *SE, GEXP* and *OTR* are significant at the 1 per cent level, while *INFL* and *FDI* appear to be insignificant.

In the case of developing countries, the reported mis-specification diagnostics seem to favour the random effects model both over the fixed effects model and the pooled model. All the coefficients have their respective predicted signs in the random effects model as well as in the fixed effects model. In the random effects model, *FSDI* appears significantly at the 1 per cent level with the coefficient estimate of 0.6167, and *SE, OTR* and *FDI* are significant at the 1 per cent level, while *GEXP* is significant at the 10 per cent level, and *INFL* is insignificant.

From a financial perspective, the different results of β_1 – that is, 0.2370 for industrial countries and 0.6167 for developing countries – have an economically significant interpretation. First, the slope coefficient measures the change in Y for a given change in the regressors X. In our case, the changes in Y for X in developing countries are larger than in industrial countries. Thus, the lower value of β_1 for industrial countries

Table 3.3 Regression results from estimation of panel data models using two subgroups: 24 industrial countries and 41 developing countries, 1960–99

Dependent variable: Y_{it}	Industrial countries			Developing countries		
	Pooled model	Fixed effects model	Random effects model	Pooled model	Fixed effects model	Random effects model
Constant	10.212889	–	2.122235	9.549002	–	7.264956
	(0.0000)		(0.0006)	(0.0000)		(0.0000)
FSDI	−0.925303	0.237076	0.241965	0.346977	0.616216	0.616757
	(0.0000)	(0.0000)	(0.0000)	(0.0294)	(0.0000)	(0.0000)
lnSE	0.278059	1.015387	0.981914	−0.066555	0.245518	0.243823
	(0.0000)	(0.0000)	(0.0000)	(0.1499)	(0.0000)	(0.0000)
GEXP	−6.951311	1.665672	1.726740	6.125087	0.181131	0.183888
	(0.0005)	(0.0000)	(0.0000)	(0.0000)	(0.0869)	(0.0822)
INFL	0.085219	0.001154	0.001169	0.004745	−0.000243	−0.000241
	(0.0000)	(0.2245)	(0.2188)	(0.0078)	(0.1209)	(0.1243)
OTR	0.548999	0.758296	0.763931	−0.494136	0.131022	0.132089
	(0.0616)	(0.0000)	(0.0000)	(0.0581)	(0.0003)	(0.0002)

FDI	−0.085572	− 0.003907	− 0.003524	−0.006691	0.010930	0.010986
	(0.0702)	(0.3080)	(0.3574)	(0.8608)	(0.0019)	(0.0018)
No. of obs.	936	936	936	1599	1599	1599
DF	929	906	929	1592	1552	1592
R^2	0.1255	0.9961	–	0.0303	0.9934	–
F_1 test	22.24	8017.41	–	8.32	5080.44	–
	(0.0000)	(0.0000)		(0.0000)	(0.0000)	
F_2 test	–	8834.44	–	–	5663.77	–
		(0.0000)			(0.0000)	
LR test	–	5070.61	–	–	7979.41	–
		(0.0000)			(0.0000)	
LM test	–	–	13416.63	–	–	28509.28
			(0.0000)			(0.0000)
Hausman test	–	–	25.85	–	–	7.17
			(0.0002)			(0.3049)

Note: Parentheses reports *P*-value of *t*-statistic.

indicates that industrial countries have developed at faster growth rates, together with a higher financial development process. Developing countries have been through relatively slower financial development processes compared to the speed of economic growth, resulting in a relatively higher value of β_1. This basically tells us that higher financial development is credited with (stimulating) faster economic growth.

On the other hand, the slope coefficient β_1 represents the output elasticity of financial-sector development. Accordingly, the result illustrates that, in the industrial countries, one standard deviation increase in *FSDI* would be predicted to increase annual real per capita GDP by 0.23 per cent, while in the case of developing countries it would raise output by 0.61 per cent. In other words, a change in financial-sector development encourages more effective economic growth in developing countries compared to industrial countries.

The impact of other variables

In this part we discuss the economic implications following from the results of the variables related to the conditioning information set:

(i)   *Scale effects*: the theories of endogenous growth imply some benefits from larger scale. In particular, if there are significant setup costs at the country level for inventing or adapting new products or production techniques, then larger economies would perform better. We test for the existence of a worldwide scale effect by adding to the regressions. The variable *SE* is logarithmic; thus, its coefficient indicates the output elasticity of the labour force. The relevant coefficient estimate seems to be significantly positive. The magnitude of the coefficient tells us that a 1 per cent increase in the labour force leads on average to about a 0.2923 per cent increase in real output (random effects in Table 3.2). The result supports the theoretical arguments of the scale effects in the endogenous growth model, namely, that an expansion of the aggregate labour force raises the per capita growth rate in the economy. When we run regressions by dividing our sample into two country groups, the estimated coefficient for *SE* of the industrial country group is 1.0153 (fixed effects in Table 3.3), which is larger than 0.2438 (random effects in Table 3.3) of the developing country group. It implies that the output elasticity of the labour force is higher in industrial countries than in developing countries.

(ii) *Government expenditure*: the estimated coefficient of *GEXP*, which is the ratio of government expenditure to GDP, is positive (0.6664), as reported in Table 3.2. The magnitude of the effect is considerable; that is, a 1 per cent change in *GEXP* increases real per capita GDP by 0.66 per cent. It is notable that government expenditure could affect economic growth both positively or negatively. *GEXP* affects economic growth through its impact on both the assets market and the goods market. In our result, the significantly positive coefficient seems to suggest that government expenditure has a positive impact on the growth process in the full sample of 65 countries.

(iii) *Inflation*: the relationship between inflation and economic growth is more complex, because inflation affects economic growth indirectly through real money balances in saving or investment functions, rather than directly. Our empirical results seem to suggest that, for the full sample, the estimated coefficient on *INFL* is negative – −0.00028 – as shown in Table 3.2. The result supports the argument that inflation has a negative effect on growth, even if the magnitude of the impact is small. After allowing for different levels of development (see our two subgroups of industrial and developing countries), the developing country group reveals a negative coefficient estimate of −0.0002, as shown in Table 3.3. In contrast to the result found for the developing country group, the industrial country group shows a positive coefficient estimate of 0.0011, as reported in Table 3.3.

(iv) *Open economy*: as far as open economy variables are concerned, the estimated coefficient of *OTR* is positive (0.3058) and highly significant, as shown in Table 3.2. We recall that *OTR* is the ratio of total export and import to GDP. So, on average, a 1 per cent change in the ratio of total foreign trade to GDP raises real per capita GDP by 0.3 per cent. The positive coefficient means that openness to trade is positively related to economic growth. This result is consistent with the theory that openness to trade increases real income in a country by increasing economic efficiency. In the case of industrial countries, the estimated coefficient is 0.7639: larger than the 0.1320 of developing countries. In other words, the growth rate of industrial countries seems to be more sensitive to trade openness compared to the case of developing countries. With regard to the other open economy variable used in this chapter, *FDI*, it has a coefficient estimate of 0.0138, with the expected sign in Table 3.2. Since *FDI* is the ratio of foreign direct investment to GDP, GDP is increased by about 0.01 per cent for each 1 per cent rise in *FDI*. In the case of developing countries, the result is consistent with the hypothesis that *FDI* can increase the rate of growth in the host economy through technology transfer and spillover effects. In contrast, industrial countries show a negative coefficient of (−0.0035).

Financial variables and sources of growth

In this part we also examine the relationship between *finance and sources of growth*. Levine (1992) and King and Levine (1993) have argued that financial services can accelerate growth by improving the allocation of capital and by enhancing the productivity of firms. To test the above hypothesis we can rewrite Lucas's (1993) endogenous growth model, adopting Cobb–Douglas technology, as

$$Y_{it} = A_{it}\, K_{it}^{\alpha}\, E_{it}^{\beta} \tag{3.31}$$

In the neoclassical model and the endogenous-growth specification, including Lucas's (1993) model, the factor parameters are constrained to levels consistent with constant returns to scale, so that $\alpha + \beta = 1$, and usually $\alpha = 0.3$ and $\beta = 1 - \beta = 0.7$ are assumed. However, we tried to calibrate the values of α and β using the method of Benhabib and Spiegel (2000). After taking natural logarithms of both sides of Equation (3.31) we can rewrite it as

$$\ln Y_{it} = \ln A_{it} + \alpha \ln K_{it} + \beta \ln E_{it} + \mu_i + v_{it} \tag{3.32}$$

which is a one-way error component model. In order to calibrate the values of parameters α and β, we run a regression to obtain the estimation results reported in Table 3.4. The dataset remains the same as before. On the basis of the mis-specification test results we chose the GLS estimator associated with the random effects model:

$$\ln Y = 9.5917 + 0.1512 \ln K + 0.5599 \ln E \tag{3.33}$$

This result gives the parameters $\alpha = 0.1512$ and $\beta = 0.5599$; that is, decreasing returns to scale with $\alpha + \beta < 1$.

We can examine the relationship between finance and capital growth by using the following functional form:

$$\ln K_{it} = \beta_1 FSDI_{it} + X_{it}\beta_k' + \mu_i + v_{it} \tag{3.34}$$

where $\ln K$ represents the natural-log level of real gross fixed capital formation. The estimation results are reported in Table 3.A1 in Appendix 2 on pages 66–7. The LM test and Hausman test suggest that the fixed effects

Table 3.4 Base growth regressions: full sample, 65 countries, 1960–99

Dependent variable: y	Pooled model	Fixed effects model	Random effects model
Constant	9.241477	–	9.591717
	(0.0000)		(0.0000)
K	0.273596	0.151366	0.151222
	(0.3521)	(0.0000)	(0.0000)
E	0.193133	0.559210	0.559915
	(0.0000)	(0.0000)	(0.0000)
No. of observations	2535	2535	2535
DF	2532	2468	2532
R^2	0.0502	0.9936	0.0261
F_1 test	66.91	5930.04	–
	(0.0000)	(0.0000)	
F_2 test	–	5708.48	–
		(0.0000)	
LR test	–	12685.5	–
		(0.0000)	
LM test	–	–	46569.20
			(0.0000)
Hausman test	–	–	2.77
			(0.2504)

Note: Parentheses reports P-value of t-statistic.

model is preferred over both to the random effects model and the pooled model.

In the fixed effects model (see Table 3.A1, column 2) all the variables appear significant, apart from *FDI*. The coefficient for *FSDI* in particular is highly significant, with a positive sign. This result provides robust evidence of a positive role for financial development in encouraging physical-capital accumulation. The coefficient estimate implies that a 1 per cent point increase of *FSDI* would result in a 0.5185 per cent higher real physical-capital accumulation per year. Consequently, our results seem to support King and Levine's (1993) argument that financial services can accelerate growth by improving the allocation of capital.

Next, in order to examine the relationship between finance and productivity growth, we adopt the values of $\alpha = 0.1512$ and $\beta = 0.5599$ above. Using these values for α and β, we can obtain the data for total factor productivity growth, φ, since

$$\varphi = \frac{A}{A} = \frac{Y}{Y} - 0.1512 \frac{K}{K} - 0.5599 \frac{E}{E} \qquad (3.35)$$

To examine the relationship between finance and productivity growth, we use the following functional form:

$$\varphi_{it} = \beta_1 FSDI_{it} + X_{it}\beta_k' + \mu_i + v_{it} \tag{3.36}$$

where φ represents the increase rate of productivity, and the other variables are the same as described previously. Table 3.A2 in Appendix 2 (see pp. 68–9) reports the estimation results of the panel regressions for productivity growth, φ. Unlike the results related to the dependent variables of economic growth and capital accumulation, the financial variables appear positive and significant in the pooled model, but not in the error components models. The coefficients for financial variables *FSDI* are positive and significant at the 1 per cent level. The value of F_1-test for testing overall significance rejects the null hypothesis at the 1 per cent level. Thus this result can provide evidence that financial development can accelerate growth by enhancing the productivity of firms. Nevertheless, the LM test and the Hausman test suggest the existence of individual effects in the specifications, so the evidence of the specification without individual effects is not compelling.

Conclusions

Using panel data analysis in this chapter we attempted to examine empirically the links between financial-sector development and economic growth. We used the widely adopted econometric approaches of the pooled model, the fixed effects model and the random effects model, but in the context of a new panel dataset comprising both industrial and developing countries spanning the period 1960–99, and also by using a more appropriate approach to measure financial development. A particular effort was made to derive the best estimators (in an econometric sense) by testing for fixed effects and random effects in the model on the basis of exhaustive mis-specification testing.

Our empirical results seem to suggest that financial development has a significant positive impact on real per capita GDP growth. The two different estimated coefficients on the financial indicators of industrial and developing countries also show that (i) higher financial develop-ment stimulates faster economic growth, and (ii) the impact of financial sector development on growth will be stronger in developing countries compared to industrial countries. Furthermore, we found evidence that financial-sector development can accelerate growth by improving the allocation of capital. Regarding the impact of other variables used in the analysis on growth, our results seem to indicate: (i) the existence of a worldwide scale effect in the endogenous growth model – and, the output elasticity of the labour force was found to be higher in industrial countries compared to developing countries; (ii) government expenditure has a positive impact on growth; (iii) inflation has a negative effect on growth; (iv) openness to trade is positively related to economic growth; and (v) foreign direct investment has a favourable correlation with growth in the case of developing countries, whereas in industrial countries it seems to have a more negative correlation.

Needless to say, correlation does not necessarily imply causation, and most importantly, even in the case of causation, as far as the relationship between financial sector development and growth is concerned the direction of causation is of paramount importance for policy purposes. This is clearly an issue for further research at both global and country level, so that significant policy lessons can be derived. Last, but definitely not least, further work needs to be done on a central issue related to the overall finance–growth–poverty reduction relationship, of crucial importance for many developing countries undertaking financial-sector reforms.

Notes

1 The finance–growth relationship has been the subject of a rather voluminous literature, both theoretical and empirical, going back to the seminal contribution by Goldsmith (1969) and the money–growth literature of the 1960s – In particular, Gurley and Shaw (1960), Tobin (1965), Patrick (1966), and the financial repression literature of the early 1970s associated with the works of McKinnon (1973) and Shaw (1973).
2 Honohan (2004) provides a comprehensive discussion on this issue.
3 See Appendix 1 for a list of countries included in the sample.
4 The employed method of estimation is $CPI(t) = CPI(t+1)/[CPI(t+4)/CPI(t+1)]^{1/3}$.
5 First, learning-by-doing works through each firm's investment. Specifically, an increase in a firm's capital stock leads to a parallel increase in its stock of knowledge. Second, each firm's knowledge is a public good that any other firm can access at zero cost. In other words, once discovered, a piece of knowledge spills over instantly across the whole economy. This assumption allows us to replace A_i by K.
6 The reasons for this popularity are: (i) its ability to handle databases of any size; (ii) the estimation and hypothesis testing methods are derived from well-known classical procedures; (iii) most of the problems and difficulties can be handled in the traditional framework; (iv) the model has been investigated most thoroughly on theoretical frontiers; and (v) the estimation results are easily interpreted (Matyas and Sevestre, 1996).

7   When an F_1-test is performed for testing the overall significance of the fixed effects model, the number K of df for the numerator is added to the number of $N-1$. It is because fixed effects subtract the individual means from their variables, so that df is $K+N-1$ for the numerator and $NT-K-N$ for the denominator as testing H_0: $\mu = \mu_i$ $\forall i$ and $\beta_1 = \beta_2 = \cdots = \beta_K = 0$. Thus the value of $F_1(70,2464) = 5635.35$ rejects the null hypothesis at the 1 per cent level of significance.

References

Arestis, P. and Demetriades, P. (1997) 'Financial Development and Economic Growth: Assessing the Evidence', *Economic Journal*, 107(May): 783–99.

Baltagi, B. H. (1995) *Econometric Analysis of Panel Data* (New York: John Wiley).

Bandiera, O., Caprio, G., Honohan, P. and Schiantarelli, F. (2000) 'Does Financial Reform Raise or Reduce Saving?', *The Review of Economics and Statistics*, 82(2): 239–63.

Barro, R. J. (1991) 'Economic Growth in a Cross-Section of Countries', *The Quarterly Journal of Economics*, 56: 407–43.

Barro, R. J. and Sala-i-Martin, X. (1995) *Economic Growth* (New York: McGraw-Hill).

Beck, T., Demirgüç-Kunt, A. and Levine, R. (1999) 'A New Database on the Financial Development and Structure', Policy Research Paper 2146, World Bank; Washington, DC.

Beck, T., Levine, R. and Loayza, N. (1999) 'Finance and the Sources of Growth', Policy Review Working Paper 2057, World Bank; Washington, DC.

Benhabib, J. and Spiegel, M. M. (2000) 'The Role of Financial Development in Growth and Investment', *Journal of Economic Growth*, 5(December): 341–60.

Breusch, T. and Pagan, A. (1980) 'The Lagrange Multiplier Test and Its Applications to Model Specification in Econometrics, *Review of Economic Studies*, 47: 239–53.

Demetriades, P. and Luintel, K. (1996) 'Banking Sector Policies and Financial Development in Nepal', *Oxford Bulletin of Economics and Statistics*, 58(2): 355–72.

Demirgüç-Kunt, A. and Levine, R. (eds) (2001) *Financial Structure and Economic Growth* (Cambridge, Mass.: MIT Press).

Fry, M. J. (1988) *Money, Interest, and Banking in Economic Development*, (Baltimore, Md.: Johns Hopkins University Press).

Goldsmith, W. (1969) *Financial Structure and Development* (New Haven, Conn.: Yale University Press).

Green, C. J. and Kirkpatrick, C. (2002) 'Finance and Development: An Overview of the Issues', *Journal of International Development*, 14(2): 207–10.

Green, C. J., Kirkpatrick, C. and Murinde, V. (2005) (eds) *Finance and Development: Surveys of Theory, Evidence and Policy* (Cheltenham: Edward Elgar).

Gurley, G. J. and Shaw, E. S. (1960) *Money in a Theory of Finance* (Washington, DC: Brookings Institution).

Hausman, J. (1978) 'Specification Tests in Econometrics', *Econometrica*, 46: 1251–71.

Hermes, N. and Lensink, R. (eds) (1996) *Financial Development and Economic Growth: Theory and Experience from Developing Countries* (London: Routledge).

Honohan, P. (2004) 'Financial Development, Growth and Poverty: How Close Are the Links?', World Bank Policy Research Working Paper 3203, February, World Bank, Washington, DC.

Johnston, J. (1991) *Econometric Methods*, 3rd edn (New York: McGraw-Hill).

Kelly, R. and Mavrotas, G. (2003) 'Financial Sector Development: Futile or Fruitful? An Examination of the Determinants of Saving in Sri Lanka', WIDER Discussion Paper 2003/14, UNU-WIDER; Helsinki.

King, R. G. and Levine, R. (1993) 'Finance, Entrepreneurship, and Growth: Theory and Evidence', *Journal of Monetary Economics*, 32: 513–42.

Levine, R. (1992) 'Financial Structures and Economic Development', World Bank Working Paper, WPS 849, World Bank, Washington, DC.

Levine, R. (1997) 'Financial Development and Economic Growth: Views and Agenda', *Journal of Economic Literature*, 35: 688–726.

Lucas, R. E., Jr. (1993) 'Making a Miracle', *Econometrica*, 61(2): 251–72.

Matyas, L. and Sevestre, P. (eds) (1996) *The Econometrics of Panel Data: A Handbook of the Theory with Applications*, 2nd rev. edn (Dordrecht: Kluwer).

McKinnon, R. I. (1973) *Money and Capital in Economic Development* (Washington, DC: Brookings Institution).

Patrick, H. T. (1966) 'Financial Development and Economic Growth in Under-developed Countries', *Economic Development and Cultural Change*, 14: 174–89.

Shaw, E. S. (1973) *Financial Deepening in Economic Development* (New York: Oxford University Press).

Tobin, J. (1965) 'Money and Economic Growth', *Econometrica*, 33: 671–84.

Wachtel, P. (2004) 'How Much Do We Really Know About Growth and Finance?', *Research in Banking and Finance*, 4: 91–113

Wachtel, P. and Rousseau, P. (1995) 'Financial Intermediation and Economic Growth: A Historical Comparision of the US, UK and Canada', in M. Bordo and R. Sylla (eds), *Anglo-American Financial Systems: Institutions and Markets in the Twentieth Century* (New York: Irwin): 329–82.

World Bank (2001) *Finance for Growth: Policy Choices in a Volatile World* (New York: Oxford University Press).

Appendix 1

Countries included in the sample (65)

Industrial countries (24)

1. Australia
2. Austria
3. Belgium
4. Canada
5. Cyprus
6. Denmark
7. Finland
8. France

9. Germany
10. Greece
11. Iceland
12. Ireland
13. Italy
14. Japan
15. Luxembourg
16. Malta
17. Netherlands
18. New Zealand
19. Norway
20. Portugal
21. Sweden
22 Switzerland
23. UK
24. USA

Developing countries (41)

Africa (15)

25. Burundi
26. Cameroon
27. Côte d'Ivoire
28. Ethiopia
29. Gabon
30. Ghana
31. Kenya
32. Morocco
33. Niger
34. Nigeria
35. Rwanda
36. Senegal
37. Sierra Leone
38. South Africa
39. Tanzania

Middle East (2)

40. Egypt
41. Iran

Asia and Pacific (10)

42. Fiji
43. India
44. Indonesia
45. South Korea
46. Malaysia
47. Nepal
48. Pakistan
49. The Philippines
50. Sri Lanka
51. Thailand

South America (14)

52. Colombia
53. Costa Rica
54. Dominican Republic
55. Ecuador
56. El Salvador
57. Guatemala
58. Haiti
59. Honduras
60. Jamaica
61. Mexico
62. Panama
63. Paraguay
64. Trinidad and Tobago
65. Venezuela

Appendix 2

Table 3.A1 Regression results from the estimation of panel data models I (dependent variable ln K)

Dependent variable ln K	65 countries			24 industrial countries			41 developing countries		
	Pooled	Fixed	Random	Pooled	Fixed	Random	Pooled	Fixed	Random
Const.	0.003734	–	−8.350973	3.583132	–	−6.624648	−2.952615	–	−7.448208
	(0.9890)		(0.0000)	(0.0000)		(0.0000)	(0.0000)		(0.0000)
FSDI	0.126272	0.518554	0.561338	0.881132	0.241497	0.326515	0.102893	1.322667	1.342380
	(0.0774)	(0.0000)	(0.0000)	(0.0000)	(0.0000)	(0.0000)	(0.4093)	(0.0000)	(0.0000)
lnSE	0.255525	1.384773	1.176346	−0.141685	1.455286	0.956696	0.517776	1.189005	1.068847
	(0.0000)	(0.0000)	(0.0000)	(0.0000)	(0.0000)	(0.0000)	(0.0000)	(0.0000)	(0.0000)
GEXP	1.391721	1.418837	1.562747	−3.893429	0.306622	1.198013	6.011570	1.649943	1.778419
	(0.0222)	(0.0000)	(0.0000)	(0.0000)	(0.3742)	(0.0003)	(0.0000)	(0.0001)	(0.0000)
INFL	0.002687	−0.003107	−0.002914	0.052207	0.007147	0.007278	−0.000479	−0.002742	−0.002646
	(0.0364)	(0.0000)	(0.0000)	(0.0000)	(0.0000)	(0.0000)	(0.7313)	(0.0000)	(0.0000)
OTR	0.352984	1.061428	1.207309	−1.050279	0.756635	0.827742	1.252638	0.971815	1.073281
	(0.0082)	(0.0000)	(0.0000)	(0.0000)	(0.0000)	(0.0000)	(0.0000)	(0.0000)	(0.0000)

FDI	0.102731 (0.0000)	-0.013107 (0.1341)	-0.008359 (0.3381)	0.137516 (0.0000)	0.004615 (0.3702)	0.010782 (0.0353)	0.082011 (0.0061)	-0.011802 (0.3867)	–	0.006806 (0.6163)
No. of obs.	2535	2535	2535	936	936	936	1599	1599		1599
DF	2528	2464	2528	929	906	929	1592	1552		1592
R^2	0.0627	0.8770	–	0.3032	0.964597	–	0.1761	0.8628		–
F_1 test	28.20 (0.0000)	251.12 (0.0000)	–	67.38 (0.0000)	851.21 (0.0000)	–	56.73 (0.0000)	212.24 (0.0000)		–
F_2 test	–	255.02 (0.0000)	–	–	735.86 (0.0000)	–	–	194.25 (0.0000)		–
LR test	–	5149.3 (0.0000)	–	–	2788.95 (0.0000)	–	–	2866.72 (0.0000)		–
LM test	–	–	31465.66 (0.0000)	–	–	10674.05 (0.0000)	–	–		18828.14 (0.0000)
Hausman test	–	–	74.38 (0.0000)	–	–	149.64 (0.0000)	–	–		23.60 (0.0006)

Table 3.A2 Regression results from the estimation of panel data models II (dependent variable φ)

Dependent variable φ	59 countries			22 industrial countries			37 developing countries		
	Pooled	Fixed	Random	Pooled	Fixed	Random	Pooled	Fixed	Random
Const.	-6.330799	–	-4.353446	2.201714	–	2.704102	-6.993461	–	-6.414300
	(0.0000)		(0.0075)	(0.0955)		(0.0813)	(0.0000)		(0.0029)
FSDI	1.353767	-2.619273	0.044900	-1.253252	-2.588653	-1.622535	1.371621	-2.228859	0.514342
	(0.0000)	(0.0000)	(0.9151)	(0.0000)	(0.0000)	(0.0000)	(0.0090)	(0.0899)	(0.5030)
lnSE	0.435526	1.104451	0.418305	0.112416	-1.119010	0.122679	0.553534	1.406419	0.579859
	(0.0001)	(0.0792)	(0.0162)	(0.3127)	(0.3652)	(0.3901)	(0.0004)	(0.0925)	(0.0153)
GEXP	-2.315155	-13.899312	-9.397474	-12.936656	-14.226455	-15.061801	-9.251460	-13.773968	-11.854743
	(0.3314)	(0.0000)	(0.0008)	(0.0000)	(0.0157)	(0.0000)	(0.0051)	(0.0006)	(0.0011)
INFL	-0.032365	-0.035759	-0.033891	-0.036609	-0.038966	-0.036157	-0.026381	-0.036203	-0.029279
	(0.0020)	(0.0027)	(0.0019)	(0.0586)	(0.0668)	(0.0664)	(0.0419)	(0.0166)	(0.0313)
OTR	0.851612	1.213454	1.073081	0.770125	3.085422	0.994098	0.073402	0.508094	0.243066
	(0.1006)	(0.2237)	(0.1305)	(0.0914)	(0.0125)	(0.0854)	(0.9321)	(0.7098)	(0.8146)
FDI	-0.122203	-0.100916	-0.145106	-0.042576	-0.036399	-0.035925	0.018099	-0.146651	-0.094399
	(0.1267)	(0.2481)	(0.0788)	(0.5689)	(0.6728)	(0.6382)	(0.8840)	(0.2696)	(0.4556)

No. of obs.	2301	2301	2301	858	858	858	1443	1443	1443
DF	2294	2236	2294	851	830	851	1436	1400	1436
R^2	0.0284	0.1504	–	0.0464	0.1118	–	0.0256	0.1082	–
F_1 test	11.21	6.19	–	6.91	3.87	–	6.30	4.05	–
	(0.0000)	(0.0000)		(0.0000)	(0.0000)		(0.0000)	(0.0000)	
F_2 test	–	5.536	–	–	2.911	–	–	3.602	–
		(0.0000)			(0.0000)			(0.0000)	
LR test	–	308.75	–	–	60.978	–	–	127.83	–
		(0.0000)			(0.0000)			(0.0000)	
LM test	–	–	242.06	–	–	10.99	–	–	74.54
			(0.0000)			(0.0009)			(0.0000)
Hausman test	–	–	59.74	–	–	21.95	–	–	17.62
			(0.0000)			(0.0012)			(0.0072)

4
Excess Credit and the South Korean Crisis

Panicos O. Demetriades and Bassam A. Fattouh

Introduction

A number of recent theoretical papers, including McKinnon and Pill (1997), Corsetti *et al.* (1999), Huang and Xu (1999) and Schneider and Tornell (2004) have analysed the role of over-investment and over-borrowing in financial crises. McKinnon and Pill (1997) argue that, in an inadequate regulatory framework, banks can inflate entrepreneurs' expected payoffs, knowing that, in case of default, the government will be forced to bail out distressed borrowers. The entrepreneurs, lacking sufficient information to assess banks' signals, tend to consider them as being correct, thus they bid eagerly for funds and a lending-investment boom ensues. In Corsetti *et al.* (1999) analysis, a financial crisis erupts as a result of potential future fiscal deficits that are implied by moral hazard behaviour in private corporate and financial investment. The latter leads to over-investment, which can persist for as long as domestic firms are able to refinance their unprofitable projects and cash shortfalls through foreign borrowing – a process known as 'evergreening'. Only when international reserves fall below a certain threshold,[1] does foreign investors' willingness to roll-over credit cease, causing a financial crisis. In a similar vein, Huang and Xu (1999) argue that over-investment in South Korea was caused by soft budget constraints, which enabled large industrial conglomerates (*chaebols*) to have continuous access to subsidized policy loans. In such an economy, there is no mechanism to ensure that bad projects are terminated, because negative signals are not revealed either to investors or depositors, creating unduly optimistic expectations. Hence, loss-making projects may be hidden for a long time by over-borrowing, and these problems only become apparent when an exogenous shock hits the economy.

This chapter provides an empirical investigation of the over-borrowing hypothesis in South Korea using a novel approach. Specifically, our modelling strategy takes into account the institutional characteristics of the South Korean credit market, including the direct effects of financial repression that were prevalent until the late 1980s. Additionally, we utilize time-series econometric techniques that allow us to construct a measure of short-run disequilibrium in the credit market.[2] Unlike previous attempts to model disequilibrium behaviour in the credit market that rule out the presence of a realized excess supply by assumption, our approach allows the actual stock of credit to be above or below its long-run equilibrium value.

Our results show that, with few exceptions, the Korean credit market had been characterized by excessive credit creation since the late 1960s. That is, the actual stock of credit was found to be greater than its long-run equilibrium level predicted by economic fundamentals, such as real economic activity and the cost of credit. Our estimates of excess credit may be interpreted as measures of 'unproductive credit' in the sense that it was not used to finance productive economic activity. The presence of excess credit indicates the existence of loss-making projects that were being refinanced continually by banks. Thus our empirical findings are consistent with the theoretical predictions of Huang and Xu (1999) and Corsetti *et al.* (1999).

Methodological issues

In evaluating whether a credit market is characterized by disequilibrium conditions, previous empirical studies, such as Laffont and Garcia (1977) and Pazarbasioglu (1996), have used the model of supply and demand from Maddala and Nelson (1974). This approach assumes that, in some markets, prices are not perfectly flexible and hence disequilibrium might occur. In the absence of any information concerning the price-adjustment process, the probability with which each observation belongs to the demand or supply function is determined by assuming that the short side of the market is never rationed. Maddala and Nelson (1974) derive the appropriate maximum likelihood method for this class of models.

By stipulating that the long side of the market is the one that *is* rationed, the traditional disequilibrium approach, while allowing for *notional* excess supply, rules out the possibility of an *effective* excess supply of credit. That is, in the traditional approach, an excess supply of credit can only represent the case in which banks would like to supply more credit than firms are willing to accept; thus, without coercion, an excess supply of credit can never be realized. In practice, however, excessive credit creation may refer to the possibility that firms take on more credit than is predicted by the long-run determinants of the demand for credit – which typically include the cost of credit and an indicator of real economic activity. Excess credit – which we define to be the excess of actual credit to the amount predicted by the long-run demand for credit – may be the result of loss-making projects that are being refinanced continually by banks. The main reason why banks refinance unprofitable projects is their reluctance to admit publicly that they have problematic assets, which would reduce their stock market value and hamper their ability to raise capital. In extreme cases, when the amount of non-performing assets exceeds shareholders' capital, admitting the presence of problematic loans is tantamount to declaring insolvency. In such circumstances, it is not unusual for banks to postpone taking action, in the hope that an economic upturn will allow firms eventually to repay their loans. Ultimately, of course, there is also the hope that when the problem threatens the soundness of many financial institutions and the stability of the financial system, some large corporates may be bailed out by the government. Thus, our notion of excess credit corresponds closely to the notion of over-borrowing, reflecting soft budget constraints and/or moral hazard (Corsetti *et al.* 1999; Huang and Xu 1999).

The preceding analysis suggests that the *effective* or short-run stock of credit may well exceed the long-run desired demand for credit. It is therefore vital to allow for the possibility that a *short-run* observation may belong to neither the *long-run* demand nor the *long-run* supply function. In spite of the short-run deviations from long-run equilibrium, it is nevertheless plausible to expect to see some adjustment towards long-run market equilibrium for *both* demand and supply functions.[3] This is consistent with both theoretical and empirical work. For example, despite the presence of information asymmetry, Laffont and Garcia (1977) find that the real interest rate has the tendency to adjust upwards when there is excess demand for credit. On the other hand, when there is an excess supply of credit, there is no reason why the interest rate should not fall, to equilibrate the credit market (Greenwald *et al.* 1993).

Thus, in order to allow for the presence of unproductive credit, our estimation strategy differs from the traditional disequilibrium approach outlined above, in the following four important respects:

(i) It assumes that in the *long-run*, the interest rate adjusts to equilibrate the credit market while allowing for departures from long-run equilibrium to occur in the short-run.

(ii) It does not impose a priori restrictions on the speed of adjustment, which admits the possibility that the credit market may take a very long time to clear. Thus, the assumption that in the long-run market equilibrium prevails is not a restrictive one because the length of the long-run is determined by the data.

(iii) It does not depend on estimating a set of probabilities which are then used to locate an observation on the long-run demand or supply function. Instead, it identifies excess supply or demand by measuring the difference between the actual stock of credit and its predicted long-run equilibrium value, utilizing standard techniques in applied time-series econometrics.

(iv) It allows for the possibility that the actual stock of credit may exceed the long-run demand for credit, representing an excess supply of credit in the short-run, which the traditional disequilibrium approach does not admit.

Empirical specification, data and results

In this section we specify a model for the *long-run* demand for and supply of bank credit, which takes into account the institutional characteristics of the South Korean credit market.

The long-run supply of credit equation

The real supply of loans in the long-run is assumed to be determined by the real lending interest rate (r), the current level of economic activity, measured by real gross domestic product (GDP) (y), and the institutional characteristics of the credit market, measured by the degree of financial repression. The first two variables are widely used in empirical studies to capture, respectively, the profitability of banks' lending activities and their expectations about the state of the economy (Laffont and Garcia 1977; Pazarbasioglu 1996). The third variable has not been addressed in the empirical literature on credit markets (Pazarbasioglu 1996; Ghosh and Ghosh 1999), despite the presence of financial restraints in almost all developing countries and some developed countries. Since the early 1960s, one of the most important institutional characteristics of the South Korean credit market has been the direct intervention of the state in the allocation and pricing of credit.[4] This was achieved mainly through controls on lending and deposit interest rates. Interest rate deregulation, which began in 1979, was only completed in the early 1990s. The impact of interest rate controls on the real supply of credit is not straightforward. In principle, lending rate controls, by limiting banks' profitability, may reduce the real supply of credit to the private sector. However, as noted by Caprio (1994), in the presence of higher interest rates, which usually follow financial liberalization, banks may choose to hold larger amounts of riskless assets, and hence supply fewer loans to the private sector. Hence the impact of the relaxation of lending rate controls on the supply of credit is ambiguous. The same conclusion holds for the impact of deposit rate controls on the supply of real credit, even though the reasoning is different. On the one hand, these controls limit the cost of funds for banks and therefore increase the willingness of banks to supply increased amounts of credit. On the other hand, however, deposit rate controls limit the supply of funds to the banking system which, unless counteracted by other means, such as increased branching or marketing, are likely to reduce the ability of banks to supply increased amounts of credit.

In addition to interest-rate controls, the South Korean government imposed reserve requirements on bank deposits (demand and/or time and savings deposits). Usually, the definition of bank reserves includes short-term government paper and/or central bank deposits, which typically yield a lower rate of return than bank loans. Hence, increases in reserve requirements raise the average cost of loanable funds and are therefore expected to result in an inward shift of the supply of credit to the private sector.

Thus we use the following specification for the long-run supply of credit (C^s):

$$C^s = \beta_0 + \beta_1 y + \beta_2 r + \beta_3 IRL + \beta_4 RR + u_t \tag{4.1}$$

where IRL is an index of interest rate restraints, RR is the required reserve ratio, and u_t is a white noise error term.

The long-run demand for credit equation

We assume that the long-run demand for (productive) credit depends positively on the level of real economic activity, measured by real GDP(y), and negatively on the cost of credit, measured by the real lending rate (r). Formally, we use the following specification for the long-run demand for credit (C^d):

$$C^d = \alpha_0 + \alpha_1 y + \alpha_2 r + v_t \tag{4.2}$$

where v_t is a white noise error term.

Reduced form

We assume that, in the long-run, the real interest rate is flexible enough to equate to the real supply and demand for credit; that is, the exchanged quantity of credit is such that

$$C = C^d = C^s \tag{4.3}$$

We next solve for the reduced form equation by substituting the value of r from Equation (4.2) in Equation (4.1) to obtain the following:

$$C = \gamma_0 + \gamma_1 y + \gamma_2 IRR + \gamma_3 RR + w_t \tag{4.4}$$

where $\quad \gamma_0 = (\alpha_2\beta_0 - \alpha_0\beta_2/\alpha_2 - \beta_2)$

$\qquad \gamma_1 = (\alpha_2\beta_1 - \alpha_1\beta_2/\alpha_2 - \beta_2) \qquad \gamma_1 > 0$

$\qquad \gamma_2 = (\alpha_2\beta_3/\alpha_2 - \beta_2) \qquad \gamma_2 > 0 \text{ or } \gamma_2 < 0$

$\qquad \gamma_3 = (\alpha_2\beta_4/\alpha_2 - \beta_2) \qquad \gamma_3 < 0$

Data

The dependent variable is measured by (the logarithm of) broad claims on the private sector deflated by the GDP deflator. Real broad credit constitutes claims on the private sector by deposit money banks, trust accounts of commercial banks, development banks and non-bank financial institutions. The data source for these variables, as well as for real GDP and the GDP deflator, is *International Financial Statistics* (IMF 1998: 6).

The construction of the index of interest rate restraints utilizes the detailed information about financial reforms summarized in the Appendix (see pp. 82–6), obtained from Bank of Korea Annual Reports (various issues). The index is assumed to take a value of unity prior to any relaxations, and decreases in value whenever restrictions on interest rates are relaxed or removed; it is therefore *increasing* with the severity of financial restraints, and *decreasing* as financial liberalization progresses. Initially, we constructed separate indices for controls on deposit rates, lending rates and money market rates. Since these indices were found to exhibit a strong positive correlation between them, we averaged them out into a single measure, which we call 'the interest rate restraints index'. This measure is plotted in Figure 4.1. Its movements reflect the changes in the underlying policy variable reasonably well. The relaxation of lending controls in 1979 is reflected in a drop in the measure for that year. The measure then exhibits relative stability

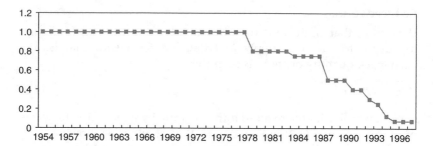

Figure 4.1 Summary measure of interest rate restraints
Source: Bank of Korea *Annual Report* (various issues).

until 1988, when it drops sharply following the liberalization of interest rates on lending and certain types of time and savings deposits. Further drops are observed in the early 1990s, reflecting further deregulation in deposit rates and lending rates on policy loans.

Data on required reserve ratios on (i) demand and (ii) time and saving deposits were collected from Bank of Korea Annual Reports (various issues).[5] Because of the very high correlation between the two ratios, we use their arithmetical average as a summary measure of reserve requirements (RR). This measure, illustrated in Figure 4.2, registers an upward jump during 1966–7, which coincides with the first wave of reforms, which saw large increases in interest rates and reserve requirements, resulting in increased state control over the banking system (Harris 1988). RR exhibits a decline during 1968–71 and fluctuates widely in the 1970s. In the early 1980s, the index shows a sharp decline, which coincides with the relaxation of lending rate controls, while the 1987–9 period registeres a considerable increases in reserve requirements. In the 1990s, RR exhibits relative stability, to decline significantly in 1997 when reserve requirements on all types of deposits were set at 2 per cent.

To test the robustness of our results to the measurement of financial repression, we also use (i) the actual ratio of bank reserves to bank deposits; and (ii) the inflation rate as alternative proxies of the degree of financial repression (Roubini and Sala-i-Martin 1992, 1995; Haslag and Koo 1999). The ratio of actual bank reserves to bank deposits differs from the required reserve ratio by the amount of excess reserves. Banks may hold excess reserves when there are regulatory restrictions limiting the development of inter-bank markets, or when other regulatory structures push them to do so (Roubini and Sala-i-Martin 1992, 1995). Thus the ratio of bank reserves to deposits can serve as a useful proxy of the degree

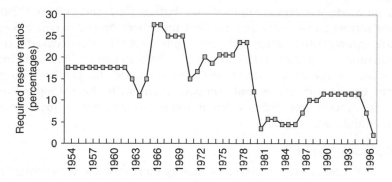

Figure 4.2 Summary measure of reserve requirements
Source: Bank of Korea *Annual Report* (various issues).

of financial repression (Haslag and Koo 1999). We expect increases in the ratio of actual reserves to deposits to result in an inward shift of the supply of credit to the private sector. The inflation rate acts like a tax on financial intermediation as it reduces the real rate of return on bank reserves. As noted by Fry (1995), substantial use of the inflation tax has usually been accompanied by high reserve requirements. We measure inflation as the percentage change in the GDP deflator. The data source for bank reserves, demand deposits and the GDP deflator is *International Financial Statistics* (IMF 1998:6).

Method of estimation

All variables were initially subjected to unit root tests, which suggested that the measure of the stock of credit, as well as real GDP, the index of interest rate restraints, reserve requirements, and the ratio of bank reserves to bank deposits, are non-stationary. Since these variables contain unit roots, we use a cointegration estimator to estimate the reduced form relationship between them given by Equation (4.4). Specifically, we apply the dynamic ordinary least squares (DOLS) estimator (Saikkonen 1991; Stock and Watson 1993). This estimator is asymptotically equivalent to Johansen's (1988) maximum-likelihood estimator in the case where variables are integrated of order one and there is a single cointegrating vector. Moreover, it has been shown to perform well in finite samples relative to other asymptotically efficient estimators (Stock and Watson 1993). In these circumstances it is known that the Engle–Granger (1987) estimator may exhibit substantial bias (Banerjee *et al.* 1986; Stock and Watson 1993). DOLS has a further advantage over the Engle–Granger estimator. While the latter suffers from a non-standard asymptotic distribution (Park and Phillips 1988), the former allows valid and efficient inferences on the parameters of the cointegrating vector. We first apply DOLS to the reduced-form equation – (Equation 4.4) – and obtain estimates of the cointegrating vector for the credit market. We next compute the predicted long-run equilibrium values and compare them with the corresponding actual stock of real credit, which allows us to construct our measure of disequilibrium credit.

Empirical results

Table 4.1 reports the results of estimating Equation (4.4) using different sets of explanatory variables. In Model A, we include the index of interest rate restraints and the reserve requirement ratio as indicators of the degree of financial repression. The explanatory variables appear with the expected signs and are statistically significant. The estimated coefficient of real GDP has the expected positive sign, takes a plausible value, and is statistically significant. The interest rate restraints index appears with a negative sign, indicating that relaxation of interest rate controls results in an increase in the equilibrium stock of real credit to the private sector. The reserve requirement ratio appears with the expected negative sign and is also statistically significant at the 5 per cent level, indicating that higher required reserve ratios are associated with lower credit to the private sector. The equation performs well, as reflected in high R^2, and passes various diagnostic tests. Finally, according to the Dickey–Fuller and Augmented Dickey–Fuller statistics, the hypothesis of a unit root in the residuals is rejected at the 5 per cent level. Thus, Model A represents a cointegrating relationship.

In Model B, we use the inflation rate and the ratio of bank reserves to deposits as alternative indicators of the degree of financial repression. The estimated coefficient of real GDP increases marginally and is statistically significant. The ratio of bank reserves to deposits appears with the expected negative sign and is statistically significant at the 1 per cent level. On the other hand, the inflation rate is not significant at conventional levels. Model B performs reasonably well and passes various diagnostic tests. Furthermore, the hypothesis of a unit root is rejected at the 5 per cent level, indicating that Model B forms a cointegrating vector.

In Model C, in addition to the ratio of bank reserves to deposits and inflation, we include the index of interest rate restraints. Interestingly, both bank reserves to deposits and the interest restraints index appear with a significant negative coefficient, indicating that these two measures may be

Table 4.1   Cointegrating vector for the credit market, 1954–97

Regressors	Model A	Model B	Model C	Model D
Intercept	−14.825*	−19.744*	−13.158*	−13.407*
	(2.256)	(1.632)	(1.979)	(2.495)
LY_t	1.431*	1.580*	1.387*	1.394*
	(0.068)	(0.051)	(0.059)	(0.074)
IRL_t	−0.463*		−0.577*	−0.535*
	(0.166)		(0.161)	(0.198)
RES/DEP_t		−0.468*	−0.512*	−0.446*
		(0.221)	(0.118)	(0.120)
RR_t	−0.006**			
	(0.003)			
INF_t		0.068	0.212	
		(0.421)	(0.223)	
No. of observations	37	37	37	37
Diagnostic tests				
Adj-R^2	0.995	0.995	0.996	0.996
J-B	2.518[0.283]	4.35 [0.108]	5.844 [0.755]	1.007 [0.604]
Q(10,0)	7.660[0.568]	14.44 [0.110]	0.988 [0.610]	7.214[0.614]
Cointegration test				
DF	−4.070*	−4.273*	−5.208*	−5.038*
ADF(1)	−3.401ᴬ	−4.028ᴬ	−4.771ᴬ	−4.649ᴬ

Notes and Sources: The dependent variable is (the logarithm of) real broad claims on private sector by deposit money banks, development banks, non-bank financial institutions and trust accounts of commercial banks. The GDP deflator deflates this variable.

LY denotes the logarithm of real GDP; *IRL* is the index of interest rate liberalization; *RR* is the index of required reserve ratios; *RES/DEP* is the ratio of bank reserves to deposits, and *INF* is the inflation rate measured by the percentage change in the GDP deflator. The equation also includes a dummy variable for year 1968 onwards to account for the structural break in the real broad claims series. Figures in parentheses are the adjusted-standard errors for long-run variance (see Hamilton 1994).

The method of estimation is DOLS (Stock and Watson 1993). Given the small number of observations, to avoid over-parameterization we only retain significant lags and leads (Inder 1995).

J-B is Jarque-Bera's test for normality; Q is the Ljung–Box test for autocorrelation. Figures in brackets are the P-values.

* significant at the 1% level; ** significant at the 5% level.

capturing different aspects of financial repression. The estimated coefficient of real GDP retains a positive sign and is statistically significant. The inflation rate, on the other hand, remains statistically insignificant at conventional levels. Model C performs better than the previous models, in

Table 4.2   Estimates of excess supply of credit

Period	EXC_B (% of real broad claims)
1961–5	16.6
1966–70	27.4
1971–5	18.9
1976–80	15.7
1981–5	6.66
1986–90	14.5
1991–5	10.9

Note: EXC_B is excess supply of credit estimated using Model D in Table 4.1.

that it passes various diagnostic tests comfortably and shows very strong evidence of cointegration. In Model D, we drop the inflation rate, which was found to be insignificant in all the other specifications. Dropping this variable does not alter the results in any significant way.

Table 4.2 contains five-year averages of the measure of the credit market disequilibrium from 1961 to 1995, based on Model D of Table 4.1. This measure is obtained by subtracting the predicted long-run equilibrium value of credit from the actual stock of real credit, and expressing this difference as a proportion of real total claims. According to our estimates, the South Korean credit market has been characterized by excess supply of credit in all these periods. Interestingly, the average proportion of excess credit was higher in the 1970s than in the 1980s and 1990s. Also note that, during the first half of the 1980s, excess credit declined significantly to 6.66 per cent, but increased again to 14.5 per cent in the second half of the 1980s. Notably, in the period that preceded the crisis, excess credit declined to less than 11 per cent, lower than the average in the 1970s and almost equal to that of the 1980s. Thus, while our results are consistent with the over-borrowing hypothesis, they warn against an over-simplification of the links between excess credit and the South Korean financial crisis, as our results suggest that the problem of excess credit persisted for a long time before the crisis. Nevertheless, the existence of excess credit provides some clues, especially if it is examined in conjunction with other developments (Huang and Xu 1999).

We next assess whether the credit market disequilibrium could act as an indicator of capital productivity growth. Models of over-borrowing and over-investment predict that over-borrowing will ultimately be reflected in lower productivity growth, perhaps with some lag. The main reason is that borrowed funds are usually used to finance unproductive or even unprofitable projects. To test this implication, we employ a simple

Table 4.3 Granger causality tests

	F-test	F critical at 5%	Interpretation
3 Lags			
EXCESS → GPRODUCT	F(3,23) = 4.99	3.05	Uni-directional
GPRODUCT → EXCESS	F(3,23) = 1.28	3.05	causality from excess credit to change in capital productivity
4 Lags			
EXCESS → GPRODUCT	F(4,20) = 4.44	2.87	Bilateral causality
GPRODUCT → EXCESS	F(4,20) = 5.14	2.87	between excess credit and capital productivity

Notes: GPRODUCT is the growth in the average productivity of capital where average productivity is measured by the ratio of the flow of current output to the capital stock; *EXCESS* is excess credit measured by the ratio of real excess supply of credit, estimated using the cointegrating vector of Model D – Table 4.1 – to real broad credit; the Granger causality test was carried out over the period 1963–95. In the *EXCESS → GPRODUCT* line, the F-statistic tests the null hypothesis that the set of estimated coefficients on the lagged *EXCESS* is not statistically different from zero. In the *GPRODUCT → EXCESS* line, the F-statistic tests the null hypothesis that the set of estimated coefficients on the lagged *GPRODUCT* is not statistically different from zero.

Granger causality test between our estimates of credit market disequilibrium and the growth in the average productivity of capital.[6] It is well known that Granger causality tests are very sensitive to the number of lags used in the analysis. Thus, in Table 4.3, we report the results with three and four lags.[7] As can be seen from Table 4.3, in the case of three lags, we find uni-directional causality from our estimates of credit market disequilibrium to growth in capital productivity. The results in the case of four lags are slightly different where we find causality running in both directions. While the latter results are difficult to interpret, the evidence of causality from our estimates of credit market equilibrium to growth in capital productivity is consistent with models of over-investment.

Concluding remarks

The empirical analysis presented in this chapter reveals the existence and persistence of excess credit in the South Korean credit market. These findings are consistent with the hypotheses of over-borrowing or over-investment, which may reflect soft budget constraints and/or moral hazard. Our results are also consistent with the hypothesis that over-borrowing can persist as long as firms are able to refinance their unprofitable projects and cash shortfalls. In the 1980s, when most of the debt was in local currency, the Korean monetary authorities were able to avert a crisis in spite of the presence of a large volume of non-performing loans, by inflating their way out of the problem (Choi 1993; Nam 1994). By the mid-1990s, this was no longer possible, as most of the debt was in foreign currency, while international reserves that might cover for them were very low. The unwillingness of foreign banks and investors to renew or roll-over credit meant that many firms could no longer finance their unprofitable projects. A conjecture that emerges from our analysis is that, while excess credit and over-investment were not *by themselves* responsible for the crisis, their conjunction with high levels of foreign debt and low foreign reserves might have contributed significantly to the South Korean financial crisis.

Appendix: summary of the main financial reforms in Korea

Interest rates

6 September 1979. The Monetary Board abolished the existing maximum interest rate on bank loans to make it possible for banks to alter their interest rate on loans. However, the Bankers Association of Korea, considering that banks themselves are not used to determining interest rates, decided to link interest rates on loans to the central bank's rediscount rate.

6 September 1979. The Monetary Board abolished the maximum interest rate on free instalment savings deposits and the maximum interest rate on personal chequing deposits.

17 May 1984.   The Board allowed seven nationwide commercial banks, local banks and the Korea Exchange Bank to engage in the negotiable certificate of deposit (CDs) from 1 June.

23 July 1984.   A narrow band for loan rates was introduced, so that banks could charge different rates according to the creditworthiness of borrowers.

5 December 1988. Interest rates on loans from banks and non-bank financial intermediaries were fully liberalized.

5 December 1988. Interest rate on time deposits of a maturity greater than two years at banks, postal savings and credit unions were liberalized.

5 December 1988. Interest rates on time and savings deposits of a maturity greater than one year at mutual savings and finance companies were liberalized.

21 November 1991. Lending rates liberalized further. Lending rates liberalized were those on bank overdrafts; on the discount of commercial bills by banks, mutual savings, and finance companies; on the discount of commercial and trade bills by investment and finance companies; on the purchase of firms' guaranteed papers by banks' trust accounts; and on overdue loans by all financial institutions.

21 November 1991. The liberalization of deposit rates applied to those on short-term, large-denomination marketable instruments such as CDs, the sale of large denomination trade bills, commercial paper (CP), and repurchase agreements (RPs).

21 November 1991. The scope of initial liberalization was extended to cover rates on long-term deposits with a maturity of three years offered by banks, mutual credit facilities, and credit unions, and mutual time deposits with a maturity of two years or more offered by mutual savings and finance companies.

21 November 1991. The issue rates of corporate bonds with a maturity of two years or more were deregulated.

1 November 1993. All lending rates (apart from those financed by the government and the Bank of Korea's rediscounts) were liberalized.

1 November 1993. Rates on long-term deposits with a maturity of at least two years were completely liberalized.

1 November 1993. Interest rates on debentures and corporate bonds with a maturity of less than two years were liberalized.

1 December 1994. Interest rates on bank and non-bank time deposits with a maturity of one year or more but less than two years were liberalized.

1 December 1994. Banks were permitted to set freely the interest rates on policy loans financed through the aggregate credit ceilings system within their respective prime rates.

24 July 1995. Interest rates on policy-based loans through the aggregate credit ceilings system of the Bank of Korea were liberalized.

20 November 1995. The Bank of Korea and the government freed the remaining regulated interest rates on bank and non-bank time deposits with a maturity of less than six months, and on their instalment deposits with a maturity of less than one year.

19 January 1996. The Bank of Korea lifted restrictions on the size of the premium a bank could charge over its prime lending rate, which had originally been imposed to prevent a sharp rise in bank lending rates in the course of interest rate deregulation.

Developments in money markets

7 March 1986. The Monetary Board liberalized the rates on negotiable CDs, secured corporate bonds and bank debentures.

13 February 1987. The Monetary Board reduced the denomination of CDs from 100 million to 50 million won.

5 December 1988. Interest rates on repurchase agreements, CP of a face value greater than 30 million won and maturity more than 91 days, financial debentures and corporate bonds were fully liberalized.

5 December 1988. New CP and conventional CP were merged into one.

4 October 1989. The Bank of Korea and the government merged the call markets, previously segmented into an inter-bank market (mainly for banks) and the over-the-counter market between non-bank financial institutions (NBFIs), which expanded the size of the money market (call markets, CP, CDs, RPs, treasury bills (TBs) and Bankers' Acceptance). After the merger, the inter-bank rate was fully liberalized.

19 October 1989. The Bank of Korea adjusted the maturity period of CDs issued by banks to other banking institutions from between 91 days and 180 days to between 30 days and 180 days.

21 November 1991. The liberalization of deposit rates applied to those on short-term, large-denomination marketable instruments such as CDs, the sale of large-denomination trade bills, CP and RPs.

21 November 1991. The issue rates of corporate bonds with a maturity of two years and more were completely deregulated.

19 December 1992. The Bank of Korea extended the maximum maturity of CDs from 180 days to 270 days.

1 November 1993. Interest rates on financial debentures and those corporate bonds with a maturity of less than two years were liberalized. Government and public bonds and monetary stabilization bonds were also to be issued at prevailing market rates.

3 September 1993. The Bank of Korea lowered the minimum denomination of CDs from 50 million to 30 million won.

18 July 1994. The minimum maturities of CDs and high denomination RPs were shortened from 91 days to 60 days.

24 July 1995. The minimum maturities of short-term financial instruments including CDs, high-value RPs and high-value CP were shortened from 60 to 30 days.

Reserve requirements on demand deposits

Effective 23 November 1987. The Monetary Board raised the minimum reserve requirement from 4.5 per cent to 7 per cent.

20 April 1989. A marginal reserve requirement ratio of 30 per cent on the average increment of demand deposits, and time and savings deposits, was imposed. The marginal reserve requirements were abolished in February 1990.

15 February 1990. The Bank of Korea raised reserve requirement ratios on time deposits, instalment savings deposits with a maturity of two years or more, and household instalment savings deposit from 7 per cent to 8 per cent. On all other deposits, the reserve requirement ratio increased from 10 per cent to 11.5 per cent.

8 February 1991. The Bank of Korea introduced reserve requirements against mutual instalment deposits.

23 April 1996.   The reserve requirement on time and savings deposits of more than two years was brought down from 8 per cent to 6 per cent.

23 April 1996.   The reserve requirement on chequing deposits, pass book deposits, saving deposits, time and savings deposits with a maturity of less than two years was lowered from 11.5 per cent to 9 per cent.

8 November 1996.   The reserve requirement on time and savings deposits of more than two years was brought down from 6 per cent to 4 per cent.

8 November 1996.   The reserve requirement on chequing deposits, pass book deposits, savings deposits, time and savings deposits with maturity of less than two years was lowered from 9 per cent to 7 per cent.

Acknowledgements

We have benefited from discussions with a number of International Monetary Fund and World Bank economists, especially Charles Adams, Tomás José Boliño, Eduardo Borensztein, Jim Gordon, Giovanni Ferri, Tae-Soo Kang and Joe Stiglitz. Naturally, all views expressed in this chapter, as well as any errors, are solely our own. We are grateful to the Economic and Social Research Council (Award reference: R000222773) and South Bank University for financial support.

Notes

1 In Corsetti *et al.* (1999), the threshold is expressed as a fraction of implicit government liabilities which arise mainly because of excessive foreign borrowing by the private sector and over-investment in low productivity projects. It is interesting to note that these implicit government liabilities can coexist with a low public debt and budget deficit.
2 See, for example, Hendry (1995), or the papers in the Engle and Granger (1991) edited volume.
3 In a way, this implies that any government policy providing financial guarantees to firms is eventually removed.
4 For a detailed discussion of the extent of financial repression in South Korea and its impact on financial development, see Demetriades and Luintel (2001).
5 Laurens and Cardoso (1998) argue that indices based only on the reserve requirement ratio and that do not take into account the continued changes in the tax base cannot capture accurately the restrictiveness of reserve requirements. This argument applies to the Chilean case, where authorities have continuously changed the tax base to close loopholes and make the controls more restrictive. In the case of Korea, however, there have been no attempts to change the tax base and as such the index we use in this chapter is not subject to this problem.

6 We measure the average productivity of capital by the ratio of the flow of current output to the capital stock. Data on the capital stock for the period 1963–90 were obtained from the World Bank Database compiled by Nehru and Dareshwar (1993). Capital stock figures from 1991 to 1997 were constructed following the perpetual inventory method, assuming a depreciation rate of 4 per cent and uprating the price of capital goods in line with the GDP deflator. Investment and GDP data were obtained from *International Financial Statistics* (CD-ROM, 1998: 6). Excess credit is measured by the ratio of real excess supply of credit, estimated using the cointegrating vector of Model D – see Table 4.1 – to real broad credit.

7 Granger tests with 2 lags produce similar results as with 3 lags and hence are not reported here.

References

Banerjee, A., Dolado, J. J., Hendry, D. F. and Smith, G. W. (1986) 'Exploring Equilibrium Relations in Econometrics through State Models: Some Monte Carlo Evidence', *Oxford Bulletin of Economics and Statistics*, 48: 253–78.

Caprio, G. (1994) 'Banking on Financial Reform? A Case of Sensitive Dependence on Initial Conditions', in G. Caprio, I. Atiyas and J. Hanson (eds), *Financial Reform: Theory and Experience* (New York: Cambridge University Press).

Choi, B. S. (1993) 'Financial Policy and Big Business in Korea: The Perils of Financial Regulation', in S. Haggard, C. H. Lee and S. Maxfield (eds), *The Politics of Finance in Developing Countries* (New York: Cornell University Press).

Corsetti, G., Pesenti, P. and Roubini, N. (1999) 'Paper Tigers? A Model of the Asian Crisis', *European Economic Review*, 43:1211–36.

Demertriades, P. O. and Luintel, K. B. (2001) 'Financial Restraints in the South Korean Miracle', *Journal of Development Economics*, 64: 459–79.

Engle, R. F. and Granger, C. W. J. (1987) 'Cointegration and Error Correction: Representation, Estimation and Testing', *Econometrica*, 55: 251–76.

Engle, R. F. and Granger, C. W. J. (eds) (1991) *Long-run Economic Relations* (Oxford: Oxford University Press).

Fry, M. (1995) *Money, Interest and Banking in Economic Development*, 2nd edn (London: Johns Hopkins University Press).

Ghosh, S. R. and Ghosh, A. (1999) 'East Asia in the Aftermath: Was There a Credit Crunch?', Paper presented at conference, 'The Credit Crunch in East Asia', World Bank, Washington, DC.

Greenwald, B. C., Levinson, A. and Stiglitz, J. E. (1993) 'Capital Market Imperfections and Regional Economic Development', in A. Giovannini (ed.), *Finance and Development: Issues and Experience* (Cambridge: Cambridge University Press).

Hamilton, J. D. (1994) *Time Series Analysis* (Princeton, NJ: Princeton University Press).

Harris, L. (1988) 'Financial Reform and Economic Growth: A New Interpretation of South Korea's Experience', in L. Harris (ed.), *New Perspectives on the Financial System* (London: Croom Helm).

Haslag, J. H. and Koo, J. (1999) 'Financial Repression, Financial Development and Economic Growth', Federal Reserve Bank of Dallas Working Paper 99–02.

Hendry, D. F. (1995) *Dynamic Econometrics* (Oxford: Oxford University Press).

Huang, H. and Xu, C. (1999) 'Financial Institutions and the Financial Crisis in East Asia', *European Economic Review,* 43: 903–14.

IMF (1998) *International Financial Statistics* (CD-ROM) (Washington, DC: IMF).

Inder, B. (1995) 'Finite Sample Arguments for Appropriate Estimation of Cointegrating Vectors', Mimeo, Monash University, presented at the 7th World Congress of Econometric Society, Tokyo.

Johansen, S. (1988) 'Statistical Analysis of Cointegrating Vectors', *Journal of Economic Dynamics and Control,* 12: 231–54.

Laffont, J. J. and Garcia, R. (1977) 'Disequilibrium Econometrics for Business Loans', *Econometrica,* 45(5):1187–204.

Laurens, B. and Cardoso, J. (1998) 'Capital Flows – Lessons from the Experience of Chile', IMF Working Paper WP/98/168, International Monetary Fund, Washington, DC.

Maddala, G. S. and Nelson, F. D. (1974) 'Maximum Likelihood Method for Models of Markets in Disequilibrium', *Econometrica,* 42:1013–30.

McKinnon, R. and Pill, H. (1997) 'Credible Economic Liberalization and Overborrowing', *American Economic Review,* 87:189–93.

Nam, S. W. (1994) 'Korea's Financial Reform since the Early 1980s', in G. Caprio, I. Atiyas, and J. Hanson (eds), *Financial Reform: Theory and Experience* (New York: Cambridge University Press).

Nehru, V. and Dareshwar, A. (1993) 'A New Database on Physical Capital Stock: Sources, Methodology and Results', *Revista de Analisis Economico,* 8: 37–59.

Park, J. Y. and Phillips, P. C. B. (1988) 'Statistical Inference in Regressions with Integrated Processes: Part 1', *Econometric Theory,* 4: 468–97.

Pazarbasioglu, C. (1996) 'A Credit Crunch? A Case Study of Finland in the Aftermath of the Banking Crisis', IMF Working Paper 96/135, International Monetary Fund, Washington, DC.

Roubini, N. and Sala-i-Martin, X. (1992) 'Financial Repression and Economic Growth', *Journal of Development Economics,* 39: 5–30.

Roubini, N. and Sala-i-Martin, X. (1995) 'A Growth Model of Inflation, Tax Evasion and Financial Repression', *Journal of Monetary Economics,* 35: 275–302.

Saikkonen, P. (1991) 'Asymptotically Efficient Estimation of Cointegrating Regression', *Econometric Theory,* 7: 1–21.

Schneider, M. and Tornell, A. (2004) 'Balance Sheet Effects, Bailout Guarantees and Financial Crises', *Review of Economic Studies,* 71(3): 883–913.

Stock, J. H. and Watson, M. W. (1993) 'A Simple Estimator of Cointegrating Vectors in High Order Integrated Systems', *Econometrica,* 61: 783–820.

5
Financial Sector Development and Growth: The Chinese Experience

Iftekhar Hasan and Mingming Zhou

Introduction

Since the mid-1990s, considerable interest has focused on the link between the financial sector and economic growth. Most empirical studies have concluded that development of the financial sector accelerates economic growth (for example, Levine 1997; Thiel 2001; Wachtel 2001). However, in the transition countries, the link between financial sector development and economic growth seems to be ambiguous at best (see, for example, Berglöf and Roland 1995; Krkoska 2001; Berglöf and Bolton 2002). These studies note that most investment in transition countries has been financed from cash inflows, foreign direct investment (FDI) has substituted for domestic financing, and the level of loans granted to the private sector is considerably lower than the European Union (EU) average.

In most countries, especially the transitional economies, financial development has been accompanied by structural institutional changes and it can be very hard to separate their impact in terms of promoting economic growth. Among the transitional economies that have transformed from centrally planned systems to market systems, China is probably the most successful in the late twentieth century, as the country has maintained an approximately 10 per cent average annual growth rate in real gross domestic product (GDP) since the mid-1980s. Unlike the 'big bang', which was characterized by economic liberalization preceded by a massive force of democratization, China's transition has been characterized by a market economy developed without democratization, liberalization that has proceeded incrementally, and privatization delayed until almost two decades after the reforms began.

Compared with China's apparent success in terms of economic growth, the engine that has been providing such spectacular growth remains a mystery, especially from the perspective of the finance–institutions–growth nexus. Part of the reason might be the lack of reliable and accessible data to facilitate such an investigation. Although it might be tempting to examine Chinese experiences by generalizing from the experiences of European and former Soviet transition countries, there are important differences in economic structure and institutional development that make the Chinese experience unique (Qian and Xu 1993; Qian 1999a, 1999b). Moreover, cross-country studies are sometimes criticized for being unable to distinguish between the proximate determinants of growth and country specific idiosyncrasies (Wachtel 2003).

An alternative approach to the empirical analysis of growth in China is to examine the variation of experiences within the Chinese economy itself. Allen *et al.* (2005) follow this approach by looking at how institutional development affects different sectors of the Chinese economy. Similarly, Cull and Xu (2005) use a survey of managers to examine differences in institutional development. They find that there are surprisingly large variations across regions within China in managers' perceptions of legal protection and property rights. These studies indicate that institutional development has not occurred across China at the same pace, and that regional differences may contribute to regional differences in growth.

In this chapter we use panel data from the Chinese provinces to study the relationship between economic growth and measures of, or proxies for, financial-sector and institutional development. There are wide differences in economic growth among the 31 provinces in the period examined (1986–2002). Our evidence indicates that those regions with more developed financial markets and institutions, more open and easy environments for private and foreign investors, more protection of property rights, more investment opportunities, and more complete market institutions, are associated with stronger growth.

Financial sector development in China

In this chapter we focus on some important aspects of financial-sector development in China since the 1980s. Initially, we discuss some fundamental aspects of institutional changes in China.

Fiscal and financial system reform

Financial liberalization in China since 1978 has taken two forms: the internal and the external dimensions (Li and Liu 2001). Internally, marketization and privatization have resulted in a decline of the state sector, while decentralization has seen the reallocation of the fiscal budget between the state and local government. In 1979, the Chinese government began to substitute state budget allocation by bank loans. From 1980, profit tax began to substitute for profit remittances in the state sector. The 'soft budget' problem reflected the weakness in budgetary control as budget deficits coexisted with 'extra-budgetary' surpluses in some years (Qian and Roland 1996). Furthermore, the various tax reform measures were complicated and subject to abuse, resulting in a decrease in the tax rate (Donnithorne 1986; Wu 1989; Blejer and Szapary 1990).

In 1984, the nature of centrally planned financial resource allocation was revised. Local governments and departments were able to decide their own resource allocation via domestic loans and self-raised funds. During the 1980s, a process of revitalization of banking institutions took place (Li 1994; Yi 1994). In the case of monetary policy, a 'stop–go' strategy has been used, but interest rates have been adjusted on various occasions since the 1993 Austerity Plan (Qian 1994). Since 1988, enterprises have had the right to decide their own investments and a bidding system has been established (Cheng 1997). In January 1994, China introduced major tax and fiscal reforms which brought in a clear distinction between national and local taxes, thus making it very difficult for local governments to reduce national taxes as they had done in the past. In 1995, the new Budget Law came into effect. This law prohibited central government borrowing from the central bank and from running a deficit to finance its current account, required local governments to balance their budgets, and restricted local governments from bond issuance or borrowing on the financial market.

Further legislation that reduced substantially the influence of local governments on monetary policy and credit allocation decisions was the Central Bank Law passed in 1995. In 1998, the Central Bank closed thirty provincial branches and replaced them with nine cross-province regional branches in order to centralize macroeconomic control and supervision. This served to further minimize local government influence over monetary policies. Another important financial regulation reform introduced in 1998 was the separation of the supervisory regulation of commercial banks, investment banks and insurance companies. The supervisory regulation of the equity market and insurance market gained independence from the Central Bank, and two supervisory bodies (the China Securities Regulatory Committee – CSRC, and the China Insurance Regulatory Committee) were established to supervise the equity market and insurance market, respectively. These reforms appear to mirror the 1933 Glass–Steagall Act in the USA, and they may reduce systematic risk in China's developing financial industry.

Banking reform

In the 1980s, reform of financial institutions and regulations was characterized by a process of revitalization of banking institutions (Li 1994; Yi 1994). However, major banking reforms did not take place until 1994, when the central government decided to separate the policy-lending banks from the commercial banks (three policy-lending banks and four specialized commercial banks were set up), thus establishing the so-called three-tier system. These major banking reforms include, among others;[1] (i) establishing a central bank; (ii) transforming the urban credit co-operatives into commercial banks (1996–8); (iii) granting licences to some foreign banks; (iv) granting licences to non-state commercial banks; (v) reducing government intervention in credit allocation; (vi) loosening interest-rate controls; and (vii) recommending accounting standards and prudential norms. Since China joined the World Trade Organization (WTO) at the end of 2001, a new set of rules has begun to take effect. The agenda indicates that further liberalization of interest rates, fair treatment of tax rates between players, fewer restrictions on takeovers, mergers and acquisitions, and greater freedom of operational and geographical scope can be expected.

As the reforms have taken place, the banking sector has been playing a major role in supporting investment in industry and economic growth in China, and the banking sector itself has experienced remarkable growth since the 1980s. However, some deep-rooted problems still persist in the Chinese banking system. Such problems include under-capitalization, a large percentage of bad loans, the continuing practice of distributing low-interest policy loans to low-efficiency state sectors, and bribe-taking and abuse of duties on the part of bank loan officers.

Corporate bond market

Since China first embarked on its policy of opening up to the rest of the world in the late 1970s, the country's stock and government bond sectors have developed rapidly. Corporate bonds, however, lag far behind stocks and government bonds. In 1986, corporate bonds were issued for the first time, with amounts averaging about RMB 8 billion (Kumar 1997). For a long time the corporate bonds listed in the stock market were all of a small-scale and unitary type, which failed to meet the issuer's demand for capital, and the curb exchange of corporate bonds was explicitly prohibited. In 1999, the total corporate bonds issued amounted to RMB 42 billion, representing just 0.51 per cent of China's GDP of RMB 8205.4 billion (*People's Daily*, 1 September 2000). However, the corporate bond market began to expand from the year 2000, following the implementation of new rules governing corporate bond issuance.[2] Although state-owned enterprises still dominated in terms of the total value of corporate bonds issued, following the implementation of the reforms, private enterprises began to catch up. Reasons for the development of the corporate bond market being so slow include, among others, stringent restrictions on issuers' qualifications, the pricing of corporate bond issues, inadequate supervision and the legal framework.

However, as the Chinese government is paying increasing attention to the importance of corporate bonds in the capital market, some progress has been observed recently. Moves to improve the functioning of the corporate bond market include: (i) the right to issue corporate bonds has been extended from large state-owned enterprises to local enterprises; (ii) controls governing fund usage have been eased to the extent that non-project fund-raising methods are allowed, such as issuing corporate bonds to repay bank loans; (iii) the process of issuing corporate bonds is more streamlined, moving towards a paperless issuance procedure; (iv) interest rates for corporate bonds are increasingly being determined by market forces, and institutional investors now play a dominant role in the corporate bond investment sector; (v) risk control mechanisms for corporate bonds are improving, as more and more issuers have opted for bank guarantees instead of guarantees from related enterprises; and (vi) encouraging the participation of foreign institutions as underwriters (Fung and Leung 2001; *China Daily, HK Edition* 2003).

The establishment of the stock market

The establishment of the Shanghai Stock Exchange (SHSE) in December 1990 and the Shenzhen Stock Exchange (SZSE) in July 1991 was designed to support state-owned enterprise (SOE) reforms. Provincial governments were not allowed to sponsor companies to come to the market. In early 1992, tens of thousands of SOEs nationwide sought permission to restructure into shareholding companies, following the late Deng Xiaoping's comment that there was a need to push forward with economic reform and to experiment with securities. During the period 1993 to 1996, local leaders retained significant influence over the listing process and the enforcement of secondary market regulation, which has been blamed for triggering some stock market crises during this period (see, for example, Green 2004). During 1997–8, power was centralized in the CSRC, and in July 1999, the Securities Law came into force, laying the legislative foundation for the development of the stock market. Under this law, brokers were banned from using client funds to finance their own operations, and foreigners were prevented from buying A-shares. By 2000, the CSRC had become equivalent to a ministry in bureaucratic rank, with its own local offices and wide-ranging policy-making powers. With the influence of local government significantly reduced, public investors regained confidence in the stock market and it has enjoyed rapid expansion since then.

Other institutional developments

Reform of Chinese state-owned enterprises (SOEs)

The restructuring of the SOEs began in 1978. Instead of privatizing the SOEs, the Chinese government chose to restructure them by increasing the autonomy of managerial decision-making and creating financial incentives at the enterprise level (Xiang 1998). During 1978–80, a system of entrepreneurship and profit-retaining was implemented, and in the following two years, a 'profit–loss' contract system was put in place under which SOEs could negotiate with the local or upper-level government on the share of profit to be retained. By early 1982, over 80 per cent of SOEs were operating under the 'profit–loss' contract system (Cheng 1997, 2000). In the years that followed, the state experimented with various approaches to rejuvenate the SOEs. These approaches can be grouped broadly under two headings: the contract responsibility system (CRS) and corporatization (Xiang 1998). The experiment with corporatization began in 1984, and remained low-key until late 1991, when it was promoted significantly by the establishment of the two stock exchanges in mainland China. In 1997, a 'differential treatment' strategy was introduced to aid SOE reform, involving the 'protection of the large and release of the small'. Smaller SOEs were asked to 'find their own solutions', and since then the privatization of Chinese SOEs has grown substantially. In essence, the process of SOE reform since 1978 can be viewed as a gradual decentralization of the management of state enterprises; management authority has shifted from government bureaucrats to SOE managers. However, after nearly thirty years of reform, SOEs remain one of the most intractable problems in the

Chinese economic system, hindering the country's transitional process towards a market economy.

The emergence and blossoming of the private sector

Since the 1980s, the private sector has grown from being an extremely restricted sector into one of the most powerful engines of growth of the Chinese economy. Market-focused economic reforms and the privatization of SOEs have nurtured the growth of the non-state sector (Liu and Li 2001). Zhejiang Province has played a leading role in privatization since the early 1980s, when the Wenzhou model was first developed. This was an early form of privatization based on capital accumulation, in a family and village environment, of small and non-professionally-managed enterprises. From 1992, enterprises were offered the chance to convert to a limited liability structure in anticipation of the Company Law. When the Company Law was finally promulgated in 1994, provincial and local authorities supported its implementation as a province-wide policy. According to interviews conducted by Krug and Hendrischke (2003, 2004), local authorities could ask enterprises under their jurisdiction to convert to being limited liability companies. Therefore, the enforcement of the incorporation under Company Law differed in different areas. A further move towards privatization and the confirmation of private property rights came in 2000, when provincial authorities introduced a 'deepened system reform' for the years 2000 and 2001. This reform aimed to reduce all public enterprise shares to less than 50 per cent, effectively giving private entrepreneurs a majority share in local enterprises.

Foreign direct investment and the 'open door' policy

The Chinese economy had been closed to Western countries since 1949, but in 1979, the government decided to 'open the door' to welcome foreign investment. Two coastal provinces, Guangdong and Fujian, were allowed to adopt 'special policies' to attract more international business. In 1980, four special economic zones (Shenzhen, Zhuhai, Shantou and Xiamen) were established, and these enjoyed a special institutional and policy environment. Their success led the central government to grant special autonomy in 1984 to an additional fourteen coastal cities (Lardy 1992, 1994; Nyaw 1997). In 1988, Hainan was added as the largest special economic zone when it became a separate province. In 1992, most cities along the Yangtze River and the country's borders were also granted special privileges as coastal cities. Even many inland cities that did not enjoy the special policies established numerous development zones within their regions to take advantage of tax benefits. As a result, FDI increased sharply in the early 1990s, from US$4.4 billion in 1991 to US$28 billion in 1993 (Qian 1999b). China's 'open door' policy allowed trade expansion in product markets and an inflow of foreign investment in the capital market (Liu and Li 2001).

While it is outside the scope of this chapter to describe every important aspect of the transition in detail, it should be stressed that while many acute problems remain unsolved in the system, the country has been undergoing highly dynamic, profound yet smooth institutional change over the years since 1978. This should lay solid foundations for a modern market economy in China.

Literature review

Both theoretical and empirical evidence suggest that a strong financial sector promotes economic growth. In the 1930s, Schumpeter (1934) stressed the role of the banking sector as a financer of productive investments and thus as an accelerator of economic growth. Pagano (1993) suggests that the financial sector might affect economic growth in the sense that it increases the productivity of investments, reduces transaction costs, and affects savings. Greenwood and Jovanovic (1990), Bencivenga and Smith (1991), Levine (1991) and Saint-Paul (1992) have all constructed theoretical models in which efficient financial markets improve the quality of investments and enhance economic growth.

Meanwhile, a number of studies also investigate empirically the link between finance and growth. Goldsmith's (1969) work provides the earliest evidence that the development of financing accelerates economic growth. King and Levine (1993) studied cross-country data for eighty countries and found a strong positive relationship between financial development indicators and economic growth. Also based on the cross-country analysis, Levine and Zervos (1996, 1998) researched the role of stock markets and the banking sector, and concluded that stock market liquidity and bank development are robustly correlated with economic growth. What is more interesting to financial economists is the role of market institutions, and in the sense that market institutions define property rights,[3] a complex set of institutions must be created to ensure that use and trading in these rights is fair and transparent, and that abuses are punished appropriately (Green 2004). At the same time, the weakness of institutions in developing countries is well identified, for example, Aron (2000) argues that institutions in some developing countries are weak because such rules are simply absent, suboptimal, or poorly enforced when the costs of monitoring and enforcement prove to be too high. Aron argues that, in such an environment, transaction costs may be too high when property rights or the rule of law are not reliable.

As Williamson (1996: 377–9) argues, creating effective institutions and the rules that govern economic transactions lie at the heart of a successful transition. Institutional studies in settings of transitional and developing economies have gained more attention in recent years (World Bank 1993, 1997; Stiglitz 1998). For example, Johnson *et al.* (2002) examined the relative importance of property rights and external finance in several Eastern European countries. They found property rights to be overwhelmingly important, while external finance explains little in terms of firm reinvestment. Acemoglu and Johnson (2003) separated proxies for the security of property rights into two groups: those measuring the risk of expropriation by the government, and those measuring the ease and reliability of contract enforcement. Their cross-country results suggest that risk of expropriation is the more severe impediment to economic development.

Following the same definition of security of property rights while using Chinese firm-level data in 2002, Cull and Xu (2005) indicated that, at China's current stage of development, expropriation risk, contract enforcement, access to finance, and ownership structure all appear to matter for Chinese firms' reinvestment decisions. Allen *et al.* (2005), also based on firm-level data in China, compared growth in the formal sector (state-owned and publicly-traded firms) and the informal sector (all other firms). They found that the informal sector grew much faster than the formal sector, and provided most of the economy's growth, despite the informal sector being associated with much poorer legal and financial mechanisms. They argue that effective informal financing channels and governance mechanisms exist to support this growth, such as those based on reputation and relationships.

Although these studies are based on firm-level data, they shed some light on the relationship between financial markets, and institutional development and growth at the macro level. There are a number of studies on regional disparities among the Chinese provinces (Borensztein and Ostry 1996; Hu and Khan 1997; Park and Prime 1997; Sachs and Woo 1997), but very few have made any effort to incorporate the role of institutions.[4] In particular, Chen and Feng (2000) found that the growth of private and semi-private enterprises leads to an increase in economic growth, while the presence of SOEs reduces growth rates among the provinces based on their sample of twenty-nine Chinese provinces from 1978 to 1989. Similarly, based on a provincial level sample during the period 1986–2001, Biggeri (2003) found that the level of aggregate output in each province was influenced negatively by the presence of SOEs, which proxies for the non-marketization of Chinese provincial economic systems. Although these works tend to study some aspects of institutions, their analysis and measure of institutional development is incomplete and unsystematic. Moreover, when they incorporate both institutional development and other explanations to explain economic growth, the role of institutions is blurred or contaminated by the endogeneity of these other factors on institutional development.

Unlike these earlier provincial studies, we try to present a complete framework to examine and measure the role of financial markets and institutional development in explaining regional growth disparities across China since 1986.

Sample and methodology

Our sample consists of panel data including relevant variables observed in 31 provinces[5] in mainland China during 1986–2002. These 31 provinces are (alphabetically) Anhui, Beijing, Chongqing, Fujian, Gansu, Guangdong, Guangxi, Guizhou, Hainan, Hebei, Heilongjiang, Henan, Hubei, Hunan, Jiangsu, Jiangxi, Jilin, Liaoning, Neimenggu, Ningxia, Qinghai, Shaanxi, Shandong, Shanghai, Shanxi, Sichuan, Tianjin, Xinjiang, Xizhang, Yunnan and Zhejiang. Our data is collected from various sources, including *China Statistics Yearbook*, *China Almanac of Banking and Finance* and *China's National and Provincial Census* (1982, 1990, 2000). Growth is measured by real GDP growth in natural logarithm form, and this serves as the dependent variable in our study.

As this study investigates the role of financial-sector development on a cross-provincial basis, all the variables are measured at the provincial level. As we argued earlier in this chapter, investigating the role of financial institutions and markets at the provincial level can give more insights into China's experience than studying the country as a whole. Even though the Chinese political system is unitary rather than federal – in that all the provincial leaders are appointed directly by the senior political leadership (Green 2004) – it is recognized that provinces in China are quite heterogeneous in terms of their institutions as well as their economic development. For example, Krug and Hendrischke (2003: 33) clearly refute the assumption that China can be treated as a country with a homogeneous culture, because 'political leaders at different levels of local government (province, county, township, village) enjoy considerable discretion in timing and method of implementing privatization and related reforms'.

Similarly, Xie (2004) also remarked that it is necessary and worthwhile to study regional differences between financial markets and institutions in China, because they represent substantially different investment risks across the regions.

In an attempt to capture financial-sector development at the provincial level, we construct the following four proxies:

(i) *Loan by state banks to GDP*. Because China's state banks represent more than 90 per cent of the total banking industry (in terms of both savings or loans), the ratio of state banks' loans to GDP is a valid proxy for total bank lending to GDP. This variable captures the degree of bank loan financing at the provincial level.

(ii) *Private lending to total loans*. That is, the ratio of total bank loans made by non-state banks to total loans made by all financial institutions. This variable signifies the degree of private financing from non-state financial institutions.

(iii) *Corporate bonds issuance to GDP*. This variable measures the relative scale of financing through corporate bonds in the economy at the provincial level.

(iv) *The number of listed firms to total firms*. As China began to establish its stock market institutions in the early 1990s, many SOEs were restructured in order to go public in the domestic stock market. Private equity thus won the opportunity to invest in SOEs through buying and trading shares in the open market. This ratio captures the degree of development of stock-market-associated institutions, including investment banks, accounting professionals, supervisory bodies, and so on. As the development of these institutions should serve both to clarify the definition of and to protect property rights, this ratio also indicates the extent of property-rights-related institutional development.

Our model also includes some other institutional variables:

(v) *The extent of foreign involvement*, as proxied by FDI/GDP (per cent). As well as FDI in the direct sense, this measurement also reflects the extent to which local governments are willing to attract foreign investment, and accept new ideas, technology and increased competition in a broader sense.

(vi) *The proportion of private (and individually-owned) enterprises in the economy*. This is proxied by the ratio of the output of private enterprises in the secondary industry to total output of all enterprises in the second industry. This measurement captures the degree of privatization at the provincial level. It may also provide an additional signal of the quality and nature of the institutions: the degree of protection of property rights, the fairness of the legal system, the attitude of local government to the private sector, and the spirit of and incentives driving local entrepreneurship. Our views here are partly consistent with Cull and Xu (2005), who argue that the extent of private ownership is another aspect of property rights. Aron (2000) also points out that the scale of private firms typically correlates positively with the strength of the institutions in place.

Finally, we include three control variables in the model:

(vii) ln *(real GDP level, with one-year lag)*. This controls for the scale of each province's economy.
(viii) *Secondary school enrolment ratio*. This controls for the education quality at the provincial level.
(ix) *Fixed assets investment to GDP*. This controls for the capital input of the economy that may provide economic growth.

Our descriptive statistics are presented in Tables 5.1 and 5.2. Table 5.1 presents the summary statistics for the whole sample, including the number of observations and the mean, standard deviation, and minimum and maximum values of each variable in the sample. All these variables are measured at the provincial level.

Table 5.2 provides the mean and standard deviation (in parentheses) of the variables in selected years (not all the years are presented here because of limits of space). Looking at the statistics, we notice that real GDP growth at the provincial level has maintained an average level of 8.59 per cent. In particular, during the period 1996–2002, GDP reached an average growth rate of almost 10.5 per cent[6] across the country. Meanwhile, loans by state banks/GDP, private lending, the ratio of listed firms, the secondary school enrolment ratio, and fixed assets investment/GDP follow a generally rising pattern. Other variables, however, are mixed in the direction of their changes.

Table 5.3 presents the correlation matrix of the independent variables in the regression. Among the variables, the pairs 'private output/total output' and 'FDI/GDP', 'private output/total output' and 'real GDP level', and so on seem to be most strongly correlated.

Table 5.1 Summary statistics

Variable		N	Mean	Median	Std Dev.	Min	Max
LHS	Real GDP growth, logged	516	0.086	0.094	0.058	−0.243	0.435
RHS							
1	Loan by state banks/GDP	558	0.857	0.823	0.282	0.315	2.924
2	Private lending/total loans	516	0.129	0.150	0.118	0.000	0.622
3	Corporate bond issuance/GDP	471	0.003	0.002	0.005	0.000	0.036
4	Listed firms/total firms	513	0.005	0.001	0.009	0.000	0.067
5	FDI/GDP	508	0.025	0.009	0.038	0.000	0.244
6	Private output/total output	498	0.299	0.262	0.173	0.000	0.811
7	ln(real GDP level), one-yr lag	546	24.319	24.487	1.093	21.045	26.651
8	Secondary school enrolment ratio	547	0.846	0.886	0.124	0.396	1.000
9	Fixed assets investment/GDP	543	0.331	0.313	0.097	0.153	0.688

Notes: This table presents summary statistics of variables used in the regression analysis of this chapter. The left-hand-side variable (LHS) – that is, the dependent variable of the regression, is the natural logarithm of real GDP growth. The right-hand-side (RHS) of the regression includes nine variables. Loan by state banks/GDP is defined as the ratio of state banks' loans to GDP. Private lending/total loans is defined as the ratio of total bank loans made by non-state banks to total loans made by all financial institutions. Corporate bond issuance/GDP is defined as the ratio of issuance of corporate bond to GDP. Listed firms/total firms is defined as the ratio of number of listed firms in the stock market to the number of total firms in the economy. FDI/GDP is defined as the ratio of foreign direct investment to GDP. Private output/total output is defined as the ratio of the output of private enterprises in the secondary industry to total output in the secondary industry. ln(real GDP level), one-year lag is defined as the natural log of initial real GDP level in RMB. Secondary school enrolment ratio is defined as the ratio of students enrolled in secondary school to students graduating from primary school. Fixed assets investment/GDP is defined as the ratio of fixed assets investments made by all sectors to GDP. All variables are measured at the province level.

Table 5.2 Summary statistics by selected years

	1986	1988	1990	1992	1994	1996	1998	2000	2002
Real GDP growth, logged	0.057	0.044	0.104	0.125	0.074	0.091	0.097	0.113	0.110
	(0.040)	(0.039)	(0.077)	(0.059)	(0.050)	(0.077)	(0.026)	(0.029)	(0.017)
1 Loan by state banks/GDP	0.728	0.693	0.791	0.852	0.772	0.812	0.913	0.985	1.038
	(0.252)	(0.247)	(0.287)	(0.274)	(0.270)	(0.254)	(0.266)	(0.309)	(0.369)
2 Private lending/total loans	0.073	0.088	0.103	0.128	0.152	0.162	0.148	0.153	0.157
	(0.136)	(0.125)	(0.125)	(0.109)	(0.103)	(0.106)	(0.101)	(0.104)	(0.119)
3 Corporate bond issuance/GDP	.	0.002	0.004	0.016	0.004	0.002	0.002	0.001	0.003
		(0.002)	(0.006)	(0.009)	(0.004)	(0.002)	(0.002)	(0.001)	(0.004)
4 Listed firms/total firms	0.000	0.000	0.000	0.001	0.002	0.002	0.011	0.014	0.015
	(0.000)	(0.000)	(0.000)	(0.003)	(0.003)	(0.003)	(0.009)	(0.012)	(0.012)
5 FDI/GDP	0.004	0.008	0.008	0.020	0.052	0.043	0.039	0.026	0.027
	(0.008)	(0.014)	(0.013)	(0.033)	(0.063)	(0.051)	(0.042)	(0.026)	(0.026)
6 Private output/total output	0.218	0.200	0.216	0.266	0.350	0.423	0.500	0.258	0.348
	(0.077)	(0.093)	(0.089)	(0.110)	(0.167)	(0.172)	(0.175)	(0.171)	(0.188)
7 ln(real GDP level), one-yr lag	23.755	23.893	23.898	24.092	24.342	24.502	24.688	24.876	25.092
	(0.933)	(0.962)	(0.968)	(0.986)	(1.036)	(1.083)	(1.083)	(1.071)	(1.068)
8 Secondary school enrolment ratio	0.754	0.751	0.793	0.821	0.869	0.906	0.922	0.915	0.943
	(0.144)	(0.138)	(0.114)	(0.104)	(0.075)	(0.081)	(0.073)	(0.085)	(0.059)
9 Fixed assets investment/GDP	0.317	0.320	0.253	0.302	0.353	0.340	0.352	0.362	0.407
	(0.066)	(0.066)	(0.083)	(0.078)	(0.107)	(0.103)	(0.086)	(0.092)	(0.118)

Notes: This table presents mean values of variables used in this chapter by selected years and respective standard deviations in parentheses. Definitions of variables are as Table 5.1.

Table 5.3 Correlation matrix

	1	2	3	4	5	6	7	8	9
1 Loan by state banks/GDP	1.000								
2 Private lending/total loans	-0.032	1.000							
3 Corporate bond issuance/GDP	0.008	0.050	1.000						
4 Listed firms/total firms	0.398	0.199	-0.131	1.000					
5 FDI/GDP	0.101	0.299	0.033	0.241	1.000				
6 Private output/total output	-0.230	0.374	0.002	0.043	0.626	1.000			
7 ln(real GDP level), one-yr lag	-0.215	0.210	-0.055	0.039	0.210	0.547	1.000		
8 Secondary school enrolment ratio	0.285	0.245	0.004	0.237	0.305	0.418	0.470	1.000	
9 Fixed assets investment/GDP	0.441	0.062	-0.028	0.390	0.390	0.043	-0.260	0.276	1.000

Notes: This table presents correlation coefficients between the independent variables used in the regression analysis of this chapter. Definitions of variables are same as in Table 5.1.

Results

Table 5.4 presents the results of two groups of regressions: the fixed-effects regression results (first five columns) and fixed-effects regressions with AR(1) correction for error terms (the right-hand columns); t-statistics are reported in parentheses.

Table 5.4 shows that the development of financial markets and institutions (bank loans, private lending, corporate bonds and the stock market) is strongly and positively related to growth. Combining the role of lending activities – at both state and private-sector levels – it is obvious that the increased availability of loans is instrumental in promoting economic development. Increased competition from private banks and foreign affiliated banks has also encouraged the public banks to compete for customers, resulting in a substantial growth in lending activities. But it is the newly available private lending activities in China that have fuelled the new phenomenon of economic growth. Coefficients associated with both the 'loan by state banks to GDP' and 'private lending to total loans' show a significant impact on economic growth. In the case of the private lending variable, the impact is not only statistically significant but also significant in the sense of its economic effect on growth. The development of the stock exchange and the process of new companies issuing equity is an important development in institutional building within the financial and capital market arena. The growth of new firms seems to affect economic growth significantly, as can be seen from the coefficient of the 'listed firms to total firms' variable. Another financing source – debt – also seems to have an important affect on growth as the 'corporate bond to GDP' ratio is associated with growth at the 1 per cent statistical significance level. FDI/GDP is also strongly correlated with growth, which is consistent with other studies (for example, Biggeri 2003). In sum, these results indicate that those regions with more developed financial markets and institutions, more investment opportunities, and a more open and easy environment for private and foreign investors are associated with stronger growth.

Conclusions

China's economic success is not only one of the most remarkable in recent history; the transitional reform path the country has followed is also unique. Thus it is important to see whether and how these institutional transitions have had an impact on economic growth in

Table 5.4 Fixed effects regressions

	Fixed effects regressions					Fixed effects regressions with AR(1)				
	1	2	3	4	5	1	2	3	4	5
Constant	0.231	0.406*	0.521**	0.215	0.840***	0.085	0.154	0.160	0.040	0.105
	(1.10)	(1.75)	(2.23)	(0.83)	(2.77)	(0.79)	(1.43)	(1.34)	(0.29)	(0.79)
Loan by state banks/GDP		0.035*	0.084***	0.071***	0.066***		0.064***	0.076***	0.077***	0.059**
		(1.76)	(3.93)	(3.19)	(3.02)		(2.74)	(3.17)	(3.26)	(2.44)
Private lending/total loans			0.077**	0.081**	0.097***			0.086*	0.093**	0.098*
			(2.14)	(2.13)	(2.59)			(1.91)	(2.03)	(2.16)
Corporate bond issuance/GDP				2.270***	2.321***				2.496***	2.758***
				(4.36)	(4.55)				(4.58)	(5.08)
Listed firms/total firms					1.752***					1.269***
					(3.85)					(2.75)
FDI/GDP	0.361***	0.435***	0.445***	0.368***	0.473***	0.210	0.316**	0.336**	0.395***	0.435***
	(2.79)	(3.21)	(3.41)	(2.76)	(3.53)	(1.38)	(2.03)	(2.24)	(2.68)	(2.98)
Private output/total output	0.012	0.013	0.035	0.038	0.053*	0.015	0.015	0.023	0.042	0.042
	(0.44)	(0.51)	(1.30)	(1.38)	(1.92)	(0.52)	(0.55)	(0.76)	(1.40)	(1.42)
ln(real GDP level), one-yr lag	−0.012	−0.021*	−0.028**	−0.015	−0.042***	−0.005	−0.010	−0.012*	−0.009	−0.011
	(1.22)	(1.89)	(2.55)	(1.23)	(2.98)	(0.77)	(1.44)	(1.67)	(1.19)	(1.41)
Secondary school enrolment ratio	0.134***	0.160***	0.166***	0.133**	0.155***	0.110**	0.115**	0.125**	0.170**	0.140**
	(2.82)	(3.22)	(3.39)	(2.54)	(2.98)	(2.10)	(2.21)	(2.32)	(3.05)	(2.52)
Fixed assets investment/GDP	0.078*	0.055	0.045	0.066	0.044	0.100*	0.061	0.042	0.037	0.027
	(1.74)	(1.18)	(1.03)	(1.43)	(0.98)	(1.89)	(1.12)	(0.81)	(0.70)	(0.52)

(Continued)

Table 5.4 Continued

	Fixed effects regressions					Fixed effects regressions with AR(1)				
	1	2	3	4	5	1	2	3	4	5
N	475	475	450	426	423	445	445	420	396	393
R^2 – within	0.0946	0.1010	0.1665	0.2021	0.2308	0.0518	0.0685	0.1100	0.1944	0.2122
– between	0.0035	0.0215	0.0219	0.0051	0.0296	0.0414	0.0043	0.0019	0.0137	0.0176
– overall	0.0372	0.0121	0.0164	0.0469	0.0200	0.0545	0.0198	0.0317	0.0824	0.0935
P-value of F-test of regression	0.0000	0.0000	0.0000	0.0000	0.0000	0.0005	0.0001	0.0000	0.0000	0.0000
P-value of F-test that all $u_i = 0$	0.6910	0.5620	0.0029	0.0007	0.0000	0.9506	0.6974	0.1462	0.0095	0.0051

Notes: This table presents regression results for real GDP growth with province fixed effects. The five right-hand columns of regressions also control for the AR(1) process of error terms. Definitions of variables are as Table 5.1. Absolute values of t-statistics are included in parentheses. *, ** and *** correspond to the coefficients significant at 10%, 5% and 1%, respectively.

China. In this chapter, we have reviewed financial sector and institutional development in China since the ideological reforms of 1978. We have also examined empirically the role played by the development of financial institutions in economic growth by employing our cross-province sample. Our evidence indicates the strong role of financial markets and institutions in promoting economic growth. Four proxies were used to capture the degree of financial-sector development at the provincial level in China: 'loan by state banks to GDP' was used to capture the degree of bank loan financing at the provincial level; 'private lending to total loans' showed the extent of private financing from non-state financial institutions; 'corporate bonds issuance to GDP' measured the relative scale of financing by means of corporate bonds in the economy at the provincial level; and the 'number of listed firms to total firms' captured the extent of the development of stock market-associated institutions. Our model also included two institutional variables: the 'degree of foreign involvement', as proxied by FDI/GDP (per cent) and the 'proportion of private (and individually-owned) enterprises in the economy', proxied by the share of private enterprise output to total output in manufacturing industries.

Overall, our evidence suggests that those regions with more developed financial markets and institutions, a more open and easy environment for private and foreign investors, more protection of property rights, better investment opportunities, and more complete market institutions are associated with stronger growth. Further research on the role of institutional developments – following Hasan *et al.* (2007) – is warranted in order to gain a more conclusive understanding of the finance–growth nexus in a transitional country such as China.

Notes

1 See Shirai (2002) for a more detailed description of Chinese banking reforms.
2 In September 2000, new rules governing corporate bond issuance were brought in. These aimed to serve the development of China's floor exchange and prepare for the curb exchange. The 2000 rules introduced the listing recommender system, and specified more stringent qualifications for bonds to be listed in the stock market (*People's Daily*, 1 September 2000).
3 Demsetz (1967) defines the 'bundle of rights' as the use, revenues and transfer of assets.
4 Chen and Feng (2000) and Biggeri (2003), however, may be a few of the exceptions.
5 This includes the four municipalities that enjoy the same level of authority as the provinces: Beijing, Shanghai, Tianjin and Chongqing.

6 It should be noted, however, that the number here is the simple average of the GDP growth rate in the thirty-one provinces. Without being weighted by provincial output, this number does not equate to GDP growth at the national level.

References

Acemoglu, D. and Johnson, S. (2003) 'Unbundling Institutions', Unpublished working paper 9934, National Bureau of Economic Research, Cambridge, Mass.

Allen, F., Qian, J. and Qian, M. (2005) 'Law, Finance and Economic Growth in China', *Journal of Financial Economics*, 77: 57–116.

Aron, J. (2000) 'Growth and Institutions: A Review of the Evidence', *The World Bank Research Observer*, 15(1): 99–135.

Bencivenga, V. R. and Smith, B. (1991) 'Financial Intermediation and Endogenous Growth', *Review of Economic Studies*, 58: 195–209.

Berglöf, E. and Bolton, P. (2002) 'The Great Divide and Beyond – Financial Architecture in Transition', *Journal of Economic Perspectives*, 16: 77–100.

Berglöf, E. and Roland, G. (1995) 'Bank Restructuring and Soft Budget Constraints in Financial Transition', Centre for Economic Policy Research Discussion Paper 1250, CEPR, London.

Biggeri, M. (2003) 'Key Factors of Recent Chinese Provincial Economic Growth', *Journal of Chinese Economic and Business Studies*, 1(2): 159–83.

Blejer, M. I. and Szapary, G. (1990) 'The Evolving Role of Tax Policy in China', *Journal of Comparative Economics*, 14(3): 452–72.

Borensztein, E. and Ostry, J. D. (1996) 'Accounting for China's Growth Performance', *American Economic Review: Papers and Proceedings*, 86: 224–8.

Chen, B. and Feng, Y. (2000) 'Determinants of Economic Growth in China: Private Enterprises, Education, and Openness', *China Economic Review*, 11: 1–15.

Cheng, C.-Y. (1997) *The Process and Effects of China's Economic Reform* (Taipei: Chinese Association for Eurasian Studies).

Cheng, C.-Y. (2000) *China's Economic Reform and the Relationship with Taiwan* (Taipei: LianJin).

China Daily HK Edition (2003) 'Huge Potential of China's Corporate Bond Market', 25 July.

Cull, R. and Xu, L. C. (2005) 'Institutions, Ownership, and Finance: The Determinants of Profit Reinvestment among Chinese Firms', *Journal of Financial Economics*, 77(1): 117–46.

Demsetz, H. (1967) 'Toward a Theory of Property Rights', in H. Demsetz, *Ownership, Control, and the Firm* (Oxford: Basil Blackwell), 104–16.

Donnithorne, A. (1986) 'Banking and Fiscal Changes in China since Mao', Conference on China's System Reforms, Paper 31, Center for Asian Studies, University of Hong Kong.

Fung, H.-G. and Leung, W. K. (2001) 'Financial Liberalization and Corporate Governance in China', *International Journal of Business*, 6(2): 3–32.

Goldsmith, R. (1969) *Financial Structure and Development* (New Haven, Conn.: Yale University Press).

Green, S. (2004) 'Equity Politics and Market Institutions: The Development of Stock Exchange Governance in China, 1984–2003', Asia Programme Working Paper 12: 1–36.

Greenwood, J. and Jovanovic, B. (1990) 'Financial Development, Growth and the Distribution of Income', *Journal of Political Economy*, 98: 1076–107.

Hasan, I., Wachtel, P. and Zhou, M. (2007) 'Institutional Development, Financial Deepening, and Economic Growth: Evidence From China', *Journal of Banking and Finance*, doi: 10.1016/j.jbankfin.2007.11.016

Hu, Z. F. and Khan, M. S. (1997) 'Why Is China Growing So Fast?', IMF Staff Paper 44: 103–31, International Monetary Fund, Washington, DC.

Johnson, S., McMillan, J. and Woodruff, C. M. (2002) 'Property Rights and Finance', *American Economic Review*, 92(5): 1335–56.

King, R. G. and Levine, R. (1993) 'Finance and Growth: Schumpeter Might Be Right', *Quarterly Journal of Economics*, 108: 717–38.

Krkoska, L. (2001) 'Foreign Direct Investment Financing of Capital Formation in Central and Eastern Europe', European Bank for Reconstruction and Development Working Paper 67, EBRD, London.

Krug, B. and Hendrischke, H. (2003) 'China Incorporated: Property Rights, Networks, and the Emergence of a Private Business Sector in China', *Managerial Finance*, 29(12): 32–44.

Krug, B. and Hendrischke, H. (2004) 'Entrepreneurship in Transition: Searching for Governance in China's New Private Sector', Erasmus Research Institute of Management Report Series Reference ERS-2004-008-ORG, ERIM, Rotterdam.

Kumar, A. (ed.) (1997) *China's Emerging Capital Markets* (Hong Kong: FT Financial Publishing Asia Pacific)

Lardy, N. R. (1992) *Foreign Trade and Economic Reform in China 1978–1990* (Cambridge: Cambridge University Press).

Lardy, N. R. (1994) *China in the World Economy* (Washington, DC: Institute for International Economics).

Levine, R. (1991) 'Stock Markets, Growth and Tax Policy', *The Journal of Finance*, 46: 1445–65.

Levine, R. (1997) 'Financial Development and Economic Growth: Views and Agenda', *Journal of Economic Literature*, 35(2): 688–726.

Levine, R. and Zervos, S. (1996) 'Stock Market Development and Long-run Growth', *The World Bank Economic Review*, 10(2): 323–42.

Levine, R. and Zervos, S. (1998) 'Stock Markets, Banks and Economic Growth', *American Economic Review*, 88: 537–58.

Li, K.-W. (1994) *Financial Repression and Economic Reform in China* (Westport, Conn.: Praeger).

Li, K.-W. and Liu, T. (2001) 'Financial Liberalization and Growth in China's Economic Reform', *World Economy*, 24(5): 673–87.

Liu, T. and Li, K.-W. (2001) 'Impact of Liberalization of Financial Resources in China's Economic Growth: Evidence from Provinces', *Journal of Asian Economics*, 12: 245–62.

Nyaw, M.-K. (1997) 'The Development of Direct Foreign Investment in China', in K.-W. Li (ed.), *Financing China Trade and Investment* (Westport, Conn.: Praeger).

Pagano, M. (1993) 'Financial Markets and Growth: An Overview', *European Economic Review*, 37: 613–22.

Park, J. H. and Prime P. B. (1997) 'Export Performance and Economic Growth in China: A Cross-Provincial Analysis', *Applied Economics*, 29: 1353–63.

People's Daily (2000) 'Corporate Bond Listing Phase in Standardization', 1 September.

Qian, Y. (1994) 'Financial System Reform in China: Lessons from Japan's Main Bank System', ch. 16 in M. Aoki and H. Patrick (eds), *The Japanese Main Bank System: Its Relevance for Developing and Transforming Economies* (New York: Oxford University Press).

Qian, Y. (1999a) 'The Institutional Foundations of China's Market Transition', Paper prepared for the Annual World Bank Conference on Development Economics, Washington, DC.

Qian, Y. (1999b) 'The Process of China's Market Transition (1978–98): The Evolutionary, Historical, and Comparative Perspectives', Working Paper 99012, Department of Economics, Stanford University.

Qian, Y. and Roland, G. (1996) 'The Soft Budget Constraint in China', *Japan and the World Economy*, 8: 207–223.

Qian, Y. and Xu, C. (1993) 'Why China's Economic Reforms Differ: The M-form Hierarchy and Entry/Expansion of the Non-state Sector', *Economics of Transition*, 1(2): 135–70.

Sachs, J. and Woo, W. T. (1997) 'Understanding China's Economic Performance', National Bureau of Economic Research Working Paper 5935, NBER, Cambridge Mass.

Saint-Paul, G. (1992) 'Technological Choice, Financial Markets and Economic Growth', *European Economic Review*, 37: 763–81.

Schumpeter, J. A. (1934) *The Theory of Economic Development* (Cambridge, Mass.: Harvard University Press).

Shirai, S. (2002) 'Banking Sector Reforms in India and China: Does India's Experience Offer Lessons for China's Future Reform Agenda?', Japan Bank for International Cooperation Institute Discussion Paper 2, JBICI, Tokyo.

Stiglitz, J. (1998) 'More Instruments and Broader Goals: Moving Towards the Post-Washington Consensus', WIDER Annual Lecture 2, UNU-WIDER, Helsinki.

Thiel, M. (2001) *Finance and Economic Growth – A Review of Theory and the Available Evidence* (Brussels: European Commission).

Wachtel, P. (2001) 'Growth and Finance: What Do We Know and How Do We Know It?', *International Finance*, 4: 335–62.

Wachtel, P. (2003) 'How Much Do We Really Know about Growth and Finance?', *Federal Reserve Bank of Atlanta Economic Review* (first quarter): 33–47.

Williamson, O. E. (1996) *The Mechanisms of Governance* (New York: Oxford University Press), 377–9.

World Bank (1993) *The East Asian Miracle: Economic Growth and Public Policy* (New York: Oxford University Press).

World Bank (1997) *World Development Report 1997: The State in a Changing World* (New York: Oxford University Press).

Wu, C. (1989) 'China's Reform of the Financial and Tax System', in C. Kessides *et al.* (eds), *Financial Reform in Socialist Economies*, Economic Development Institute Seminar Series (Washington, DC: World Bank), 64–72.

Xiang, B. (1998) 'Institutional Factors Influencing China's Accounting Reforms and Standards', *Accounting Horizons*, 12(2): 105–19.

Xie, P. (2004) 'Differences of Financial Risks among Provinces in China', Speech at Financial Innovations and Macroeconomic Risks Symposium, 7 March, Beijing.

Yi, G. (1994) *Money, Banking and Financial Markets in China* (Boulder, Col.: Westview Press).

6
Institutional Analysis of Financial Market Fragmentation in Sub-Saharan Africa: A Risk–Cost Configuration Approach

Machiko Nissanke and Ernest Aryeetey

Introduction

Financial markets in Sub-Saharan Africa (SSA) have played a very limited role in the mobilization of resources to facilitate growth-enhancing private investments. Despite various efforts through financial sector reforms, financial markets remain largely fragmented, with substantial gaps in the financing of economic activities by private agents. Based on findings from surveys of formal and informal financial institutions and their clients in Ghana, Malawi, Nigeria and Tanzania,[1] we argued elsewhere (Aryeetey *et al.* 1997; Nissanke and Aryeetey 1998) that the continuous poor performance of financial systems can be partly explained by the high degree of financial market fragmentation.

The growing literature on institutional economics provides clues to possible sources of this market condition. In contrast to the Walrasian notion of markets, institutional economics views markets as broad institutional structures and arrangements that support and govern the process of exchange with the aim of minimizing transaction costs. Like any other institutions, markets exist to reduce uncertainty by establishing a stable structure for human exchange and interaction (North 1990). Specifically, as social institutions, markets structure, organize and legitimize contractual agreements, and the exchange of property rights. In this context, Coase (1992) outlines the concept of efficient property rights, since the institutional setting that governs the exchange process, including an appropriate system of property rights, becomes an important prerequisite for the efficient functioning of markets. In Coase's view, an efficient system of property rights is one that results in minimizing transaction costs for market operations.

Advancing the theory of imperfect information, Stiglitz (1989) also defines markets as an important set of institutions. In particular, it is emphasized that markets operate in environments characterized by imperfect, costly and incomplete information, and therefore appropriate governance mechanisms are required to eschew the agency problems arising from opportunistic behaviour, including moral hazard and adverse incentives. Thus institutions are seen as being created and refined to deal with various forms of market failure.

Indeed, Stiglitz's theory of imperfect information is in many respects comparable to the analysis advanced by institutional economists such as Williamson (1985, 1995), North (1990) and Coase (1992). Both schools criticize the conventional neoclassical model for failing to include the role of transaction costs in exchange, and for its inability to explain the role of institutions in the formation and operation of markets by minimizing transaction costs and reducing uncertainty. Both schools emphasize the costliness and incompleteness of information and enforcement upon which agents in the real world have to act.

Indeed, emphasizing the presence of perverse market failures, other institutional economists such as Young (1998) and Aoki (2001) conduct their institutional analysis more-or-less exclusively on agents' behaviour and their strategic interactions in a game-theoretic framework, providing a 'behavioural' micro-analytic perspective of institutions. Thus they focus more on the dimension of institutions as outcomes of game equilibria; in particular, as those of repeated games.

Arrow (1998) further notes that the role of non-market institutions is to co-ordinate expectations as well as to enforce incentives in the presence of asymmetry of information, market failure (in particular with regard to contingent future markets), and the need for co-ordination resulting from externalities and increasing returns. In this sense, institutions could be seen as serving as mechanisms and means to deal with a whole set of market failures (for example; public goods, externalities, imperfect and costly information, and the wedge between social and private benefits/returns). As Bardhan (2005) notes, one of critical functions of institutions is to correct co-ordination failures.

Institutional economics has comparative advantages over the standard static economic theory in dealing with the determinants of change over time, as it places the nature and sources of dynamism at the centre of analysis (Bardhan 1989; Harriss *et al.* 1995).[2] It can offer a coherent account of institutional changes necessary for economic development and market transformation. For example, North (1989, 1990) suggests that the sources of low growth are associated with the inability of economies to transform institutional structures in response to new technological and market opportunities. More specifically, he explains the evolution and transformation of markets as social institutions in terms of a trade-off between transaction costs and economies of scale, as increasing specialization (division of labour) proceeds.

North (1989) sees the evolution of markets as a movement from personal exchange towards the impersonal exchange of modern economies. Personal exchange involves local trade, where specialization (division of labour) is extremely limited, and individuals often engage in repeated dealings among themselves in a geographically and socially confined community setting. Transaction costs in personal exchanges are low, because transactions are governed by social codes and norms, with minimum monitoring and enforcement costs. Personal exchange then evolves into limited impersonalized exchange that involves some long-distance and cross-cultural trade. This type of exchange requires governance mechanisms, which, in historical terms, would involve dependence on kinship links, the bonding of labour, the exchange of hostages, or a merchant code of conduct.

Finally, the advanced impersonal exchange of modern economies emerges. This requires third-party enforcement rules and other elaborate institutional structures to reduce transaction costs, with effective formal systems of monitoring and mechanisms for enforcing contracts and property rights. An extensive informational network that can provide market participants with timely and comprehensive information is another critical prerequisite for market development. For markets to operate efficiently, access to information should not be discriminatory, and rules governing market operations should be transparent and comprehensible to all market participants.

Importantly, North emphasizes that market transformation from the stage of personalized exchange towards the modern impersonal mode of exchange does not necessarily take place automatically. For markets to transform and graduate to a higher stage, an appropriate institutional environment and governance structure should be developed to reduce uncertainties and transaction costs. The history of commerce illustrates how this requirement led to the formation and rise of city-states initially, and to nation-states later on, which were capable of specifying property rights and enforcing contracts (North 1989, 1990). There was a need for self-enforcing institutions and sanctions for free riding and the breach of norms as foundations for impersonal exchanges, trade, credit and markets, as shown in the examples of the differences in guilds and business coalitions between the medieval Maghrebi and Genoese traders (Greif 1993; Greif *et al.* 1994). These studies underscore the importance of establishing credibility in institutional environments and arrangements.

In our view, this analytical perspective of market evolution provides a refreshing framework for understanding the institutional sources and constraints of market fragmentation observed in SSA. One of the critical questions to be raised in the context of Sub-Saharan economies is why informal financial institutions find it hard to transform and graduate into becoming formal institutions that could handle more impersonal financial transactions. What are the institutional constraints for their successful graduation? What kinds of costs are involved in their transformation (transformation costs), so that the process of market expansion and deepening could take place within the supporting institutional structure?[3] What is a real impediment that hinders institutional innovation for market development in Africa?[4]

A further interesting twist comes from the fact that the market structure prevailing in these economies is not an outcome of the natural course of market evolution, with the realization of higher rates of return through the gradual formalization of markets as the channel. In SSA economies, as in many other developing economies, formal institutions coexist alongside informal traditional institutions as a result of modern institutional structures being superimposed on traditional societies, often without necessary adaptations. This condition could result in an extreme form of market fragmentation and segmentation, with few effective linkages between formal and informal institutions.[5] Consequently, the financial system as a whole is unable to deal with the risks inherent in SSA economies.

Distinguishing fragmentation conceptually from segmentation-cum-specialization, this chapter, based on our fieldwork data collected in the early 1990s, examines the institutional source of market fragmentation by analysing how financial risks are managed in different market segments, and what sorts of transaction costs are incurred by formal and informal institutions in the process of loan screening, loan monitoring and contract enforcement.[6] It evaluates the implications of the prevailing state of managing financial risks for market structures, and it addresses the institutional constraints facing financial systems for market transformation and development.

Risk characteristics of African financial markets and institutional performance

Lenders are generally exposed to two types of risk in their dealings with borrowers: systemic and idiosyncratic. The high systemic risk originates from unpredictable variations in income as a result of exogenous factors. The high idiosyncratic risk stems from the costly acquisition and asymmetric distribution of information, which can lead to the pervasive problem of moral hazard and adverse selection. Both types of risk are high in SSA countries. Systemic risks are high, as the economies are exposed continuously to large, aggregate, externally and policy-generated shocks as well as to high political instability and civil strife (Collier 1996; Adam and O'Connell 1999). Consequently, economic transactions are conducted in highly uncertain and risky environments, which engender eminently more volatile returns to investment and highly variable income streams than in other parts of the world.

The high-risk environment and frequent incidence of large income shocks heighten demand for mechanisms and institutions for risk management, even if only for sheer survival. Indeed, in many low-income, agriculture-based economies, where possibilities of risk management through upward diversification of economic activities have not been exploited, a variety of institutional arrangements such as share-cropping or labour migration have often served as risk-coping and risk-sharing as well as insurance mechanisms (Mordoch 1995; Bardhan and Udry 1999). However, where aggregate systemic risk is high, effective insurance against large income fluctuations is difficult to achieve through community-based risk-pooling mechanisms (Townsend 1995; Dercon 2004; Conning and Udry 2005). Many recent empirical studies reveal only limited risk-sharing, even in small village communities.[7] When insurance markets are missing and insurance possibilities limited, an act of inter-temporal trade to effect resource transfers over time such as saving and credit becomes vitally important for consumption-smoothing (Besley 1995a, 1995b). Credit transaction is seen as an insurance substitute in such circumstances, when market opportunities for risk-sharing are limited (Besley 1995b).[8] Seasonal variability of agricultural production and income in rural areas provides an added imperative for short-run savings–credit facilities as a liquidity management device over the production cycles (Besley 1995b; Conning and Udry 2005). Thus there is potentially immense demand for financial intermediation as an effective device for risk-pooling and risk-sharing in SSA.

However, financial markets in SSA have been unsuccessful in meeting this potential demand for consumption-smoothing beyond spatially confined community levels, as well as in serving the financial needs of real sector activities economy-wide. This condition partly reflects a typical dilemma associated with a vicious circle in under-developed and less-diversified economies. The portfolio structure of both lenders and borrowers is constrained by low-risk diversification in their asset composition, making it difficult to offset financial loss in one activity against the gains from another through spatial risk-pooling. A wave of loan defaults triggered by an increase of systemic risk can be propagated nationwide as a result of the high risk-covariance of economic activities. At times of negative aggregate shocks, a general crisis could ensue rapidly, because the severely impaired net worth borrowers could lead to distress in the financial sector because lenders are incapable of dealing with high aggregate systemic risks.

The underdeveloped financial markets in SSA may also be attributed to the high idiosyncratic risk that lenders face when financial transactions are conducted beyond community levels, because of poor endowments of information capital. This condition can be analysed effectively with the aid of the recent theoretical advancement in information economics. Pioneered by Stiglitz and Weiss (1981), a large number of theoretical papers have explored the implications of imperfect information and incomplete markets for contracts in credit markets in low-income environments.[9]

For example, Hoff and Stiglitz (1990) and Conning and Udry (2005) explain segmentation into formal and informal markets typically observed in developing countries by the structural differences in the cost and risk characteristics of different types of transaction. This is a clear elevation from the previous, almost exclusive, reliance on the policy-based explanation embedded in the financial repression hypothesis (Fry 1982, 1988; Roe 1991) for this critical issue in finance and development. The financial repression hypothesis is concerned mainly with parallel market activities induced by pervasive government controls and regulations. While the new understanding derived from information economics points to a possibility of segmentation leading to market specialization, where each market segment serves specific market niches by exploiting comparative advantage for assessing borrower-specific idiosyncratic risks in an environment of imperfect information. In the following sections, this theoretical perspective is adopted to explain the prevailing financial market structure in SSA.

Performance of formal financial institutions

By the early 1980s, the formal financial sector in many SSA countries had typically achieved a certain degree of diversity as a result of the efforts of the newly independent governments to reshape the post-independence financial landscape. As part of their independent nation-building programme, they established indigenous formal institutions and attempted to diversify the institutional structure of the financial system and extended banks' branch networks. However, the risk-management capacity of these formal financial institutions remained very restricted indeed. There is little doubt that the long history of widespread political interference and control of banks' operations impaired the risk-handling capacity of these institutions.

Critically, the manner in which 'repressive' policies were implemented in SSA hindered the development of institutional capacity among financial institutions. The rationale of commercial viability was largely subsumed by the dictates of other government policy objectives, as well as political goals or capture (Brownbridge and Harvey 1998; Nissanke and Aryeetey 1998). Many banks – and in particular those government-owned banks operating on a soft budget – failed to develop the capacity for risk assessment and monitoring of their loan portfolio. Savings mobilization was often not actively pursued. There was neither active liquidity and liability management nor any incentive to increase efficiency, often resulting in increased costs of financial intermediation. The regime of financial repression discouraged banks from investing in information capital, crucial for the development of financial systems. Institutions have typically been burdened with severe agency problems in dealing with idiosyncratic risks; that is, the problems caused by costly and imperfect information such as adverse selection, moral hazard and contract enforcement (Nissanke and Aryeetey 1998).

Financial-sector reforms have been implemented to address the problems arising from repression, guided largely by policy prescriptions advanced by the financial repression school. Under the two fundamental premises of liberalization and balance-sheet restructuring, interest rates and credit allocation have been decontrolled, and efforts have been made to strengthen the regulatory framework. Extensive restructuring and recapitalizing operations have been mounted for distressed banks.[10] Despite the differences in initial conditions, policy sequence and the pace of reform, the expected positive effects from liberalization (in terms of savings mobilization and private-sector credit availability) have been slow to emerge in all our case-study countries.

Banks' balance sheets remain precarious. In places such as Ghana and Malawi, where reforms have been relatively orderly, most banking institutions have not yet developed the capacity for risk management. Instead, they continue to operate in an extremely constrained environment with an underdeveloped institutional infrastructure and a poor information base. The portfolios of banking institutions have been dominated continuously by two characteristics: an extremely high incidence of non-performing loans, and excess liquidity.[11] The persistence of these conditions, despite radical changes in the policy environment, can be explained by the institutional environment that has restricted banks' risk management and prevented improvement in their operational practice.

The lack of changes in institutional environments explains the paucity of savings mobilization efforts, the 'low-lending trap' in the presence of latent excess demand for credit and loans, and the de facto crowding out of private finance by public financial requirements. These factors have combined to form a general post-liberalization credit crunch in many countries, encouraged by the presence of high-yielding government paper or bank bills.[12]

Informal finance

Informal financial transactions can be grouped into non-commercial, such as transactions between relatives and friends or small-scale group arrangements, and commercially-based, conducted by savings collectors, estate-owners, landlords, traders and money-lenders.[13] In SSA, most informal financial agents/arrangements tend to specialize in either lending or savings mobilization, while arrangements engaging in both activities typically provide their services to members only.

Informal financial units have been developed in response to the demand from a distinct clientele, and each unit tends to serve a particular market niche (Aryeetey and Udry 1997). Thus, the relative importance of different categories of the informal sector varies widely between countries in SSA. Furthermore, all four of our country studies suggest that the informal sector may far exceed the formal sector in coverage, influence, and even value transacted. Rather than a contraction in response to reform, as predicted by the financial repression hypothesis, there has been a rapid increase in demand for informal savings and credit facilities in the more liberalized environment of the early 2000s.

The recent increase in demand for informal finance is related to the greater trading opportunities that emerged in the adjustment period.

It can also be explained by an increase in unsatisfied demand for formal-sector credit, which has been restrained continuously as part of stabilization efforts. While formal institutions have continued to find it hard to overcome their inherent constraints during the reform process; it is the informal financial sector, demand-driven by its nature, that has responded first to the growing demand for financial services.

However, informal activities continue to specialize in small and short-term transactions or seasonal requirements, such as cash-flow and liquidity management for consumption smoothing at a low-income equilibrium. Saving cycles are very short. For example, the facilities of savings collectors are used primarily to keep deposits secure and savings are returned to the depositors in the shortest possible time. Thus, in spite of the acknowledged potential of informal units as deposit mobilizers, they have never been seen as having a key role in financial intermediation in the region. While many informal segments grew with the demand for their services, they face difficulties in moving beyond their particular sphere of specialization. Compared to other developing regions, informal operations in SSA have been more confined to traditional forms of activities without transforming into higher modes of operation.

Institutional arrangements for risk management

With limited opportunities for risk management through income smoothing, borrowing in SSA is largely occasioned by the need to smooth consumption in the face of erratic income flows. As borrowers seek to cushion themselves against imminent consumption risk, they may choose to smooth consumption across time and space. Spatial consumption smoothing amounts to pooling idiosyncratic risks of people/households and co-insuring against risks (Besley 1995a, 1995b; Townsend 1995; Dercon 2004). The search for other households as an insurance often embraces such social features as ethnicity, religion, business relations, neighbourliness, kinship and family, because the effectiveness of mechanisms for containing idiosyncratic risk depends on the amount and quality of information on the part of both insurers and insured, and the insurers' ability to enforce the contracts.

Dealing with idiosyncratic risks in lender–borrower interactions can be characterized effectively by a principal–agent relationship within a game theoretic framework (Conning and Udry 2005). In this relationship, lenders are preoccupied with the question of whether they will be repaid. When the effectiveness of formal legal enforcement mechanisms remains in doubt, the question of why borrowers bother to repay gains greater importance. If the relationship between borrower and lender is exclusive and repeat transaction is critical, as we find in many rural credit markets and most group arrangements, the promise of repeat borrowing and social sanctions serve as effective incentives for borrowers not to default. Social sanctions could include exclusion from other financial transactions (such as informal insurance) or other economic or social penalties. Social sanctions are available only in reasonably cohesive social groups, providing yet another reason for the propensity to transact credit within community-based groups.

However, as credit relationships are extended beyond this 'exclusive' relationship and repeated personalized transactions, other institutional arrangements become necessary to sustain transactions. Collateral is one such institutional innovation to deal with the incentive problem. Collateral pledged in exchange for loans serves three important functions: (i) directly reducing the cost to the lender of a loan default; (ii) adding an incentive for the borrower to repay, thereby reducing the moral hazard; and (iii) mitigating the problem of adverse selection by enabling the lender to screen out the borrowers most likely to default (Udry 1990).

Hence, a collateral asset should possess several attributes: (i) it must be easily appropriable by the lender; (ii) it should have a secondary market; and (iii) it should not itself be subject to moral hazard problems or other collateral-specific risk (Binswanger *et al.* 1989). Although land is a preferred asset as collateral, land markets are often underdeveloped. Other assets commonly used as collateral in rural credit transactions include jewellery or other household items as well as economic trees and standing crops, livestock and farm equipment (Bardhan and Udry 1999). As these assets are not perfect as collateral assets with the moral hazard problems, collateral substitutes such as third-party loan guarantees, interlinked transactions and a joint liability are also widely used for risk diffusion.

With spatially limited and costly information as well as costly and time-consuming contract enforcement in SSA, lenders operating beyond a community have to devote considerable resources to screening and monitoring borrowers to mitigate the problems of adverse selection and moral hazard. 'Outside' formal agents are not able to access the social sanctions that are available to informal localized lenders in this type of setting.

Because of all these institutional conditions, both formal and informal lending institutions attempt to minimize risk through loan administration practices that place greater emphasis on screening than on

monitoring or contract enforcement. Further, in such extreme institu-
tion- and information-constrained economies, lenders' perceptions
about different categories of borrowers are frequently used as a first
step towards screening.

We now turn to the key features of the risk management methods
adopted by formal and informal lenders that we found in our survey.[14]

Risk perception, screening and monitoring

Formal finance

Risk perception and loan screening. It is more difficult and costly for
formal institutions to obtain accurate information about smaller
borrowers. Our fieldwork confirms that banks' risk perceptions are less
favourable for small borrowers, which is well known by such small
borrowers. So these small borrowers are less likely to overcome the first
hurdle in accessing formal credit. Furthermore, many banks confirmed
that the higher interest rates charged for smaller borrowers are attributed
to differences in perceived risk. The increased centralization of loan
administration under reform programmes to achieve greater control
over loan quality has often led to increased risk aversion, contrary to the
hope that market liberalization would expand the scope of banking
operations to a wider group of private agents.

Equally, in screening, banks are disadvantaged in acquiring information on personal integrity. While they try to obtain information about
potential borrowers and their current indebtedness from third parties
(including approaching other banks for references), their attempts are
usually unsuccessful. The most reliable information banks can access is
borrowers' account history available at their own branches. Given this
situation, judgements are based largely on project documentation and
bankers' personal knowledge of the proposed projects. They can carry
out major feasibility studies, which inevitably increase screening costs.
As standard practice in the screening process, project sites of small
agricultural and large enterprise clients are visited. Indeed, time spent in
verifying information for project analysis, with its associated salary and
support costs, was cited to be the largest single impediment to lending to
small borrowers, as the fixed costs of acquiring information that is
independent of loan size are viewed as being too high. In assessing
project creditworthiness, the return on projects was mentioned as the
most important criterion by all the bankers surveyed.

Many banks, especially those undergoing reform, recognize the
problems caused by the absence of credit reference bureaux and poor

interbank co-operation. The lack of good market information on supply, demand and costs also hinders project assessment. Increasingly, banks recognize the need to pursue more character-based assessments for small borrowers who cannot supply the documentation and financial inform-ation demanded for project appraisal. Despite this, reforms have not yet led to any major changes in the assessment of creditworthiness. Banks have begun to look for alternative securities, such as blocked accounts and letters of undertaking, but landed property remains the dominant form of collateral.

The mention of collateral in the lending criteria of nearly all lenders suggests that it is used as a substitute for effective appraisal of the entrepreneur and project. Interestingly, while banks insist that they consider the viability of projects to be the most important criterion in assessing applications, many small borrowers believe that their loan applications were rejected because of a lack of collateral. The foreclosure of collateral property is difficult in many African countries, in view of the ambiguities surrounding property rights. Thus collateral requirement and restricted options for collateral assets and substitutes are likely to act as a credit-rationing device, excluding many otherwise creditworthy small borrowers from formal credit.

As loan screening is costly, there is some evidence from our fieldwork to confirm the theoretical prediction that lenders are more likely to enter into repetitive games. In Nigeria, banks tend to have a long-standing relationship with their large clients. For both commercial and merchant banks, there were far fewer first-time borrowers than repeat borrowers. This situation was repeated in Ghana for large borrowers, and in Malawi for all types of borrowers. Other forms of 'tests', such as the provision of a small initial loan, were rarely applied. Fewer than 10 per cent of bank managers in Ghana indicated they had provided initial advances to any type of borrower. This may be explained by the screening methods, whereby greater emphasis is given to the quality of projects than to borrower characteristics.

Loan monitoring We found little evidence of extensive loan monitoring in our bank branch surveys in Ghana, Nigeria and Tanzania.[15] Monitoring was more often conducted through accounts than via projects. This failure of banks to make extensive project visits does not necessarily indicate a lack of concern about moral hazard. Rather, it was the result of pressures to cut costs. Also, many banks in SSA, particularly government-owned banks, lack the transport facilities for regular project visits. In Malawi alone did loan monitoring dominate the loan administration process, mainly because agricultural borrowers are usually owners of large plantations within easy reach of urban bank branches.

Informal finance

Risk perceptions and loan screening.   Informal lenders generally contend that they do not attach different risks to borrowers within their usual clientele. In group-based arrangements, borrowers are pre-selected by membership requirements. Traders lend only to people with whom they have a trading relationship. Moneylenders are the only informal lenders who do not lend to distinct groups of clients. Given the lack of competitive pressure, moneylenders respond to possible risk variations by charging uniformly high risk premiums for all loans, rather than charging different interest rates to different borrowers. They rationalize their high rates as reflecting socially acceptable norms.

Screening in the informal sector relies extensively on personal knowledge of borrowers, as suggested by Udry (1990, 1994) and Yotopoulos and Floro (1991). The development of personal ties and proximity are mechanisms for countering the effects of adverse selection and moral hazard. Such familiarity with a borrower reduces the significance of repeat borrowing, and a repetitive relationship only becomes important if the lender has no other means of verifying information about a borrower. The more rural the environment, the greater the need to personalize ties in confronting information asymmetry, as observed by Udry (1990, 1994) in Northern Nigeria, where agricultural lending is, as a norm, conducted among relatives, acquaintances and neighbours.

In general, in individually-managed arrangements, more than two-thirds of successful applicants were personal acquaintances of lenders. Many West African moneylenders who do not show a preference for repeat lending, attach a great deal of importance to the recommendation of previous clients with information on the personal character of a new client rather than on his/her indebtedness. West African savings collectors are often indifferent between repeat and first-time borrowers, as the key piece of information for them is whether cash flows are sufficient to make daily deposits possible.

While interlinked credit markets are often seen as a major aspect of informal credit transactions in developing countries (Bardhan 1989; Yotopoulos and Floro 1991), we found few in our sample. This is consistent with the observation made about production relations in semi-arid Africa: that the tied market relations are limited and inefficient as a collateral substitute (Binswanger *et al.* 1989). Most moneylenders in Ghana and Nigeria did not require a business relationship with applicants before loan approval. The largest incidence of interlinked transactions was observed in Tanzania, where linking credit to land titles effectively became a way of buying land in a system where land sales were not possible. In Malawi, interlinked transactions are observed between estate owners and labourers/tenants in tobacco plantations.

In group-based arrangements such as rotating saving and credit associations (ROSCAs) or non-rotating savings and credit associations (SCAs), where only members received loans, all borrowers are known. Effectively, they do not screen loans, but screen membership based on the applicant's character, trustworthiness and commitment to the group's goals. In general, the methods of client selection used by informal lenders and groups effectively reduce the risk of dealing with small borrowers. Thus, their clientele/borrowers may be thought of as being low-risk, even though they would be perceived as high-risk by formal lenders.

Loan monitoring. It is often suggested that the opportunity for frequent and easy loan monitoring is one way by which informal lenders are able to reduce the incidence of default (Yotopoulos and Floro 1991). Contrary to this notion, we observed little attempt by informal lenders to monitor the use of loans explicitly. Our evidence supports Udry's (1990) position that informal lenders have little need to monitor loans explicitly, because of free information flow in their operating circles.

In Tanzania, only two of the nineteen savings and credit societies (SCS) reported any form of loan monitoring. For West African savings collectors, loan monitoring is taken for granted as daily visits to clients for deposit collection ensures that loans are monitored. Moneylenders in Ghana and Nigeria, and informal groups in most other countries, indicated that they did not bother with monitoring. The situation is different only for estate owners in Malawi, who provide loans as part of interlinked market arrangements that require regular interaction between lender and borrower.

Loan repayment and contract enforcement

Formal finance

Loan repayment trends. Loan repayment trends vary considerably across bank types.[16] Some of the most disappointing bank loan repayment records were in Tanzania, where poor contract enforcement characterizes the whole banking system and there was a serious deterioration in the loan portfolios of banks' in the adjustment period.[17] The proportion of non-performing loans for commercial banks in Tanzania was between 80 and 86 per cent (Bagachwa 1996).

In Nigeria, both publicly-owned and private banks are under considerable stress. Given the proliferation of financial institutions following imprudent and premature deregulation, the problems of moral hazard and adverse selection have loomed large. In 1992, 45 per cent of the total outstanding loans of the banking system were classified as non-performing. Among the distressed banks that are technically insolvent but continue to operate, 67–77 per cent of outstanding loans have been non-performing in recent years. These statistics do not cover non-performing loans of the development finance institutions (DFIs), which are believed to have non-performing loans amounting to at least 80–90 per cent of total loans. Some of the worst performances were observed in rural lending by large commercial banks and merchant banks.

In Ghana, formal-sector default rates are not low, but there was more variation by borrower type and location than we saw in Nigeria and Tanzania. Small agricultural loans accounted for over 55 per cent of delinquency in the period between 1988 and 1990. Actual defaults were most pronounced in development bank branches and the unit rural banks. Although small loans tend to default more than large loans in numerical terms, large loans accounted for 55 per cent of loan amounts in default by the end of 1991. Amounts in default by small agricultural borrowers accounted for 25 per cent.

In Malawi, poor repayment rates for small borrowers were also observed, but the scale of the problem was much more contained. Furthermore, delinquency, rather than actual default, was more of a problem, as most delinquent loans tended to be paid within twelve months of becoming overdue. Delinquency among small enterprise borrowers stood at 16 per cent for the same period. Interestingly, only 5 per cent of agricultural loans were either delinquent or in default, a figure comparable to the 2 per cent for large enterprises. The low default rates for agriculture may be because, in Malawi, these loans are directed at large plantation owners.

Contract enforcement

Under conditions of low repayment, one would expect contract enforcement to play a significant role in loan administration. However, despite a relatively large incidence of default, foreclosure of collateral or legal action was rarely observed in our case-study countries. With no legal institutions to enforce contracts effectively, and the absence of bankruptcy laws and procedures, the attitude of banks to contract enforcement is subtle. The first line of action is to persuade delinquent borrowers to resume their payments. Most Ghanaian bankers indicated that delinquency and default tended not to be wilful, but instead a result of poor returns on investments, particularly because of bad management of small enterprise projects.[18] About 85 per cent of bank managers interviewed in Ghana indicated that they often re-finance projects to revive distressed borrowers. However, these banks do not have access to sufficient information to arrange state-contingent loan contracts for borrowers who are do not default wilfully. Nor are there many effective mechanisms available to banks to enforce wilfully defaulting borrowers.

Informal finance

Loan repayment

Our surveys confirm the view that delinquency and default rates in the informal sector are relatively low (Udry 1990, 1994). In Ghana, between 70 per cent and 80 per cent of our entire sample of informal lenders reported that they had no delinquent borrowers in 1990 and 1991. Among those who had, the delinquents usually represented less than 5 per cent of borrowers. The largest proportion of defaulting borrowers was observed in rural credit unions and co-operatives with hundreds of members, where defaulters averaged 30 per cent of borrowers. While Malawian and Tanzanian default rates were also low, slightly higher delinquency rates were observed in Nigeria, where 14 per cent of borrowers from moneylenders were delinquent; 17 per cent with SCAs, and 20 per cent with *esusu* collector borrowers.[19] As in other countries, all lenders believed that delinquent borrowers would repay within three months of the loan maturing. Default rates in rural Nigeria were significantly lower than those in urban Nigeria, which is in accordance with Udry's (1990) findings.

In rural areas, non-payment is generally attributed to borrowers' cash-flow problems, while many urban lenders think it is a mixture of cash-flow problems and low commitment on the part of borrowers to settle debts. Cross-tabulating perceptions on the causes of default to loan end-use suggests, however, that lenders providing loans for consumption purposes and trading tend to be more concerned with strategic default than those lending to farmers. The latter are more concerned about failed projects, arising from random production and income shocks that lead to default. Within local communities, where the free flow of information is guaranteed, loan contracts could be structured as state-contingent contracting without a fear of moral hazard. Udry (1990, 1994) reports that, in the villages of Northern Nigeria, such state-contingent contracting is used as a risk-pooling mechanism against idiosyncratic shocks within the village. Under such arrangements, realized interest rates and repayment periods are adjusted for households who have experienced adverse shocks. Needless to say, however, such arrangements cannot be used against village-wide systemic shocks.

Contract enforcement

While repayment trends in the semi-formal and informal sectors are much better, these are seldom the result of more 'aggressive' contract enforcement procedures, as suggested by Shipton (1991). We found little evidence of litigation. To start with, informal lenders effectively screen out 'costly' borrowers in the case of non-payment. Once delinquency becomes an issue, lenders apply the most effective but least costly enforcement mechanisms at hand, case by case. Hence, contract enforcement mechanisms vary significantly depending on lender–borrower relationships. Effective tools are often embedded in the personalized relationships through the extended family, friendship and other social relationships. Among group-based arrangements and in rural areas, mechanisms such as peer pressure or the potential use of social stigmatization are effective. Udry (1990) reports a case where an appeal to community authorities by a lender in response to a perceived default resulted in a prompt repayment. Ironically, when the number of defaulters in a rural co-operative arrangement is large, the sanction of stigmatizing an individual fails to be effective. Where lenders cannot depend on moral suasion alone, they apply other mechanisms.

In Tanzania, the use of interlinked transactions enables an expansion of the control variables to influence the borrower's actions (Bagachwa 1995). An interlinked transaction can thus be treated as a disguised form of collateral.[20] Granting usufruct rights to lenders, such as tree pledging, is also common among cocoa farmers in western Africa (Adegboye 1969). In the absence of these mechanisms, collateral assumes a greater role in risk management. Thus, more Ghanaian lenders than their Tanzanian counterparts demanded collateral in the form of physical assets such as buildings, farmland, and undeveloped land or non-physical securities such as guarantees from friends, relations or employers. About 83 per cent of Ghanaian moneylenders and 76 per cent of credit unions require security against loans.

Although informal lenders do not generally resort to foreclosure on collateral or expensive legal actions, they do hold on to collateral to guarantee eventual repayment. It is certainly easier for a cocoa farmer to hold on to a confiscated cocoa farm indefinitely than for a bank to do so. Banks are not able to seize collateral, as storage or maintenance costs can be prohibitive. Hence, borrowers would not treat the threat of collateral confiscation by an informal lender as lightly as they would from a formal lender, and this could affect their attitudes to repayment between the two sectors.

Estimates of transaction costs

While the costs of acquiring information affect the choice of risk management methods, the transaction costs are determined by both the method and the effectiveness of the risk management applied. The transaction costs of lending are the sum of the costs of administering credit (loan screening, monitoring and contract enforcement) and the costs of the risk of default, defined as 'those expenses for the risk of loan default incurred by the lending institutions, for example, provision for loan losses, the loan guarantee fees paid, and the actual bad debts incurred' (Saito and Villanueva 1981). In this section, we relate risk management practices to transaction costs.

Formal finance

Although most banks base cost calculations on their standard overhead costs, in considering transaction costs for each type of lender, we measured administrative costs and default risk costs separately.[21] Our analysis shows that the cost structure reflects the relative importance attached to the different components of risk management.

In Ghana, commercial banks concentrate more on screening expenditure.[22] An exception to this is the administration of small agricultural loans, for which all banks allocated an average 40 per cent of the resources for monitoring loans, more than double that for other types of loans. In contrast, Nigerian banks spend less on screening (15 per cent of loan administration costs) but find themselves incurring higher costs for loan monitoring and contract enforcement. This may be attributed to a more pervasive fear of moral hazard and wilful default in Nigeria. The marginal cost for administering each loan is as indicated in Table 6.1.

While many small borrowers are already excluded from the sample because of screening, our survey data do not validate the popular assertion that small loans cost more to transact than larger ones. The overall administration costs are also correlated with the degree of centralization of decision-making, as greater centralization increases

Table 6.1   Loan administration costs as a percentage of loan amount

Country	Type of enterprise/applicant			
	Small-scale enterprises	Large-scale enterprises	Small-scale agriculture	Other
Ghana	1.7	0.2	3.5	1.4
Malawi*	3.4	17.6	8.9	13.5
Nigeria	12.9	18.9	12.3	11.4
Tanzania**	12.4	–	–	–

Notes: * Based only on staff time allocations; ** Not broken down by sector.
Source: Nissanke and Aryeetey (1998).

Table 6.2   Transaction costs of lending in Ghana as a proportion of total loan amount for sector, by type of bank

Bank type	Type of enterprise/applicant			
	Small-scale enterprises	Large-scale enterprises	Small-scale agriculture	Other
Commercial bank	3.2	1.8	6.4	4.1
Development bank	8.7	8.0	10.6	8.2
Unit rural bank	5.8	–	3.9	3.0
Overall	5.9	4.9	6.9	5.1

Source: Nissanke and Aryeetey (1998).

screening costs. For example, the cost differential between small enterprises and large ones in Malawi is related to the degree of centralization of decision-making between the two types of loans, as the amounts sought by small enterprises fall within the lending limits of branch managers. Much higher costs incurred by Nigerian banks across different borrower types are also attributable to more centralized decision-making, larger overheads, and larger branch networks than their Ghanaian counterparts. The high loan administration costs for the small-enterprise sector in Nigeria also reflect the greater engagement by merchant banks in this type of lending.

For Ghana, where we obtained estimates on default risk costs, total transactions costs were measured as in Table 6.2.[23]

For all types of borrowers, the transaction costs were highest for development banks, where loan administration costs per branch were lowest. Clearly, their administration methods put a premium on default risk, as it was their high provisions for bad debts that increased their transaction costs. Significant over-estimations of default risks are also common for other banks. Our estimates of the average transaction costs for small-enterprise lending and small agricultural loans are comparable to those incurred by development banks in the Philippines, reported in Saito and Villanueva (1981). The major difference arises for large enterprises: our estimate of 4.9 per cent for this category is more than twice their average of 2.1 per cent.

Further, it is worth noting that transaction costs in the range of 5–7 per cent would account for less than a half of interest rate spreads in Ghana. Thus the high and increasing spreads observed in the adjustment period cannot be explained totally by high transaction costs, and may instead reflect a lack of competition among banks. However, high spreads in the other countries may be related more closely to high transaction costs, because of their higher administration costs (see Table 6.1). The high transaction cost of arranging loans also explains why banks prefer roll-over overdraft facilities with a low cost–risk configuration, or investing in low-risk and high-return government papers and bank bills.

Informal finance

The transaction costs of informal lenders are much lower than those incurred by formal ones (see Table 6.3).[24] Most costs are incurred in the screening process, which dominates their risk management. Their screening costs are low because they rely extensively on pre-selection of clients. Any attempt to break out of their traditional segment will require new operating principles and additional information-gathering costs. This explains why all informal lenders behave as moneylenders

Table 6.3 Mean loan administration cost, 1992 (percentage of loan amount)

Country	Moneylender		Savings collector		Savings and credit association/ co-operative		Credit union	
	Urban	Rural	Urban	Rural	Urban	Rural	Urban	Rural
Ghana	1.8	2.7	0.9	0.6	0.3	0.3	2.6	4.4
Malawi	0.6	0.6	–	–	0.2	0.2	0.4	0.1
Nigeria	3.2	2.7	0.6	0.6	1.0	0.6	1.9	0.6
Tanzania	1.7	2.6	–	–	0.1	0.1	2.5	3.0

Source: Nissanke and Aryeetey (1998).

when they lend to non-members: a new risk is introduced, for which a premium has to be charged.

In general, costs increase as the operations of informal entities become more formal. Thus the cost of more formal credit unions in Accra was on average twice that of co-operatives. It is hard, however, to attribute the phenomenal differences in interest rates charged across informal lenders to the differences in loan administration costs shown here. The ability of some commercial informal lenders to extract a monopoly rent is confirmed by our survey data. For example, the mean monthly interest rates charged by moneylenders are 10 per cent, 19 per cent, 8 per cent and 48 per cent in Ghana, Nigeria, Tanzania and Malawi, respectively. Naturally, the share of monopoly rent in the interest rates is a function of the degree of competition prevailing in a particular market.[25] As markets are so fragmented, moneylenders acting as last resorts for those who do not have access to alternative credit sources face hardly any competition. Furthermore, an analysis of interest rates charged by commercial informal lenders must allow for compensation for transaction costs, risk premiums and the opportunity costs of funds, as well as monopoly rents or profits (Bottomley 1975).

For a more accurate picture on this question it is necessary to estimate the cost of funds. This requires data on interest payments on deposits and their handling costs, returns on alternative investments (the opportunity costs of lending), and interest payments on loans taken for lending. Although we have only limited data from Ghana and Malawi on some of these parameters, a number of general points can be made. First, the lack of access that informal units have to banks for on-lending means that there are few borrowed funds involved. Second, for most informal units, deposit mobilization incurs insignificant costs. For example, savings collectors who receive payments for taking deposits may have a negative cost of funds.[26] For a typical one-month loan from an *esusu* collector in Accra, the total transaction cost was equivalent to −5.3 per cent of the loan amount. Considering the monthly lending rate of 3.3 per cent, there is a substantially large spread of more than 8 percentage points.[27]

The opportunity cost of funds can also be fairly low, depending on where lenders would otherwise have invested. For ROSCA members, low opportunity costs can be inferred by the fact that their operations remain sustainable, even though no interest is paid on the funds deposited by members. The opportunity cost of funds for moneylenders may also be low, as they are known to lend out 'temporarily idle' funds in the very short term. Their loan default risks are effectively contained and the costs involved are not high.

Given these preliminary observations, the high interest rates charged by moneylenders are difficult to justify in terms of high rates of default, a high correlation among defaults and high costs of screening loan applicants and pursuing delinquent borrowers (as suggested by Aleem 1990, in relation to a rural credit market in Pakistan). In the countries studied here, the high returns realized by moneylenders could be interpreted as monopoly profit from operating in incomplete, uncompetitive markets. While it is admittedly hazardous to compare interest rates on informal credit because of the highly heterogeneous nature of loan products,[28] wide differential returns across different segments of the informal market cannot be justified by risk differentials or cost differentials alone.

Summary and conclusion: market structure and institutional constraints for market transformation

Our discussion shows that the demarcation of the boundaries of specialization is determined by each lender's attempts to mitigate the problems caused by information asymmetry, and to contain risks and transaction costs. Both formal and informal lenders largely pre-select clients on the basis of the availability of information and the means of managing risks. Each market segment thus formed serves distinct socio-economic groups with structurally differentiated financial products.

This condition is related to a variety of institutional constraints. The internal shortcomings of the formal financial sector, such as inadequate supervisory and regulatory provisions, are compounded by poor legal mechanisms for contract enforcement, inappropriate incentive environments, and restricted flows of information, the combination of which increases the riskiness of lending. Each lender's preference for a particular risk management method is shaped in this institutional environment, while attempts to confront the increased riskiness have differential impacts on transaction costs. Faced with various institutional constraints, the range of clientele served by each lender is both narrow and polarized at the extreme ends of the market.

For example, the cost of acquiring reliable information on idiosyncratic risks of potential borrowers is prohibitive for formal institutions. Hence the type of information sought by, and available to, banks about small borrowers during the screening process is less reliable and qualitatively different from that collected by informal lenders. Therefore, banks are forced to devote relatively more resources to monitoring and contract enforcement than are informal lenders or groups. Despite these efforts and the resources expended, banks' loan repayment rates continue to be poorer, and hence banks have to absorb high default-risk costs into their transaction costs.

In contrast, informal financial market segments have long-established devices and mechanisms for coping with agency problems within geographically and socially confined community settings. These mechanisms used by heterogeneous informal associations and agents are rooted firmly in indigenous social codes and norms. They are anchored in institutional arrangements tested over many decades, if not centuries.

Indeed, informal units enjoy considerable advantages in information and transaction costs when they deal with their traditional clientele. They possess a competitive edge in risk management and transaction costs in small credit provision within local networks, as well as in small and short-term savings mobilization, which are difficult for formal institutions to tap for reasons of size-sensitive costs.

This condition points to the potential in exploiting the comparative advantages of the informal financial sector to promote financial sector development. We have argued (in Nissanke and Aryeetey 1998) that the capacity of financial systems could be enhanced if integrative mechanisms between formal and informal segments are developed that can reduce operational constraints facing each sector, and at the same time capitalize on the comparative advantages conferred by each sector. Even though markets incorporate both formal and informal segments, a financial system could perform its function more efficiently if the potential benefits from the specialization of each sector could be fully exploited. Such integrative mechanisms could facilitate 'crowding-in' synergy effects between informal and formal financial institutions, as Conning and Udry (2005) suggest. For this potential to be realized there should be dynamic and operative interactions between the segments through overlapping players, and market signals should be transmitted across the sectors.[29] For example, in a number of Asian countries, a heterogeneous and dynamic informal financial sector has continued to exist as part of the financial system. Yet, in these economies, market integration has taken place and the intermediation efficiency of the system as a whole has increased over time, as specialization in financial services by each sector has progressed (Ghate 1990; Biggs 1991).[30]

Referring to some Asian economies where a continuum or a semblance of an integrated financial system is observed, Ghate (1988: 75) suggests that the two sectors are substitutes over a range of credit needs that occupy the middle range of a spectrum of credit markets and purposes. Within this range they impinge on each other's share of the market, depending on lending and borrowing rates in each sector. At both ends of the spectrum, however, each occupies a number of markets which cannot be served by the other and which are therefore complementary.

In short, the integrated financial system has a 'captive' segment and a 'contested' segment.

It may be argued that the financial system as a whole becomes more competitive if the range of demand, non-exclusive to one sector (that is, the contested segment), expands. In the presence of overlapping demand, there are also spillover effects from the formal to the informal segments. For example, Bell (1990) shows that when informal lenders act as intermediaries for formal institutions, the resulting lower cost of funds to informal lenders will be passed on to borrowers, depending on the degree of competition in the informal market. Thus, where demand is non-exclusive (that is, overlapping), direct credit links can have a positive effect on the efficiency of financial systems.

In SSA, there have been few functional linkages between and within different market segments. First, direct institutional linkages are insignificant. While there are direct deposit links between banks and some informal agents/associations, the savings of informal agents are held in non-interest-bearing demand deposits for safe-keeping, and, as such, are seldom intermediated for investment because of conservative asset management on the part of banks (Aryeetey and Steel 1992; Nissanke and Aryeetey 1998). There are few direct linkages in credit allocation between banks and traditional informal operators.

Indirect links among different market segments are also weak because of the extremely narrow range of overlapping demand for financial services. Neither complementarity nor competition are generally observed in financial market relationships. De facto financial inter-mediation, which involves on-lending by large enterprises to smaller sub-contractors, has not been observed on the scale found in some Asian countries, partly as a result of the limited scope for backward and forward linkages in real sector activities in SSA. Nor has an extensive 'credit layering' of wholesale and retail provision of services been reported.

Overall, flows of funds and information are insignificant between segments, and access by clients to financial products is extremely limited with little substitution and overlapping demand. Under such prevailing conditions, formal and informal sectors often form almost discrete financial enclaves. With few linkages among segments, the scope for information-sharing or risk-pooling/sharing has been limited. Informational advantages possessed by informal agents have not been effectively capitalized up on as a means of achieving a more efficient system of financial intermediation.

A specific market structure has emerged in which institutional arrangements have become barriers for interaction across segments. Markets are characterized by an extreme degree of fragmentation, giving agents in each segment the opportunity to exploit market power. In fragmented markets, risk-adjusted returns are not comparable across segments. Cost variations observed among different types of lenders cannot on their own account for the large differences in loan prices. Interest rates diverge significantly across and within segments, reflecting the severity of market fragmentation. As the range of the captive segment far exceeds that of the contested segment, structural characteristics of these potentially monopolistic competitive markets are skewed towards imperfect competition.

Severely constrained by institutional conditions, financial units specialize in a very narrow range of products. This has led to a situation where, not only do financial markets become too fragmented to allow risk-adjusted returns to converge, but considerable gaps in financial services have also emerged. The financing gaps absorb those potential borrowers who either fail to meet the lending criteria of various existing lenders, or find their products unattractive. They are either too large for informal lenders or too small for formal lenders.[31]

With the fundamental problems faced by formal and informal institutions/agents unresolved, each segment continues to struggle with its respective operational constraints. On the one hand, despite the flexibility and adaptability shown by some informal financial arrangements, the characteristics of informal agents/groups are such that the growth of operations *within* the informal sector is severely limited in SSA.

In effect, informal financial units operate continuously as personalized transactions, largely in a repeated-game framework. Their heavy reliance on localized, personal information often prevents them from transforming into full-scale intermediaries. Their risk management is valid as self-reinforcing contracts within a limited community/local setting. It relies extensively on traditional social institutions and mechanisms based on the village and kin groups for informal insurance arrangements. While these have provided informal social safety nets and redistributive mechanisms, local lenders are granted the opportunity of using their privileged personalized information about the borrower to bar entry to the local credit market. This has injected a more monopolistic element into the market structure.

On the other hand, formal institutions implanted externally during the colonial period or created by governments on independence do not have a firm anchor in indigenous social institutions. African states are often regarded as operating with 'soft state' institutions (Platteau 1996). The formal legal systems and the concepts of private property rights are seen as 'foreign' to many local settings, and hence lack support and legitimacy in local culture and social norms.[32] In the absence of functional institutions to support their operations, banks suffer from a legacy of either conservatism or financial distress, characterized by high transaction costs and severe loan recovery problems. This is despite their potential advantage in exploiting economies of scale in portfolio management and diversification to allow spatial risk-pooling and maturity transformation.

As outside agencies, formal financial institutions do not have access to local information about borrowers. Consequently, their methods of loan screening and monitoring are costly and imperfect. Therefore, using collateral requirements as a credit-rationing device for small borrowers, they concentrate their loan portfolio on larger, formal (often public) enterprises. The performance of these enterprises is not necessarily rigorously screened and monitored. With the weak formal systems of contract enforcement, implicit government guarantees against the failure of large formal institutions can ultimately be used as a last resort. In SSA, such guarantees have largely to be underwritten by foreign aid, and this condition could engender and perpetuate a culture of 'aid dependency'.

Thus the institutional environment prevailing in SSA is not yet fully capable of supporting transactions taking place beyond local communities. This condition has led many researchers to conclude that African economies appear to be locked into the low developmental stage, where a dense social network leads to the development of fairly stable informal structures, such as customs, trust and normative rules which give an informal institutional framework for organizing activities, as Aron (1997) argued. One of the critical questions to be addressed in relation to African economic development is to create institutional conditions where private agents operating within informal arrangements feel prepared to transform themselves into more formal units that are conducive to productive activities promising higher social and private returns. For this to happen, however, the institutional environment would need to undergo a fundamental structural transformation in order to underpin market transformation on a sustainable basis.

In Nissanke and Aryeetey (1998), we spelt out some institutional measures to accelerate the process of integration of hitherto fragmented informal and formal market segments. We emphasized the possibility of financial-sector development, building on the strengths of informal institutions in SSA. Here it may suffice to note that, broadly speaking, institutional measures for financial market transformation should address informational problems, the incentive (agency) problem and contract enforcement problems directly (Hoff and Stiglitz 1990; Conning and Udry 2005). These should therefore encompass measures aimed at strengthening legal systems related to property rights safeguards and contract enforcement; accumulating information capital; improving the governance/incentive structure; and intensifying market network development.[33] Special attention should also be paid to 'institution innovation' aimed at overcoming extreme market fragmentation through effective integration measures.

Institutions, which define and limit the set of choices facing agents by providing the incentive structure, comprise formal rules, informal constraints, and the effectiveness of their enforcement (North 1990). Hence, institutional change is a multi-faceted and complex process, involving changes in perceptions, preferences, organizational forms, and agents' behavioural patterns through the society investing in acquiring knowledge, co-ordination, and 'learning-by-doing' skills (North 1990, 1997). These cannot be effected over the short-term. However, governments could play a positive role in expediting the transformation process by understanding that the changes in formal rules governing enforcement mechanisms have to be complemented and supported by incremental changes in informal constraints and ideological constructs, to restructure human interactions and develop new conventions and norms.

Notes

1   For detailed fieldwork methodology, samples and results, see Aryeetey (1994, 1996), Bagachwa (1995, 1996), Chipeta and Mkandawire (1996a, 1996b), Soyibo (1996a, 1996b).
2   For more detailed discussion on the evolution and dynamics of institutional changes, see Nissanke and Sindzingre (2005).

3   Here, we define transformation costs in relation to market transformation as the costs involved in transforming the form and nature of modes of market exchanges. Thus they are different from those given by North (1990: 6). North's transformation costs are referred to as the traditional production costs of capital, labour, technology and natural resources.

4   Fafchamps (2004) lists innovation failure – along with authority failure and co-ordination failure – as one of the critical features of financial markets in SSA.

5   See Sindzingre (2006) for a critical assessment on a rather over-simplistic, dichotomizing application of the concepts of 'formal' and 'informal', found in institutional economics. Here, 'formal' and 'informal' finance are used following convention in the literature of financial economics.

6   Conning and Udry (2005) also discuss fragmentation of rural financial markets in low-income countries.

7   See Conning and Udry (2005) for the results of empirical tests of the efficient risk-sharing and full insurance hypotheses.

8   As Besley (1995b) notes, while the distinction between credit and insurance is often blurred, a pure credit arrangement rather than a contract with contingencies is unlikely to be optimal in many risky environments.

9   Alderman and Paxson (1992) and Conning and Udry (2005), among others, provide a useful bibliography of such studies.

10 Popiel (1994) provides estimates that the cost of bank restructuring operations in about 20 SSA countries between 1984 and 1993 was often equivalent to between 7 per cent and 15 per cent of their GDP. Deschamps and Bonnardeaux (1997) report that the direct cost of bank restructuring ranged from 20 per cent to 50 per cent of GDP in the most affected SSA countries.

11 See Chapter 4 of Nissanke and Aryeetey (1998) for a detailed analysis of these phenomena and factors explaining them.

12 A similar condition is observed across many countries in SSA. See, for example, Kasekende and Atingi-Ego (2003) for Uganda, and Ngugi (2001) for Kenya.

13 Besley (1995b) uses the term 'nonmarket institution' as a catchall for these different informal financial institutions in reference to the fact that these institutions make relatively little use of formal contractual obligations enforced through a codified legal system. For theoretical models of these non-market institutions such as group lending and credit co-operatives, see Besley and Coate (1995) and Banerjee *et al.* (1994), respectively.

14 For more detailed fieldwork methodology and results, see Chapters 5 and 6 of Nissanke and Aryeetey (1998).

15 In these three countries, commercial banks showed a greater likelihood of carrying out project visits than did development or merchant banks.

16 Deschamps and Bonnardeaux (1997) estimate that, for Sub-Saharan Africa in the mid-1980s, non-performing loans represented at times 50 per cent or more of total loans outstanding.

17 An analysis of the loan portfolio at the National Bank for Commerce (NBC) showed that about 94 per cent was substandard, doubtful, or rated as a loss by end-December 1991 (Eriksson 1993). NBC, drawing on central bank facilities, had extended loans and credit continuously to its major parastatal clientele

far in excess of deposits mobilized. The Cooperative and Rural Development Bank (CRDB) also suffered from high delinquency and default rates on loans and overdraft facilities as its main borrowers were the co-operative unions. In all these cases, from the outset there was little prospect of repayment. Yet the banks continued to provide loans, using implicit government guarantees.

18   This contrasts with the Nigerian case, where a number of bankers believe that some default is wilful, and where collusion between borrowers and some bank officials has been observed.

19   *Susu* or *esusu* is the term used in West Africa referring to informal savings arrangements organized either on the basis of a savings group or by an individual savings collector.

20   Land-based credit market interlinkages are popular in Tanzania, because these are the simplest way of acquiring the usufructuary rights to land. This situation gives rise to a lending game in which borrowers' defaults are favourable for the lender as his/her utility is enhanced. However, Udry (1990) reports that the use of collateral and interlinked contracts is absent within rural communities in Northern Nigeria, where information asymmetries are unimportant. This is the case despite the fact that each of the sample villages has active land sales markets, and land is available to serve as a collateral asset.

21   See Nissanke and Aryeetey (1998) for our estimates of the breakdown of these costs for Ghana and Nigeria, and discussions of trends in Malawi and Tanzania, based on perceptions of bank staff and research associates. See Aryeetey (1994) for a detailed description of the methodology used in our estimates.

22   Many commercial banks in Ghana insisted on a more thorough screening process. This resulted in relatively low default rates and lower enforcement costs. This, however, has led to relatively fewer loan approvals by commercial banks, indicating their high risk aversion.

23   While we expect transaction costs in Nigeria and Tanzania to be much higher than those for Ghana, Malawian transaction costs should not be much different.

24   The estimates shown in Table 6.3 cover only loan administration costs, not default risk costs. However, the latter should be low in view of low default rates for informal lenders. See Nissanke and Aryeetey (1998) for the detailed breakdown of loan administration costs.

25   In the case of interlinked credit transactions, the contestability of linked markets should be taken into account.

26   They only earn interest on their deposits (mainly demand deposits) with the bank if their balances exceed (Cedi) ¢1 million continuously for half of the year, which means that there is usually no interest forgone. Aryeetey and Steel (1992) measured the cost of funds as the implicit daily interest rate on fixed deposits accumulated over 30 days, or −0.2 per cent, representing the collectors' fee. This was equivalent to −6.3 per cent of average loan amount per month or −54.4 per cent per annum.

27   For the other informal lenders in Ghana, the cost of funds was usually between zero and 0.1 per cent, thus also giving them substantial spreads. Also in Malawi, the cost of funds for all informal lenders was estimated as being insignificant.

28   For example, Basu (1989) argues that, in rural credit markets, where open discrimination among borrowers within a community is not in accord with social norms, the interest rate structure becomes a choice variable of the lender. Interest variation in relation to the duration, size and purpose of loans

between borrowers could serve as a subtle system of price discrimination in lenders' risk management.

29 See Jain (1999) for discussion on formal–informal sector interaction in an adverse selection setting.

30 See Nissanke (1998) for more detailed discussion on comparison of market structure in Asia and Africa.

31 See Nissanke (1998) for the implication of this gap in financial services for real sector development and diversification in SSA.

32 Transaction costs associated with monitoring and enforcement could be lowered if exercising social and moral norms would lead to a reduction of opportunistic behaviour (Vandenberg 2002).

33 North (1997) lists four major variables as a means of providing low-cost transacting and credible commitment, which are regarded in turn as the institutional requirements for creating efficient factor and product markets. They are: (i) an efficient system of property rights that reduces the cost of measuring contract performance; (ii) an increased market size supported by mechanisms for constraining opportunistic behaviour; (iii) credible enforcement mechanisms through improved legal systems and impartial adjudication; and (iv) ideological attitudes and perceptions to reduce the cost of the measurement and enforcement of contract performances.

References

Adam, C. and O'Connell, S. (1999) 'Aid, Taxation and Development: Analytical Perspectives on Aid Effectiveness in Sub-Saharan Africa', *Economics and Politics*, 11: 225–54.

Adegboye, R. O. (1969) 'Procuring Loans by Pledging Cocoa Trees', *Nigerian Geographical Journal*, 12(1–2): 63–76.

Alderman, H. and Paxson, C. (1992) 'Do the Poor Insure? A Synthesis of the Literature on Risk Sharing Institutions in Developing Countries', in E. Bacha (ed.), *Economics in a Changing World: Development, Trade and Environment* (London: Macmillan).

Aleem, I. (1990) 'Imperfect Information, Screening, and the Costs of Informal Lending: A Study of a Rural Credit Market in Pakistan', *The World Bank Economic Review*, 4(3): 329–49.

Aoki, M. (2001) *Toward a Comparative Institutional Analysis* (Cambridge, Mass.: MIT Press).

Aron, J. (1997) 'Political, Economic and Social Institutions: A Review of Growth Evidence (with an African Focus)', Background paper for the World Bank World Development Report 1997, *The State in a Changing World* (Washington, World Bank, DC).

Arrow, K. J. (1998) 'The Place of Institutions in the Economy: A Theoretical Perspective', in Y. Hayami and M. Aoki (eds), *The Institutional Foundations of East Asian Economic Development* (London: Macmillan, in association with the International Economic Association).

Aryeetey, E. (1994) 'Financial Integration and Development in Sub-Saharan Africa: A Study of Informal Finance in Ghana', Overseas Development Institute Working Paper 78, ODI, London.

Aryeetey, E. (1996) 'The Formal Financial Sector in Ghana after the Reforms', Overseas Development Institute Working Paper 86, ODI, London.
Aryeetey, E., Hettige, H., Nissanke, M. and Steel, W. (1997) 'Financial Market Fragmentation and Reforms in Ghana, Malawi, Nigeria and Tanzania', *World Bank Economic Review*, 11(2): 195–218.
Aryeetey, E. and Steel, W. (1992) 'Incomplete Linkage between Informal and Formal Finance in Ghana', in W. Steel (ed.), *Financial Deepening in Sub-Saharan Africa: Theory and Innovations* (Washington, DC: World Bank, Industry Development Division).
Aryeetey, E. and Udry, C. (1997) 'The Characteristics of Informal Financial Markets in Sub-Saharan Africa', *Journal of African Economies*, 6(1) (Supplement).
Bagachwa, M. S. D. (1995) 'Financial Integration and Development in Sub-Saharan Africa: A Study of Informal Finance in Tanzania', Overseas Development Institute Working Paper 79, ODI, London.
Bagachwa, M. S. D. (1996) 'The Role of Formal Financial Institutions in Tanzania', Overseas Development Institute Working Paper 87, ODI, London.
Banerjee, A., Besley, T. and Guinnnane, T. (1994) 'Thy Neighbor's Keeper: The Design of a Credit Cooperative with Theory and a Test', *Quarterly Journal of Economics*, 109: 491–515.
Bardhan, P. (1989) *The Economic Theory of Agrarian Institutions* (Oxford: Oxford University Press).
Bardhan, P. (2005) *Scarcity, Conflicts and Cooperation: Essays in the Political and Institutional Economics of Development* (Cambridge, Mass.: MIT Press).
Bardhan, P. and Udry, C. (1999) *Development Microeconomics* (Oxford: Oxford University Press).
Basu, K. (1989) 'Rural Credit Markets: The Structure of Interest Rates, Exploitation, and Efficiency' in P. Bardhan (ed.), *The Economic Theory of Agrarian Institutions* (Oxford University Press).
Bell, C. (1990) 'Interaction between Institutional and Informal Credit Agencies in Rural India', *The World Bank Economic Review*, 4(3): 295–327.
Besley, T. (1995a) 'Savings, Credit and Insurance', in J. Behrman and T. N. Srinivason, *Handbook of Development Economics*, Vol. III (New York: North-Holland).
Besley, T. (1995b) 'Nonmarket Institutions for Credit and Risk Sharing in Low-income Countries', *Journal of Economic Perspectives*, 9(3): 115–27.
Besley, T. and Coate, S. (1995) 'Group Lending, Repayment Incentives and Social Collateral', *Journal of Development Economics*, 46: 1–18.
Biggs, T. S. (1991) 'Heterogeneous Firms and Efficient Financial Intermediation in Taiwan,' in M. Roemer and C. Jones (eds), *Markets in Developing Countries* (San Francisco: ICS Press).
Binswanger, H., McIntire, J. and Udry, C. (1989) 'Production Relations in Semi-arid African Agriculture', in P. Bardhan (ed.), *The Economic Theory of Agrarian Institutions* (Oxford: Oxford University Press).
Bottomley, A. (1975) 'Interest Rate Determination in Underdeveloped Rural Areas', *American Journal of Agricultural Economics*, 57(2): 279–91.
Brownbridge, M. and Harvey, C. (1998) *Banking in Africa* (Oxford: James Currey).
Chipeta, C. and Mkandawire, M. L. C. (1996a) 'Financial Integration and Development in Sub-Saharan Africa: Informal Financial Sector in Malawi', Overseas Development Institute Working Paper 85, ODI, London.

Chipeta, C. and Mkandawire, M. L. C. (1996b) 'The Formal and Semi-Formal Sectors in Malawi', Overseas Development Institute Working Paper 89, ODI, London.

Coase, R. H. (1992) 'The institutional Structure of Production', *American Economic Review*, 82(4): 713–20.

Collier, P. (1996) 'The Role of the State in Economic Development: Cross Regional Experiences', Paper presented at the African Economic Research Consortium Plenary Sessions, Nairobi, December.

Conning, J. and Udry, C. (2005) 'Rural Financial Markets in Developing Countries', Paper prepared for R. E., Everson, P. Pingali and T. P. Shultz (eds), *Handbook of Agricultural Economics*, Vol. 3 (North-Holland, Elsevier).

Dercon, S. (ed.) (2004) *Insurance Against Poverty*, UNU-WIDER Studies in Development Economics (Oxford: Oxford University Press).

Deschamps, J. and Bonnardeaux, J. (1997) *Bank Restructuring in Sub-Saharan Africa: Lessons from Special Case Studies*, Mimeo, World Bank, Washington, DC.

Eriksson, G. (1993) 'Incidence and Pattern of the Soft Budget in Tanzania', *Macroeconomic Studies* 44/93 (Stockholm: SIDA Planning Secretariat).

Fafchamps, M. (2004) *Market Institutions in Sub-Saharan Africa: Theory and Evidence* (Cambridge, Mass.: MIT Press).

Fry, M. J. (1982) 'Models of Financially Repressed Developing Economies', *World Development*, 10(9): 731–50.

Fry, M. J. (1988) *Money, Interest, and Banking in Economic Development* (Baltimore, Md.: Johns Hopkins University Press).

Ghate, P. B. (1988) 'Informal Credit Markets in Asian Developing Countries', *Asian Development Review*, 6(1): 64–85.

Ghate, P. B. (1990) 'Interaction between the Formal and Informal Financial Sectors', Paper presented at the UN International Conference on Savings and Credit for Development, 28–31 May.

Greif, A. (1993) 'Contract Enforceability and Economic Institutions in Early Trade: The Maghribi Traders' Coalition', *American Economic Review*, 83(3): 525–48.

Greif, A., Milgrom, P. and Weingast, B. (1994) 'Coordination, Commitment, and Enforcement: The Case of the Merchant Guild', *Journal of Political Economy*, 102(4): 745–76.

Harriss, J., Hunter, J. and Lewis, C. M. (eds) (1995) *The New Institutional Economics and Third World Development* (London: Routledge).

Hoff, K. and Stiglitz, J. E. (1990) 'Imperfect Information and Rural Credit Markets-Puzzles and Policy Perspectives', *The World Bank Economic Review*, 4(3): 235–50.

Jain, S. (1999) 'Symbiosis vs Crowding-out: The Interaction of Formal and Informal Credit Markets in Developing Countries', *Journal of Developing Economics*, 59(2): 419–44.

Kasekende, L. A. and Atingi-Ego, M. (2003) 'Financial Liberalisation and its Implication for the Domestic System: The Case of Uganda', AERC Research Paper 128 (Nairobi: AERC).

Mordoch, J. (1995) 'Income Smoothing and Consumption Smoothing', *Journal of Economic Perspectives*, 9(3): 103–14.

Ngugi, R. W. (2001) 'An Empirical Analysis of Interest Rate Spread in Kenya', AERC Research Paper 106 (Nairobi: AERC).

Nissanke, M. (1998) *Financing Enterprise Development and Export Diversification in Sub-Saharan Africa*, UNCTAD, Special Study Series 8 (Geneva: UNCTAD).

Nissanke, M. and Aryeetey, E. (1998) *Financial Integration and Development in Sub-Saharan Africa, Liberalisation and Reform in Sub-Saharan Africa* (London New York: Routledge).

Nissanke, M. and Sindzingre, A. (2005) 'Institutional Foundations for Shared Growth in Sub-Saharan Africa', Paper presented at the International Conference, 'Shared Growth in Sub-Saharan Africa', Accra, 21–22 July. See also *African Development Review* 18(3): 353–91.

North, D. (1989) 'Institutions and Economic Growth: A Historical Introduction', *World Development*, 17(9): 1319–32.

North, D. (1990) *Institutions, Institutional Change and Economic Performance* (Cambridge: Cambridge University Press).

North, D. (1997) 'The Contribution of the New Institutional Economics to an Understanding of the Transition Problem', WIDER Annual Lecture 1, UNU-WIDER, Helsinki.

Platteu, J. (1996) 'The Evolutionary Theory of Land Rights as Applied to Sub-Saharan Africa: A Critical Assessment', *Development and Change*, 27(2): 29–86.

Popiel, P. A. (1994) 'Financial Systems in Sub-Saharan Africa: A Comparative Study', World Bank Discussion Paper 260, Africa Technical Department Series, World Bank, Washington, DC.

Roe, A. R. (1991) 'Financial Systems and Development in Africa', Conference report of an EDI Policy Seminar, Nairobi, 29 January–1 February 1990.

Saito, K. A. and Villanueva, D. P. (1981) 'Transaction Costs of Credit to the Small-scale Sector in the Philippines, *Economic Development and Cultural Change*, 29(3): 631–40.

Shipton, P. (1991) 'Time and Money in the Western Sahel: A Clash of Cultures in Gambian Rural Finance', in M. Roemer and C. Jones (eds), *Markets in Developing Countries* (San Francisco: ICS Press), 113–39.

Sindzingre, A. (2006) 'The Relevance of the Concepts of Formality and Informality: A Theoretical Appraisal', in B. Guha-Khasnobis, R. Kanbur and E. Ostrom (eds), *Linking the Formal and Informal Economy: Concepts and Policies* (Oxford: Oxford University Press for EGDI and UNU-WIDER).

Soyibo, A. (1996a) 'Financial Linkage and Development in Sub-Saharan Africa: The Informal Financial Sector in Nigeria', Overseas Development Institute Working Paper 90 ODI, London.

Soyibo, A. (1996b) 'The Role of Financial Institutions in Nigeria', Overseas Development Institute Working Paper 88, ODI, London.

Stiglitz, J. E. (1989) 'Markets, Market Failures and Development', *American Economic Review*, 79(2): 197–203.

Stiglitz, J. and Weiss, A. (1981) 'Credit Rationing in Markets with Incomplete Information', *American Economic Review*, 71(3): 393–410.

Townsend, R. M. (1995) 'Consumption Insurance: An Evaluation of Risk-bearing Systems in Low-income Economies', *Journal of Economic Perspectives*, 9(3): 83–102.

Udry, C. (1990) 'Credit Markets in Northern Nigeria: Credit as Insurance in a Rural Economy', *The World Bank Economic Review*, 4(3): 251–69.

Udry, C. (1994) 'Risk and Insurance in a Rural Credit Market: An Empirical Investigation in Northern Nigeria', *Review of Economic Studies*, 61(3): 495–526.

Vandenberg, P. (2002) 'North's Institutionalism and the Prospect of Combining Theoretical Approaches', *Cambridge Journal of Economics*, 26: 217–35.

Williamson, O. (1985) *The Economics Institutions of Capitalism* (New York: Free Press).

Williamson, O. (1995) 'The Institutions and Governance of Economic Development and Reform', Proceedings of the World Bank Annual Conference on Development Economics, May 1994, Washington, DC.

Yotopoulos, P. A. and Floro, L. (1991) 'Transaction Costs and Quantity Rationing in the Informal Credit Markets; Philippine Agriculture,' in M. Roemer and C. Jones (eds), *Markets in Developing Countries* (San Francisco: ICS Press), 141–65.

Young, H. P. (1998) 'Social Norms and Economic welfare', *European Economic Review*, 42(3–5): 821–30.

7
Financial Reform and the Mobilization of Domestic Savings: The Experience of Morocco

Mina Baliamoune-Lutz

Introduction

Morocco began to implement significant financial-sector reforms from the mid-1980s.[1] Such reforms were quite fashionable in the developing world during those years and most were part of a wide range of structural adjustment programmes that extended to reforms of the exchange rate and foreign trade system, deregulation and price liberalization, and fiscal consolidation (Chowdhury 2001; Mavrotas and Kelly 2001). Morocco was one of the first Arab countries to embark on financial liberalization and reform. Early reform programmes resulted in significant changes in real interest rates, which were negative during the decades of financial repression in the 1970s and the first half of the 1980s (see Figure 7.1). During the late 1980s, soon after the early reforms had taken place, real interest rates became positive and quite high, reaching 5.80 per cent in 1987 and 6.14 per cent in 1988.

In the early 1980s, Morocco raised the average levels of lending and deposit rates by about 20 per cent and simplified the structure of administered interest. Interest rates on above-one-year deposits were liberalized in 1985, and rates on deposits above six months and above three months were liberalized in 1989 and 1990, respectively. Morocco also introduced a minimum interest rate, with the goal of promoting long-term savings. Interest rates on all time-deposits were liberalized in 1992. As interest rates rose during the first half of the 1990s, bank deposits increased significantly. The effects were also reflected in a decline in chequing deposits which, in general, do not earn interest. The Moroccan government liberalized lending rates in February 1996. In addition, Morocco introduced important institutional changes in order to protect savers and facilitate smooth transactions. These changes included the creation of the

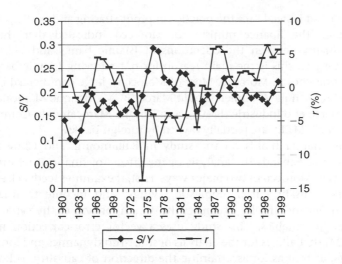

Figure 7.1 Private savings ratio (*S/Y*) and real interest rates (*r*), Morocco, 1960–99
Source: Baliamoune and Chowdhury (2003).

Deontological Council of Stocks and Bonds (Conseil Déontologique des Valeurs Mobilières), the modernization and privatization of the Casablanca Stock Exchange, and full convertibility of current-account balances in 1993. In general, these were additional strategies aimed at promoting domestic savings. These strategies resulted in stronger financial deepening, and more effective intermediaries. Finally, it is important to point out that financial liberalization in Morocco was characterized by gradualism, which may explain (at least partially) the absence of financial crises in the 1990s, when many emerging markets around the world experienced major turbulence.

As is pointed out in Baliamoune and Chowdhury (2003), financial reform involves the elimination of credit controls, deregulation of interest rates, the easing of entry into the financial services industry, development of capital markets, increased prudential regulation and supervision, and the liberalization of international capital flows. However, in Morocco, the liberalization of international capital flows has not yet been fully implemented, as capital outflows by nationals are still subject to state control and allowed only in a small number of specific cases. Moreover, the development of capital markets, despite the modernization and privatization of the Casablanca Stock Exchange, is still weak.

It is worth noting that Morocco follows, in general, French banking practices and does not use Islamic banking (Islamic banking prohibits *riba* (usury) and instead uses the practice of profit-sharing and participation). In 1998, the finance minister of Morocco indicated that there is *inconsistency* between the operations of Islamic banks and Moroccan banking law; this is the main reason for not allowing Islamic banks to open branches in Morocco. Most of Morocco's large commercial banks, including Banque Commerciale du Maroc (BCM), Banque Marocaine du Commerce et d'Industrie (BMCI), and Banque Marocaine du Commerce Extérieur (BMCE), are partially owned by foreign banks.

This chapter builds on the study in Baliamoune and Chowdhury (2003) and expands the analysis of the effects of financial reforms on savings in Morocco in two major ways. First, it examines feedback effects (reverse causality) from domestic savings[2] and income to financial reform. Second, its also examines the decomposition of the variance in the main variables. This study uses a vector error-correction model (VECM) that allows for the analysis of short-run dynamics and long-run effects, as well as for ascertaining the direction of causality. Following Baliamoune and Chowdhury, the indicators of financial reform examined in this study include real interest rates, financial depth, and the effectiveness of financial intermediation.

Financial reforms, savings mobilization and growth

The relationship between financial development and economic growth remains a major topic in the literature on financial intermediation and economic development. While many studies have stressed the important role of the financial sector in economic growth (McKinnon 1973; Shaw 1973), there is no consensus on whether financial development causes economic growth. Indeed, there are scholars who argue that causality is either non-existent, or that it runs in the opposite direction, from economic growth to financial development. Robinson (1952), Lucas (1988) and Stern (1989) have maintained that finance plays only a marginal role in economic growth.

There is currently a large body of research on the effects of financial development and financial reforms in developing countries. Since many developing countries were, in the 1980s and early 1990s, urged by international lenders and development agencies to liberalize markets, including financial markets, reasonable data is available to test the success of such policies and reforms. In addition, the financial crises in South East Asia in the 1990s and their impact on economic growth have called into question the rationale and suitability of financial market liberalization.

Recent empirical literature in support of the positive effects of financial development or reforms on savings, investment and growth includes Bencivenga and Smith (1991), King and Levine (1993a, 1993b), Beck *et al.* (2000) and Baliamoune and Chowdhury (2003). However, the results in this literature are, in general, not conclusive. For example, King and Levine (1993a: 730) argue that 'finance seems importantly to lead economic growth'. On the other hand, Demetriades and Hussein (1996) find little empirical evidence in support of the supply-leading proposition (the hypothesis that finance causes growth).

A major rationale for the push for financial liberalization centres on the role of the financial sector in promoting the mobilization of saving, facilitating access to credit, and enhancing resource allocation (McKinnon 1973; Shaw 1973). It seems that the effect of financial reforms on economic growth is through the impact of financial liberalization on investments and savings, and the resulting enhancement in capital formation. The theoretical rationale behind the idea that financial liberalization (a major component of financial development) promotes growth is fairly straightforward (see Levine 1997). For investment to occur, investors and savers must be given incentives, and savings have to be channelled to investors. Financial liberalization, which is a driving force behind financial development, ensures that this process takes place efficiently. When interest rates rise, the quality of investments is enhanced, since financial repression tends to be associated with investment of relatively poor quality. Higher deposit rates increase the supply of funds, thus the quantity of investment also rises. Calderón and Liu (2003) used pooled data from 109 developing and developed countries, and concluded that financial deepening promotes economic growth through two channels: by causing more rapid capital accumulation and through stimulating productivity growth. But the authors also find causality from growth to financial development.

Therefore, a useful approach to assess the impact of financial liberalization is to study its effects on savings. Studies that have examined such effects in developing countries include Fry (1995), Hussain (1996), Dayal-Gulati and Thimann (1997), Demetriades and Luintel (1997), Jbili *et al.* (1997), Bandiera *et al.* (2000) and Baliamoune and Chowdhury (2003). There is, however, no clear consensus on the impact of financial liberalization and reforms on savings. Hussain (1996) shows that, in the three years following financial reforms in Egypt, savings rose by about 6 per cent of gross domestic product (GDP) above the level that would have resulted if no financial liberalization had occurred. In the case of

Morocco, Baliamoune and Chowdhury (2003) found that financial reform has a positive impact on saving. Mavrotas and Kelly (2001) have demonstrated that financial reform that leads to higher interest rates and lower risk may increase the level of savings by expanding the range of available savings instruments and increasing the expected return. However, other studies have argued that financial reform may in fact decrease savings by reducing liquidity constraints through, say, improved access to consumer credit. Chowdhury (2001) shows that there was a decline in private savings following financial liberalization in Bangladesh. Similarly, Chapple (1991) has found a decline in both household and corporate savings in New Zealand following liberalization. Finally, Uygur (1993) reported that, during the 1970s and 1980s in Turkey, the negative income effect[3] from higher interest rates was stronger than the positive substitution effect, and concluded that financial liberalization had a negative impact on private saving.

There is also no consensus regarding the impact of interest rates. Some scholars have found a positive link between real interest rates and saving (see, for example, Fry 1978). Cheng (1980) contends that, in Pacific Basin Countries, 'real deposit interest rate played a critical role in setting the rate of each nation's financial growth. Positive real deposit rates maintained over a number of years, invariably led to financial deepening' (Cheng 1980: 54). However, other scholars have not found such a link. For example, Arestis and Demetriades (1997: 791) report that '[h]igh real interest rates completely failed to increase savings or boost investment – both actually fell as a proportion of GNP over the period'. Also, Modigliani (1986: 304) argues that 'despite a hot debate, no convincing general evidence either way has been produced, which leads me to the provisional view that s [the saving ratio] is largely independent of the interest rate'. Dornbusch and Reynoso (1989: 205) also note that 'virtually no study has demonstrated a discernable net effect [of real deposit rates on saving ratios]'.

Some studies have found that there is a negative and significant effect of real interest rates on investment (Greene and Villanueva 1991) or that interest rates do not necessarily have a positive effect on investment (Morisset 1993). But other studies have obtained different results. In the case of Sub-Saharan Africa, for example, Ndikumana (2000) shows that higher financial development causes higher domestic investment, which suggests that financial development can cause economic growth by enhancing capital accumulation.

Bencivenga and Smith (1991) showed how the introduction of financial intermediation shifts the composition of savings toward capital, and hence acts to promote economic growth. However, Akinboade (2000) found that, during the period of financial liberalization in Tanzania, the association between financial deepening and economic growth was negative, but no evidence of causality between the two variables was found. Finally, Baliamoune-Lutz (2003) showed that economic growth in Morocco caused financial reform, but also that financial reform had no effect on growth.

Summary of previous studies of Morocco's experience

Two existing studies have specifically explored the links between financial reforms and domestic savings in Morocco: Jbili *et al.* (1997)[4] and Baliamoune and Chowdhury (2003). The first study failed to find evidence of a significant impact of financial reforms on savings, while the second reported that financial deepening enhanced the mobilization of private savings. Jbili *et al.* (1997) use Moroccan data for 1970–95 and show that the correlation between the ratio of M2 to GDP and the savings rate was 0.37 in the entire sample and −0.86 (negative) in the reform period (1986–95). In addition, their regression results indicate that financial deepening (or the volume of intermediation) did not influence saving in Morocco. But the authors did report a significant and negative coefficient on real interest rates and on the proxy for the effectiveness of financial intermediation (the ratio of reserve money to quasi money). However, the proxy for the cost of capital (real interest rate), financial depth and financial intermediation effectiveness all showed insignificant coefficients in the reform period. This suggests that financial reform had no impact on the savings rate in Morocco. As pointed out in Baliamoune and Chowdhury (2003), the study in Jbili *et al.* (1997) suffers from major econometric problems, in addition to the short period covered by the data (only about three to five years) subsequent to major reforms.

In contrast, the second study (Baliamoune and Chowdhury 2003) used cointegration models and similar indicators of financial reforms, together with a number of control variables including income, the share of agriculture in GDP, public saving, and the dependency ratio. Using Moroccan data for 1960–99, Baliamoune and Chowdhury distinguished long-run behaviour from short-run dynamics and showed that, in the long-run, income and the ratio of broad money to GDP (M2/GDP) have a positive influence on saving, but real interest rates do not affect the savings rate. In the short run, however, the coefficients on M2/GDP and the real interest rate were significant and negative. The coefficient on the effectiveness of financial intermediaries was insignificant in the short run, and significant but with the wrong sign (positive) in the long run. The authors also found strong support for Ricardian Equivalence[5] in both the long and the short run. Overall, the authors showed that, in Morocco, financial deepening (the ratio of broad money to GDP) has caused private savings to increase. However, an important issue that was not addressed in Baliamoune and Chowdhury (2003) was feedback and reverse causality between the variables of interest.

A third study, by Odedokun (1996), used annual data for 1964–88 from a group of developing countries and found that financial intermediation did not have an effect on growth in Morocco. However, the 1964–88 period does not capture the major financial reforms undertaken by the Moroccan government in the 1990s. On the other hand, Baliamoune-Lutz (2003) shows that there is uni-directional causality from growth to financial reform in Morocco.

VECM estimation and variance decomposition

Estimation

To try to remedy some of the weaknesses in the existing studies on financial reform in Morocco, we estimate a VECM using Moroccan annual data for the period 1960–99. The data (and as shown in Tables 7.1–7.3) are from *International Financial Statistics* (IFS), published by the International Monetary Fund, and from the database of *La Direction de la Statistique* in Morocco.

Descriptive statistics and correlations among the main variables are reported in Tables 7.1(a) and 7.1(b), respectively. The dependent variable, private saving ratio (*PRIVSAV*) is defined as the ratio of private saving to GDP. Because of the lack of published reliable data on private saving in Morocco, we follow Dayal-Gulati and Thimann (1997) and Baliamoune and Chowdhury (2003), and calculate private savings as national domestic savings plus the current account balance minus public savings. Following Baliamoune and Chowdhury (2003), we use the share of agriculture in GDP (*AGR*), public saving ratio (*PUBLICSAV*), and income in log form (LOG(*Y*)) as control variables. We also use the same indicators of financial reforms that the authors use: namely, real interest rates (*REALR*) as a measure of financial liberalization; the ratio of broad money to GDP (*M2/GDP*) as a measure of financial depth or volume of intermediation; and the ratio of reserve money to total deposit (*RES/TD*) as an indicator of the effectiveness of financial intermediaries. A decline in this ratio implies higher efficiency. Andersen and Tarp (2003) argue that increased

Table 7.1(a) Descriptive statistics

	PRIVSAV	Y	M2/GDP	RES/TD	REALR	PUBLICSAV	AGR
1960–86							
Mean	0.19	8197.33	0.37	0.68	−1.80	−0.07	20.68
Median	0.18	8322.00	0.35	0.68	−0.58	−0.05	19.50
Std dev.	0.05	1559.69	0.06	0.12	4.02	0.04	3.72
Maximum	0.29	10755.00	0.46	0.86	4.51	−0.02	31.00
Minimum	0.10	5691.00	0.30	0.46	−13.84	−0.18	16.50
Observations	27	27	27	27	27	27	27
1987–99							
Mean	0.19	11351.31	0.61	0.43	3.70	−0.03	17.64
Median	0.19	11432.00	0.62	0.42	4.41	−0.03	18.00
Std dev.	0.02	491.04	0.10	0.06	2.11	0.01	2.17
Maximum	0.23	12202.00	0.79	0.52	6.36	−0.01	20.50
Minimum	0.16	10360.00	0.46	0.35	0.51	−0.05	14.90
Observations	13	13	13	13	13	13	13
1960–99							
Mean	0.19	9222.38	0.45	0.60	−0.01	−0.05	19.69
Median	0.19	9471.00	0.43	0.62	0.28	−0.04	19.10
Maximum	0.29	12202.00	0.79	0.86	6.36	−0.01	31.00
Std dev.	0.04	1983.47	0.13	0.16	4.35	0.04	3.58
Minimum	0.10	5691.00	0.30	0.35	−13.84	−0.18	14.90
Observations	40	40	40	40	40	40	40

Table 7.1(b) Correlation matrix

	PRIVSAV	LOG(Y)	M2/GDP	RES/TD	REALR	PUBLICSAV	AGR
PRIVSAV	1	0.664	0.601	−0.325	−0.473	−0.922	−0.579
LOG(Y)	0.664	1	0.836	−0.642	−0.567	−0.643	−0.737
M2/GDP	0.601	0.836	1	−0.861	−0.472	−0.697	−0.422
RES/TD	−0.325	−0.642	−0.861	1	0.360	0.4876	0.173
REALR	−0.473	−0.567	−0.472	0.360	1	0.4871	0.213
PUBLICSAV	−0.922	−0.644	−0.697	0.487	0.487	1	0.405
AGR	−0.579	−0.738	−0.422	0.173	0.213	0.405	1

Source: See text, p. 152.

competition in the banking sector (following financial liberalization) will not necessarily induce efficient financial intermediation. Thus we also need to examine indicators of financial intermediaries' efficiency and effectiveness to achieve a more complete view of the effect of financial reforms.

It is important to note that financial development in developing countries tends to be associated with the development of money and financial intermediation rather than the development of capital markets, as is more prevalent in developed economies. Thus, in developing economies, financial deepening is often associated with the growth of activity of financial intermediaries, such as savings institutions and commercial banks.

The statistics reported in Table 7.1(a) indicate that, while the mean and the median of private savings have remained almost the same in the pre- and post-reform periods, the variance (and standard deviation) have decreased significantly. At the same time, we observe that financial depth, the efficiency of financial intermediaries, and real interest rates are all higher in the post-1986 period.

The correlation coefficients displayed in Table 7.1(b) indicate that there is a strong positive association between private saving, income and financial deepening (M2/*GDP*). We also note the negative correlation between private saving and the indicator of financial intermediaries' efficiency, *RES/TD* (recall that the lower is the ratio, the higher the efficiency). Interestingly, the correlation between the savings ratio and the real interest rate is negative; suggesting that the income effect outweighs the substitution effect. The coefficients of correlation among the other variables are all statistically significant and have the expected signs. It is worth noting that there is strong correlation (-0.861) between financial deepening (M2/*GDP*) and the efficiency of financial intermediaries (*RES/TD*). Greater financial depth is associated with higher efficiency in financial intermediation.

Because of the nature of the data, it is important to ascertain their time series properties. In particular, we need to test for unit root and cointegration. Phillips–Perron unit root tests were used to test for stationarity. The variables were all non-stationary in levels but stationary in first difference. The Phillips–Perron test is more reliable than the augmented Dickey–Fuller test for unit root when the presence of structural breaks is suspected. To test for cointegration, we used the Johansen and Juselius (1992) test, and the results indicate that the variables are cointegrated and provide evidence in support of a single cointegrating vector. Wald tests were also performed, to test for the inclusion of lags in the VECM equations.[6]

The empirical results displayed in Table 7.2 indicate that, in addition to a long-run stable relationship (based on the cointegrating equation), there are some interesting short-run dynamics among the variables. Interest rates seem to have a long-run positive effect on private saving (substitution effect). However, in the short run, the effect of interest rates is negative. This seems to be a plausible relationship, given Morocco's increased

Table 7.2 Cointegration and vector error-correction equations

Cointegrating equation

PRIVSAV(−1)	1.000000
LOG(*Y*(−1))	0.011295
	[0.42814]
RES/TD(−1)	0.040308
	[0.87644]
M2/*GDP*(−1)	−0.003430
	[−0.06187]
REALR(−1)	−0.003276
	[−2.50015]
Constant	−0.319041

Error Correction	D(PRIVSAV)	D(LOG(Y))	D(RES/TD)	D(M2/GDP)	D(REALR)
CointEq1	−0.884868	−0.453748	−0.446941	0.244212	14.21622
	[−8.04306]	[−1.21743]	[−1.74414]	[1.42405]	[0.53403]
D(PRIVSAV(−1))	0.240836	−0.119606	0.294340	0.156217	−4.804945
	[2.35881]	[−0.34579]	[1.23768]	[0.98156]	[−0.19449]
D(PRIVSAV(−2))	0.079990	−0.318090	0.138313	0.273393	3.074885
	[0.69154]	[−0.81175]	[0.51338]	[1.51631]	[0.10986]
D(LOG(Y(−1))	−0.023758	−0.055408	0.049525	0.087343	−16.37543
	[−0.31440]	[−0.21644]	[0.28138]	[0.74152]	[−0.89559]
D(LOG(Y(−2)))	0.057802	−0.107494	−0.037524	0.129788	−22.09728
	[0.71963]	[−0.39504]	[−0.20057]	[1.03662]	[−1.13696]
D(RES/TD(−1))	−0.051316	0.432026	−0.120121	−0.314815	−1.603379
	[−0.53723]	[1.33507]	[−0.53990]	[−2.11436]	[−0.06937]
D(RES/TD(−2))	0.080806	0.167965	0.220414	−0.108560	−35.41812
	[0.88799]	[0.54484]	[1.03990]	[−0.76533]	[−1.60853]
D(M2/GDP(−1))	0.153985	0.935907	0.319348	−0.650543	−61.35111
	[1.02579]	[1.84035]	[0.91334]	[−2.78018]	[−1.68905]
D(M2/GDP(−2))	0.373943	0.087453	0.136396	0.229527	−69.77697
	[2.57193]	[0.17755]	[0.40275]	[1.01275]	[−1.98337]
D(REALR(−1))	−0.002407	−0.000592	0.001640	0.001824	−0.501393
	[−2.79995]	[−0.20315]	[0.81930]	[1.36144]	[−2.41052]
D(REALR(−2))	−0.001199	2.95E-05	0.000658	6.88E-05	−0.302309
	[−1.43014]	[0.01040]	[0.33672]	[0.05267]	[−1.49010]
Constant	−0.017368	−0.087669	−0.104788	0.111879	4.038624
	[−0.71558]	[−1.06620]	[−1.85356]	[2.95717]	[0.68767]
PUBLICSAV	−0.879921	−0.617559	−0.321191	0.489346	25.35791
	[−6.75160]	[−1.39871]	[−1.05807]	[2.40877]	[0.80411]
AGR	−0.001856	0.003577	0.003844	−0.004042	−0.029197
	[−1.47930]	[0.84176]	[1.31566]	[−2.06689]	[−0.09619]
Log Likelihood	280.8028				

Note: t-statistic in brackets.
Source: See text, p. 152; the estimations are performed using Eviews 5.1.

openness to international trade and integration in world markets, and the expansion in consumer lending; both of these have contributed to an increase in consumption.[7] In fact, Baliamoune and Chowdhury (2003) argue that this, indeed, has taken place in Morocco since the early 1990s, as consumer credit institutions relaxed their requirements for providing consumer loans.

In the short run, financial deepening has an effect on savings, but with a two-year lag. It is shown that the coefficient on the second lag of the variable M2/*GDP* is positive and significant, at least at the 5 per cent level, but the coefficient on its first lag is not significant. As expected, there is a significant and negative relationship between the private savings and the public savings ratios. The coefficient on the variable *PUBLICSAV* is −0.89, suggesting the presence of Ricardian equivalence (see Baliamoune and Chowdhury 2003).

VECMs are useful when trying to determine whether there are feedback effects or reverse causality, or an indirect relationship between the variables. It is clear from the results shown in Table 7.2 that such effects do exist. When discussing the coefficients of correlation earlier, we noted that there is a strong association between financial deepening and the efficiency of financial intermediaries in Morocco. The error-correction (short-run) equations indicate there is uni-directional causality from financial intermediaries' effectiveness to financial deepening. While private saving does not seem to cause financial depth, public saving seems to have a positive influence on financial depth (M2/*GDP*). In addition, there is negative causality from M2/*GDP* to real interest rates. It seems that an increase in broad money causes real interest rates to fall. This could be a result of an excess-supply-of-funds effect.

We also note that a higher share of agriculture in GDP causes M2/*GDP* to decline. This result is consistent with the low monetization in rural areas. However, in the savings equation, while the coefficient on agriculture is negative, it has low statistical significance, so we cannot conclude that the share of agriculture has a significant impact on private saving. In theory, the high uncertainty of rural income makes a strong case for higher saving rates in rural areas. Yet, low monetization may prevent higher saving. Before the 1990s, informal financial institutions were quite common, especially in Morocco's rural areas. One objective of financial reform was to increase the number and proximity of formal financial institutions. This is thought to be an important strategy in financial reform programmes. As maintained by Rosenzweig (2001: 53), 'the proximity of formal financial institutions increases financial savings and crowds out informal insurance arrangements, thus in principle better facilitating financial intermediation'. Focusing on the rural sector is beyond the scope of this chapter, but there are linkages between increases in financial activity in rural areas and both financial depth and the effectiveness of financial intermediation in general.

Variance decomposition

Table 7.3 shows the decomposition of the variance in the variables. Variance decomposition provides information about the relative importance of each random innovation in affecting the endogenous variables in the vector autoregressive (VAR) model. There seems to be an important contribution (40–45 per cent) of the innovation in real interest rates, M2/GDP and income to the variance in private saving in the long run.

Table 7.3 Variance decomposition

Period	S.E.	*PRIVSAV*	LOG(*Y*)	*RES/TD*	M2/GDP	*REALR*
Variance decomposition of *PRIVSAV*						
1	0.015059	100.0000	0.000000	0.000000	0.000000	0.000000
2	0.018198	89.02099	6.608219	1.140123	2.451100	0.779567
3	0.020152	77.92357	7.438658	1.083351	7.269652	6.284771
4	0.021963	67.20337	6.618761	2.135278	6.199153	17.84344
5	0.022703	62.89806	8.365420	2.451455	6.458304	19.82676
6	0.024071	56.06197	9.893561	3.946075	8.617110	21.48128
7	0.024855	52.58434	11.57400	3.775867	9.413786	22.65201
8	0.025832	48.70040	12.73323	4.148566	10.72599	23.69181
9	0.026506	46.31342	14.35684	4.011716	10.95113	24.36690
10	0.027342	43.61112	15.26926	4.166987	11.36120	25.59144
Variance decomposition of LOG(*Y*)						
1	0.051018	0.020803	99.97920	0.000000	0.000000	0.000000
2	0.067106	0.388122	87.37628	6.164296	5.881463	0.189842
3	0.080658	0.870798	85.14066	6.564152	4.886367	2.538027
4	0.091404	0.862250	84.78721	7.442045	4.693631	2.214868
5	0.099537	1.160711	85.56158	6.937976	4.121370	2.218362
6	0.108043	1.284326	84.61437	7.794711	4.221449	2.085146
7	0.115807	1.327008	84.97850	7.567024	3.880579	2.246889
8	0.123033	1.372116	84.61966	7.988716	3.899574	2.119931
9	0.129669	1.417159	84.84474	7.838499	3.715264	2.184340
10	0.136263	1.439097	84.57893	8.122685	3.731665	2.127624
Variance decomposition of *RES/TD*						
1	0.035077	14.08584	1.430781	84.48338	0.000000	0.000000
2	0.049423	10.18907	0.851964	82.97326	1.772031	4.213682

(Continued)

Table 7.3   Continued

Period	S.E.	*PRIVSAV*	LOG(*Y*)	*RES/TD*	M2/*GDP*	*REALR*
3	0.063646	11.05728	0.548930	81.67749	1.146430	5.569868
4	0.073058	12.89995	0.614586	79.60366	0.874303	6.007503
5	0.083082	15.36895	0.679634	76.90791	0.726867	6.316632
6	0.091969	17.03057	0.708247	75.09369	0.665813	6.501678
7	0.100185	18.35464	0.754430	73.69691	0.708130	6.485890
8	0.107768	19.21031	0.821574	72.87005	0.706191	6.391880
9	0.114862	19.78023	0.859433	72.27930	0.707066	6.373964
10	0.121544	20.15451	0.889329	71.93043	0.687176	6.338547
Variance decomposition of M2/*GDP*						
1	0.023474	15.68985	30.45018	1.315138	52.54482	0.000000
2	0.029444	32.55204	19.99662	8.181607	37.97733	1.292399
3	0.038461	37.44097	13.99614	5.865384	40.08118	2.616321
4	0.044164	39.81672	11.48499	8.768615	37.83501	2.094668
5	0.050584	41.16477	9.208401	6.977576	41.00812	1.641127
6	0.055314	42.66981	7.963002	8.840849	39.10923	1.417118
7	0.060116	42.93489	7.232729	8.013291	40.50992	1.309168
8	0.064133	43.74906	6.579957	8.919192	39.57282	1.178970
9	0.068220	44.09440	6.112096	8.354186	40.35297	1.086350
10	0.071830	44.63360	5.719852	8.907352	39.75522	0.983980
Variance decomposition of *REALR*						
1	3.643935	2.925248	9.676884	5.993551	0.978364	80.42595
2	4.074578	2.467670	9.551902	5.046101	5.466612	77.46772
3	4.593284	2.072937	15.37212	6.121186	10.04721	66.38654
4	5.060796	2.188199	17.79328	5.279629	10.75380	63.98510
5	5.445492	1.913607	18.11997	4.560460	12.08013	63.32584
6	5.777298	1.739090	19.67913	4.056269	13.13724	61.38828
7	6.106199	1.581372	20.85819	3.631097	13.60911	60.32023
8	6.409844	1.445081	21.49195	3.319035	13.84933	59.89461
9	6.703301	1.333112	22.03735	3.035075	14.19176	59.40270
10	6.981485	1.248996	22.61554	2.802421	14.42794	58.90510

Note: Cholesky ordering: *PRIVSAV* LOG(*Y*) *RES/TD* M2/*GDP REALR*.
Source: See text, p. 152; the estimations are performed using Eviews 5.1.

Interestingly, income seems to be insensitive to innovations in the other variables, including the indicators of financial reform. This is consistent with the findings in Baliamoune-Lutz (2003) where it is shown that growth leads financial reform in Morocco (demand-following proposition). On the other hand, shocks to private saving seem to have some influence on the variance of *RES/TD* in both the short and the long run. Similarly, innovations in private saving affect the variance of M2/*GDP*, in both the short and the long run. Shocks to income have a significant impact on the variance of M2/*GDP* in the short run, but the effect falls dramatically in the long run. Finally innovations in income have an important impact on the variance of real interest rates in both the short and the long run, while innovations in M2/*GDP* seem to affect the variance of real interest rates only in the long run.

Thus, based on the results in Tables 7.2 and 7.3, there are some important relationships that must be taken into account when assessing the effects of financial reform in Morocco. The causality between the efficiency of financial intermediaries and financial deepening may be viewed as complementarity between these two indicators of financial reform. In some cases, it may be easier for regulators to affect financial intermediaries' efficiency (for example, by changing the required reserve ratio) than to influence financial depth directly (which is a major goal of financial reform). In such cases, knowing that financial intermediaries' efficiency causes financial deepening to increase is a useful piece of information for policy-makers.

The finding that increases in real interest rates cause the private savings ratio to fall in the short run may suggest the presence of a strong income effect. Alternatively, it may reflect a relatively weak substitution effect. In the pre reform period in Morocco, households used various instruments for their savings, including purchasing gold and expensive jewellery, and using the informal (curb) market. To the extent that households shift funds from these instruments to bank deposits, financial depth and the efficiency of financial intermediaries may improve but the private savings ratio may not change. In fact, this ratio may even fall, because bank deposits are safer and the real return is now higher compared to using the informal market. In addition, as mentioned earlier, there was a significant expansion of consumer lending in Morocco, beginning in the 1990s, which could have contributed to this result.

Concluding comments

The discussion of financial reforms in Morocco and the empirical results derived in this study indicate that, overall, there are important effects in both the short and the long run. In the short run, financial depth (volume of intermediation) has a positive influence on private saving, while interest rates show a negative impact. On the other hand, the effectiveness of financial intermediation does not seem to have a direct effect on saving but has a significant influence on the volume of intermediation. Thus intermediation effectiveness seems to have an indirect influence on private saving. In the long run, savings have a stable relationship (co-movement) with financial reform and the influence of interest rates is positive, indicating that the substitution effect outweighs the income effect.

These findings are consistent with the behaviour of the means shown in Table 7.1(a). The positive influence on saving from increased financial depth may be offset by the negative impact of higher interest rates. In the post-reform period (1987–99) we observe that all indicators of financial reform have improved, with interest rates and financial depth registering significant increases. Yet the savings rate has remained unchanged. Perhaps the main outcome of the financial liberalization that resulted from the reforms was to move savings from the informal market and thus enhance the efficiency of financial intermediation.

Notes

1 See Baliamoune and Chowdhury (2003) for a more detailed discussion of these reforms.
2 The terms 'domestic saving' and 'private saving' are considered in this study to mean 'domestic private saving'.
3 In theory, the effect of higher interest rates is ambiguous. Higher real interest rates imply higher rates of return on savings and thus would lead to a shift of funds to savings (substitution effect). An increase in real interest rates may also lead to a decline in saving, as lower saving is required to reach a given level of funds in the future as a result of higher returns (income effect).
4 Jbili *et al.* (1997) also examine the effects of financial reforms in Algeria and Tunisia.
5 The concept of Ricardian equivalence refers to the case where an increase in government expenditures or an isolated cut in taxes leads to an equivalent rise in private saving, because individuals would expect an equivalent tax increase in the future. Thus exogenous shifts in public saving are matched by offsetting shifts in private saving. In such cases, fiscal policy is unable to affect savings directly (see Barro 1974).
6 To save space, these results are not included in the chapter, but may be obtained from the author upon request.
7 See Bayoumi (1993) for a similar explanation on the consumption boom in the United Kingdom.

References

Akinboade, O. A. (2000) 'The Relationship between Financial Deepening and Economic Growth in Tanzania', *Journal of International Development*, 12: 939–50.
Andersen, B. T. and Tarp, F. (2003) 'Financial Liberalization, Financial Development and Economic Growth in LDCs', *Journal of International Development*, 15: 189–209.

Arestis, P. and Demetriades, P. (1997) 'Financial Development and Economic Growth: Assessing the Evidence', *Economic Journal*, 107: 783–99.

Baliamoune, M. N. and Chowdhury, A. R. (2003) 'The Long-run Behavior and Short-run Dynamics of Private Savings in Morocco', *Savings and Development*, 27(2): 135–60.

Baliamoune-Lutz, M. (2003) 'Financial Liberalization and Economic Growth in Morocco: A Test of the Supply-leading Hypothesis', *Journal of Business in Developing Nations*, 7: 31–50.

Bandiera, O., Caprio, G., Honohan, P. and Schiantarelli, F. (2000) 'Does Financial Reform Raise or Reduce Private Savings?', *Review of Economics and Statistics*, 82(2): 239–63.

Barro, R. (1974) 'Are Government Bonds Net Wealth?', *Journal of Political Economy*, 82: 1095–117.

Bayoumi, T. (1993) 'Financial Deregulation and Consumption in the United Kingdom', *Review of Economics and Statistics*, 75: 536–39.

Beck, T., Levine, R. and Loayza, N. (2000) 'Finance and the Sources of Growth', *Journal of Financial Economics*, 58: 261–310.

Bencivenga, V. R. and Smith, B. D. (1991) 'Financial Intermediation and Endogenous Growth', *Review of Economic Studies*, 58: 195–209.

Calderón, C. and Liu, L. (2003) 'The Direction of Causality between Financial Development and Economic Growth', *Journal of Development Economics*, 72: 321–34.

Chapple, S. (1991) 'Financial Liberalization in New Zealand, 1984–90', United Nations Conference on Trade and Development Discussion Paper 35, UNCTAD, Geneva.

Cheng, H.-S. (1980) 'Financial Deepening in Pacific Basin Countries', *Federal Reserve Bank of San Francisco Economic Review* (Summer): 43–56.

Chowdhury, A. (2001) 'The Impact of Financial Reform on Private Savings in Bangladesh', WIDER Discussion Paper 2001/78, UNU-WIDER, Helsinki.

Dayal-Gulati, A. and Thimann, C. (1997) 'Saving in Southeast Asia and Latin America Compared: Searching for Policy Lessons', IMF Working Paper WP/97/110, IMF, Washington, DC.

Demetriades, P. O. and Hussein, K. A. (1996) 'Does Financial Development Cause Economic Growth? Time-series Evidence from 16 Countries', *Journal of Development Economics*, 51: 387–411.

Demetriades, P. and Luintel, K. (1997) 'The Direct Cost of Financial Repression: Evidence from India', *Review of Economics and Statistics*, 79(2): 311–20.

Dornbusch, R. and Reynoso, A. (1989) 'Financial Factors in Economic Development', *American Economic Review*, 79(2): 204–9.

Fry, M. (1978) 'Money and Capital or Financial Deepening in Economic Development?', *Journal of Money, Credit and Banking*, 10: 464–75.

Fry, M. (1995) *Money, Interest and Banking in Economic Development*, 2nd edn (London: Johns Hopkins University Press).

Greene, J. and Villanueva, D. (1991) 'Private Investment in Developing Countries: An Empirical Analysis', *IMF Staff Papers*, 38(1): 33–58.

Hussain, N. (1996) 'Financial Liberalization, Currency Substitution, and Investment: The Case of Egypt', African Development Bank Economic Research Papers 24, African Development Bank, Addis Ababa.

Jbili, A., Enders, K. and Treichel, V. (1997) 'Financial Sector Reforms in Algeria, Morocco, and Tunisia: A Preliminary Assessment', IMF Working Paper WP/97/81, IMF, Washington, DC.

Johansen, S. and Juselius, K. (1992) 'Testing Structural Hypotheses in a Multivariate Cointegration Analysis of the PPP and the UIP for UK', *Journal of Econometrics*, 53: 211–44.

King, R. G. and Levine, R. (1993a) 'Finance and Growth: Schumpeter Might Be Right', *Quarterly Journal of Economics*, 108: 717–37.

King, R. G. and Levine, R. (1993b) 'Finance, Entrepreneurship and Growth: Theory and Evidence', *Journal of Monetary Economics*, 32: 1–30.

Levine, R. (1997) 'Financial Development and Economic Growth: Views and Agenda', *Journal of Economic Literature*, 35: 688–726.

Lucas, R. E. (1988) 'On the Mechanics of Economic Development', *Journal of Monetary Economics*, 22: 3–42.

Mavrotas, G. and Kelly, R. (2001) 'Savings Mobilisation and Financial Sector Development: The Nexus', *Savings and Development*, 15(1): 33–65.

McKinnon, R. (1973) *Money and Capital in Economic Development* (Washington, DC: Brookings Institution).

Modigliani, F. (1986) 'Life-Cycle, Individual Thrift and the Wealth of Nations', *American Economic Review*, 76(3): 297–313.

Morisset, J. (1993) 'Does Financial Liberalization Really Improve Private Investment in Developing Countries?', *Journal of Development Economics*, 40: 133–50.

Ndikumana, L. (2000) 'Financial Determinants of Domestic Investment in Sub-Saharan Africa: Evidence from Panel Data', *World Development*, 28(2): 381–400.

Odedokun, M. O. (1996) 'Alternative Econometric Approaches for Analyzing the Role of the Financial Sector in Economic Growth: Time Series Evidence from LDCs', *Journal of Development Economics*, 50: 119–46.

Robinson, J. (1952) 'The Generalization of the General Theory,' in J. Robinson, *The Rate of Interest, and Other Essays* (London: Macmillan), 67–142.

Rosenzweig, M. R. (2001) 'Savings Behaviour in Low-income Countries', *Oxford Review of Economic Policy*, 17(1): 40–54.

Shaw, E. (1973) *Financial Deepening in Economic Development* (New York: Oxford University Press).

Stern, N. (1989) 'The Economics of Development: A Survey', *Economic Journal*, 99: 597–685.

Uyger, E. (1993) 'Liberalization and Economic Performance in Turkey', United Nations Conference on Trade and Development Discussion Paper 65, UNCTAD, Geneva.

8

The Structure and Performance of Ethiopia's Financial Sector in the Pre- and Post-Reform Periods, with a Special Focus on Banking

Alemayehu Geda

Introduction

One of the main objectives of financial institutions such as banks is mobilizing resources (in particular, domestic savings) and channelling these to would-be investors. This intermediation role of banks takes different forms in different economic systems. Ethiopia's history since the 1970s clearly shows the validity of this statement.

Under state socialism (1974–91), popularly referred to in Ethiopia as the 'Derg[1] regime', banks and other financial institutions were basically executing the economic plans outlined by the central planning organ. In that period, regulation and supervision were not critical, because the national plan regulated and directed the activities of financial institutions. Moreover, banks were directed to finance some public projects that might not have passed proper financial appraisal but were simply based on either ideological grounds or 'merit wants' arguments.

Following the demise of the Derg regime in 1991, post-1991 economic policy has witnessed a marked departure from the previous socialist system. The main difference has been in the open adoption of a market-orientated economic policy. In fact, many of the policies adopted by the new government in Addis Ababa in 1991 had already been proposed by the defunct Derg regime as it approached the end of its reign.

This new change in policy brought about a significant change in the functioning of the financial sector. Not only was this going to serve the private sector, which had hitherto been demonized, but new private financial institutions were also emerging. At the same time, the role of Ethiopia's central bank, the National Bank of Ethiopia (NBE), was also reformulated. Thus financial-sector reconstruction was at the top of the government's agenda.

In undertaking this task, the Ethiopian government adopted a strategy of (i) gradualism: the gradual opening up of private banks and insurance companies alongside public ones, the gradual liberalization of the foreign exchange market, and so on; and (ii) strengthening domestic competitive capacity before full liberalization (that is, restricting the sector to domestic investors, strengthening the regulatory and supervision capacity of the NBE, giving the banks autonomy, and opening up the inter-bank money market). In line with this strategy, various proclamations and regulations have been passed since 1992 (Geda and Dendir 2001).

A brief history of banking in Ethiopia

The history of the use of modern money in Ethiopia can be traced back more than 2,000 years (Pankhurst, cited in Gedey 1990). It flourished in what is called the Axumite era, from 1000BC to around AD975. Leaving that long history aside, modern banking in Ethiopia began in 1905 with the establishment of Abyssinian Bank, based on a 50-year agreement with the Anglo-Egyptian National Bank. In 1908, a new development bank (called Société Nationale d'Ethiope pour le Développement de l'Agriculture et du Commerce) and two other foreign banks (Banque de l'Indochine and the Compagnie de l'Afrique Orientale) were also established (Pankhurst 1968, cited in Degefe 1995). These banks were criticized for being wholly foreign-owned. In 1931, the Ethiopian government purchased the Abyssinian Bank, which was the dominant bank, and renamed it the Bank of Ethiopia – the first nationally-owned bank on the African continent (Gedey 1990: 83; Degefe 1995: 234).

During the five years of Italian occupation (1936–41), banking activity expanded. The Italian banks were particularly active. Table 8.1(a) shows most of the banks that were in operation during this period. After independence from Italy's brief occupation, where the role of Britain was paramount because of its strategic planning during the Second World War, Barclays Bank was established and remained in business in Ethiopia from 1941 to 1943 (Gedey 1990; Degefe 1995). Following this, in 1943, the Ethiopian government established the State Bank of Ethiopia. The establishment of the Bank by Ethiopia was a painful process, because Britain was against it (see Degefe (1995) for an interesting neo-colonial story). The Bank of Ethiopia operated as both a commercial and a central bank until 1963 when it was remodelled into the National Bank of Ethiopia (the Central Bank, re-established in 1976) and the Commercial Bank of Ethiopia (CBE). After this period, many other banks were

Table 8.1 Banks in operation in Ethiopia
(a) during the brief period of Italian occupation (1936–41)

Year of establishment (European calendar)	Name of bank	Number of branches
1914*	Banco di Italy	9
1914*	Banco di Roma	18
1939	Banco di Napoli	4
1939	Banco Nacionale (De's Voro)	4
1939	Casa de Credito....	1
1939	Societé Nacionale di Ethiopia	1
Total		37

(b) before the 1974 revolution

Year of establishment (European calendar)	Name of bank	Number of branches	Capital at the date of establishment (in millions Birr)
n.d.	Banco di Napoli	1	2
1963	Imperial Saving and Home Ownership Public Association	1	0.6
1963	National Bank of Ethiopia, NBE	4	10
1963	Commercial Bank of Ethiopia, CBE	65	35
1963	Addis Bank Share Co.	26	5
1964	Ethiopian Saving and Mortgage S.Co.	?	3
1964	Ethiopian Investment Corporation S.C.	1	20
1966	Banco di Roma (Ethiopia) S.C.	8	4
1969	Agricultural and Industrial Development Bank	5	100

Note: * These two banks of Italian origin were established before the Italian occupation; n.d. – no date.
Source: Gedey (1990).

established; just before the 1974 revolution the banks listed in Table 8.1(b) were in operation.

All privately-owned financial institutions, including three commercial banks, thirteen insurance companies and two non-bank financial intermediaries, were nationalized on 1 January 1975.[2] The nationalized banks were reorganized and one commercial bank (the CBE); a national bank (recreated in 1976); two specialized banks (the Agricultural and Industrial Bank (AIB) – renamed recently as the Development Bank of Ethiopia (DBE), and a Housing and Saving Bank (HSB) – renamed recently as the Construction and Business Bank (CBB)); and one insurance company (Ethiopian Insurance Company) were formed. Following the regime change in 1991 and the liberalization policy in 1992, these financial institutions were reorganized to work to a market-orientated policy framework. Moreover, new privately-owned financial institutions were also allowed to work alongside the publicly-owned ones. The rest of this chapter examines these financial institutions.

The structure and performance of the financial sector in the pre- and post-reform periods

Following the McKinnon (1973) and Shaw (1973) paradigm, financial liberalization has been high on the agenda of developing countries. The financial repression school (as it is sometimes referred to) argues that government intervention in the finance sector, in particular through subsidized interest rates and (favoured) credit allocation, not only distorts the financial market but also depresses savings and leads to inefficient investment. The policy prescription that follows is liberalization. This has been endorsed by the international financial and development institutions, such as the World Bank and the International Monetary Fund (IMF), and was high on the agenda of the reform packages prescribed for most developing countries called structural adjustment programmes (SAPs).

Many of the developing countries, with the exception of a few in Asia, that went through this agonizing reform process have been unable to enjoy the promised benefits in general, and the promised financial sector prosperity in particular. Vos (1993) noted that one of the major factors that might explain the failure of financial liberalization in Latin America and its success in Asian countries (such as South Korea and Taiwan) were the control and intervention by the state to address structural problems. Thus, for Vos, gradualism and addressing some of the gaps in financial-sector reform – such as the lack of sensible prudential supervisory capacity in place before the onset of reform – are crucial.

The pre-reform financial sector in Ethiopia

The pre-reform period here refers to the period 1974–91 (the Derg regime). During this period, all private banks were nationalized. The National Bank of Ethiopia was at the apex of the banking structure and was engaged in all the functions of a central bank. As noted earlier, CBE, AIDB (DBE), HSB (CBB) were in operation during this period. In addition to these banks, there were also two other financial institutions: the Ethiopian Insurance Corporation (EIC) and the Pension and Social Security Authority (PSSA).

The CBE, followed by the DBE, were (and remain) the most important banks in the country. Because of the dominant position of these two banks, their major activities and performance are now discussed at length. This helps to provide a picture of banking activity in the country both before and after the 1992 reform.

The Commercial Bank of Ethiopia (CBE)

The CBE was established in its present form by a merger of one of the nationalized private bank (Addis Bank) with that of the publicly-owned commercial bank by proclamation No. 184 (1980). The CBE is directed by a board and managed by three managers (one general and two deputies) appointed by the government. The management is supported by detailed monthly and quarterly reports from the bank's various branches.

Mobilization of deposits

Figure 8.1 shows the mobilization of deposits by the CBE in the pre- and post-reform periods, demonstrating that the CBE is the dominant bank, accounting for more than 90 per cent of the total deposits mobilized in the country in the pre-reform period. This share is the highest for demand deposits (100 per cent) followed by savings (96 per cent) and time (45 per cent) deposits. Thus, to study the CBE in the pre-reform period basically equates to studying the banking sector in Ethiopia.

The CBE's share of total deposits has fallen to an average of 87 per cent in the post-reform period; the figure for 2002/3 was 75.5 per cent. The sharp decline in the CBE's share of total deposits noted in 2002/3 was primarily a result of the performance of the new private banks, in particular the Awash and Dashen Banks. The share of the CBB and DBE has also increased.

Clearly, there is an evolving structural shift when deposits are observed by institutions (that is, by type of ownership). In general, the trend is to move away from a dominant public sector towards a financial structure where the role of the private sector is becoming increasingly important. In general, during the two periods (before and after the reform), demand deposits by the private sector and individuals increased; the share of co-operatives declined; and the share of public enterprises and agencies declined. Financial agencies' share also declined, while the central government's share increased. In terms of savings and time deposits, the

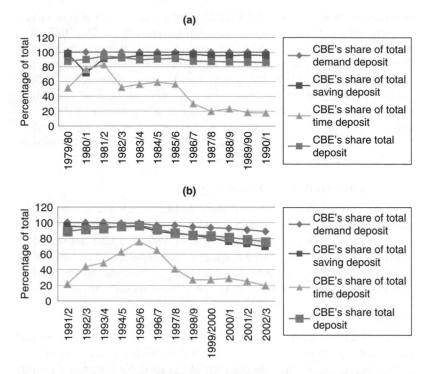

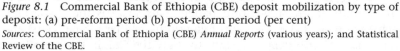

Figure 8.1   Commercial Bank of Ethiopia (CBE) deposit mobilization by type of deposit: (a) pre-reform period (b) post-reform period (per cent)

Sources: Commercial Bank of Ethiopia (CBE) *Annual Reports* (various years); and Statistical Review of the CBE.

private sector had the lion's share in both periods. This is attributed to the government's rule restricting public enterprises and agencies from holding such deposits (Geda 1999).

Loans and advances

Tables 8.2 and 8.3 show the CBE's outstanding loans disaggregated by sector and 'institution'. In the years immediately before reform (1985–91) the CBE's average outstanding loans were highest in the international trade sector (15 per cent in 1989) followed by housing and construction, and domestic trade (about 6 per cent) and industry (5.5 per cent). In the post-reform period, outstanding loans with the international trade sector grew enormously (reaching an average of 19.3 per cent for the period 1992–2003). This was followed by domestic trade (12.6 per cent), industry (7.2 per cent), and transport and communication (5.4 per cent). Loans to

Table 8.2 Commercial Bank of Ethiopia: loans and advances, by sector (per cent, unless stated otherwise)

Before reform	1985/6	1986/7	1987/8	1988/9	1989/90	1990/1	1985–91 (avg.)	1992–2003 (avg.)
Central government	61.7	58.1	53.5	59.7	65.7	70.7	61.6	36.2
Agriculture	1.9	2.7	2.6	1.9	1.5	1.3	2.0	2.6
Industry	4.4	5.0	5.9	6.7	5.6	5.3	5.5	7.2
Domestic trade	5.7	7.2	8.8	5.5	4.7	3.7	5.9	12.6
International trade	14.5	15.9	17.4	16.4	13.8	10.6	14.8	19.3
Exports	8.9	6.0	5.6	7.5	5.1	5.7	6.5	7.7
Imports	5.6	10.0	11.8	8.9	8.7	4.9	8.3	11.7
Housing & construction	7.0	6.3	6.4	6.0	5.7	5.5	6.1	4.1
Transport & communication	3.2	3.0	4.2	2.7	2.0	1.8	2.8	5.4
Hotels and tourism	0.5	0.5	0.4	0.3	0.3	0.4	0.4	1.3
Mines, power & water resources	0.0	0.0	0.0	0.0	0.0	0.0	0.0	0.0
Personal	0.4	0.4	0.4	0.3	0.3	0.4	0.4	0.2
Others	0.7	0.7	0.5	0.4	0.4	0.4	0.5	11.2
Total (millions of Birr)	2,352.7	2,500.0	2,800.0	3,130.4	3,406.2	3,721.1		
Inter-bank lending	19.4	18.6	17.7	24.2	25.9	25.1		
Grand total (millions of Birr)	2,372.1	2,518.6	2,817.7	3,154.6	3,432.1	3,746.2		

(Continued)

Table 8.2 Continued

After reform	1992/3	1993/4	1994/5	1995/6	1996/7	1997/8	1998/9	1999/2000	2000/1	2001/2	2002/3
Central government	52.3	46.8	34.5	32.2	22.0	20.9	22.4	22.1	41.5	47.1	55.9
Agriculture	0.9	1.4	2.2	2.4	3.5	3.4	3.5	3.5	2.4	2.8	2.3
Industry	11.0	8.9	6.1	6.5	7.5	7.5	7.5	7.1	6.4	5.6	5.5
Domestic trade	8.6	14.0	16.7	19.5	20.4	18.3	12.9	12.5	6.9	5.3	3.6
International trade	19.0	18.9	20.8	19.6	25.0	25.3	24.6	21.8	15.5	13.7	8.1
Exports	8.2	10.1	9.8	7.3	9.8	9.5	9.7	7.4	5.6	4.0	2.7
Imports	10.8	8.8	11.0	12.3	15.2	15.9	14.8	14.4	9.9	9.7	5.4
Housing & construction	4.1	4.1	4.1	4.0	4.5	4.0	4.3	4.5	4.0	3.3	3.8
Transport & communication	2.7	4.1	6.6	9.6	10.0	8.3	4.8	5.9	3.4	2.2	1.4
Hotels and tourism	0.9	1.3	2.4	1.8	2.0	1.9	1.2	1.1	0.7	1.0	0.5
Mines, power & water resources	0.0	0.0	0.0	0.0	0.0	0.0	0.0	0.0	0.0	0.0	0.0
Personal	0.3	0.2	0.2	0.2	0.2	0.2	0.1	0.1	0.1	0.1	0.2
Others	0.2	0.5	6.4	4.2	4.9	10.1	18.6	21.4	19.1	18.8	18.7
Total (millions of Birr)	5008.9	5596.5	7450.9	8841.7	9497.1	10486.9	11582.7	12097.9	16620.4	17338.8	17943.3
Inter-bank lending	110.6	128.0	179.5	527.6	540.8	496.7	546.9	676.9	564.3	0	456.6
Grand total (millions of Birr)	5119.5	5724.5	7630.4	9369.3	10037.9	10983.6	12129.6	12774.8	17184.7	17338.8	18399.9

Source: Commercial Bank of Ethiopia (CBE) *Annual Reports* (various years).

Table 8.3 Commercial Bank of Ethiopia: outstanding loans and advances by institutional category

	Public sector				Private sector			Total
	Central government (1)	Total (2 = 3 + 4)	Financial sector (3)	Non-financial sector (4)	Private sector (5)	Co-operatives (6)	Private enterprises and agencies (7 = 5 − 6)	
Before reform								
1985/6	1,451.1	565.8	19.4	546.4	355.2	2.8	352.4	2,372.1
1986/7	1,451.6	655.5	18.6	636.9	411.5	29.8	381.7	2,518.6
1987/8	1,497.8	846.6	17.7	828.9	473.3	20.8	452.5	2,817.7
1988/9	1,868.5	897.8	24.2	873.5	388.3	22.1	366.2	3,154.6
1989/90	2,239.3	812.1	25.9	786.2	380.7	12.7	368.0	3,432.1
Average value (1985/6–1989/90)	1,567.3	741.4	20.0	721.5	407.1	18.9	388.2	2,715.8
Average annual share (1985/6–1989/90)	57.7	27.3	0.7	26.5	15.0	0.7	14.3	100.0
End of period (1988/9) share	59.2	28.5	0.8	27.7	12.3	0.7	11.6	100.0
After reform								
1992/3	2,617.4	1,492.6	110.6	1,382.0	1,009.5	33.1	976.4	5,119.5
1993/4	2,617.2	1,616.6	128.0	1,488.6	1,490.7	65.7	1,425.0	5,724.5
1994/5	2,573.7	1,953.1	179.5	1,773.6	0.0	107.7	2,995.9	7,630.4
1995/6	2,847.2	2,403.2	527.6	1,875.5	4,418.9	107.0	4,311.9	9,669.3
1996/7	2,089.8	2,113.6	540.8	1,572.8	5,834.5	122.3	5,712.2	10,037.9
1997/8	2,193.1	1,984.5	496.7	1,487.8	6,806.0	113.0	6,693.0	10,983.6

(Continued)

Table 8.3 *Continued*

	Public sector				Private sector			
	Central government (1)	Total (2 = 3 + 4)	Financial sector (3)	Non-financial sector (4)	Private sector (5)	Co-operatives (6)	Private enterprises and agencies (7 = 5 − 6)	Total
1998/9	2,599.8	1,740.1	546.9	1,193.2	7,789.7	339.6	7,450.1	12,129.6
1999/2000	2,675.8	2,027.0	676.9	1,350.1	8,072.0	325.1	7,746.9	12,774.8
2000/1	6,901.3	1,733.9	564.3	1,169.6	8,549.7	261.2	8,288.5	17,184.8
2001/2	8,160.7	1,449.5	0.0	0.0	7,728.6	298.4	7,430.2	17,338.8
2002/3	10,038.7	986.5	0.0	0.0	6,917.9	283.9	6,634.0	17,943.1
Average value (1992/3–2002/3)	4,119.5	1,772.8	342.8	1,208.5	5,328.9	187.0	5,424.0	11,503.3
Average share (1992/3–2002/3)	35.8	15.4	3.0	10.5	46.3	1.6	47.2	100.0
End of period (2002/3) share	55.9	5.5	0.0	0.0	38.6	1.6	37.0	100.0

Source: Commercial Bank of Ethiopia (CBE) *Annual Reports* (various years).

central government, which were about 62 per cent in pre-reform period, declined by nearly half, to 36 per cent, in the post-reform period. This perhaps indicates the discipline the government was exercising in its fiscal and monetary polices.

When the outstanding loans by institution are broken down, outstanding loans to public enterprises (which were about 27 per cent during last five years of the pre-reform period) declined to an average of 15 per cent in the post-reform period, the figure for 2002/3 being 5 per cent. The share of the private sector, however, increased from 14 per cent to 47 per cent between the two periods. This is attributed to the liberalization programme, which resulted in the increasing exposure of the CBE to competition from the private sector. As for the government, as noted above, the CBE's outstanding loans to government dropped by nearly half.

Loan collection

In the pre-reform period, the highest loan collection was made from domestic trade, followed by import and exports, and industry (in order of importance). In terms of institutional disaggregation, loan collection from the private sector was significant, totalling almost 47 per cent in the pre-reform period and reaching an average figure of nearly 75 per cent in the post reform period. Loan collection from the public sector (state enter prises) had been falling steadily in the pre-reform period. This trend has continued in the post-reform period (dropping from 44 per cent to 11 per cent between the two periods). This indicates the poor financial shape the public sector was in (see Tables 8.4 and 8.5 for details).

In general, total loan collection has shown a marked improvement in the post-reform period. The growth figure, which was generally negative in the pre-reform period, became positive in the post-reform period. Thus the performance of the CBE in this regard is quite commendable. This highlights the important point that existing public banks, with proper regulation and a sound policy environment, can improve their performance enormously. Hence, privatization, as the IMF has argued, may not be the only approach that can bring about efficiency in the banking sector.

Asset quality

Table 8.6 shows the quality of assets at the CBE. The liquidity ratio in both periods is quite high – being well above the statutory requirement of 20 per cent in all periods. These figures show an increasing trend in the post-reform period. The quality of the bank's assets can also be inferred from the 'loan-to-deposit ratio' that shows a declining percentage (notwithstanding

Table 8.4 Commercial Bank of Ethiopia: loan collection by institutional disaggregation

	Central government	State enterprises	Financial sector	Non-financial sector	Private sector	Co-operatives	Private enterprises and Agencies	Total	Total less IB lending
Before reform									
1985/6	0.0	117.5	0.9	116.6	206.8	3.6	203.2	324.3	97.6
1986/7	0.0	137.4	0.0	137.4	137.0	9.0	128.0	274.4	0.0
1987/8	0.0	186.0	0.9	185.1	218.8	66.8	152.0	404.8	0.0
1988/9	0.0	143.8	0.9	142.9	174.4	49.1	125.3	318.2	0.0
1989/90	0.0	172.3	0.9	171.4	223.2	30.5	192.7	395.5	0.0
	0.0	107.1	0.9	106.2	172.8	36.7	136.1	279.9	0.0
Average annual value (1985/6 –1989/90)	0.0	151.4	0.7	150.7	192.0	31.8	160.2	343.4	19.5
Average annual share (1985/6 –1989/90)	0.0	44.1	0.2	43.9	55.9	9.3	46.7	100.0	5.7
After reform									
1992/3	0.0	160.3	1.7	158.6	373.8	49.3	324.5	534.1	0.0
1993/4	0.0	443.1	1.4	441.7	892.4	35.9	856.5	1,335.5	0.0
1994/5	0.0	283.5	1.3	282.2	1,180.0	239.4	1,516.9	2,039.8	2,038.5

1995/6	0.0	303.6	0.0	303.6	2,399.3	292.5	2,106.8	2,702.9	2,703.0
1996/7	0.0	338.7	71.9	266.8	2,418.1	243.9	2,174.2	2,756.8	2,684.9
1997/8	0.0	197.3	44.3	153.0	2,494.1	342.7	2,151.4	2,691.4	2,624.7
1998/9	0.0	187.3	75.9	111.4	2,572.6	294.5	2,278.1	2,759.9	2,684.0
1999/2000	0.0	256.6	102.4	154.2	1,916.1	365.7	1,550.4	2,172.8	2,070.3
2000/1	0.0	290.3	146.8	143.5	2,366.2	501.3	1,865.0	2,656.5	2,509.7
2001/2	0.0	93.3	0.0	0.0	2,016.4	481.4	1,535.0	2,109.7	82.7
2002/3	0.0	154.2	0.0	0.0	2,073.4	339.4	1,734.0	2,227.6	59.8
Average annual value (1992/3–2002/3)	0.0	246.2	40.5	183.2	1,882.0	289.6	1,644.8	2,180.6	1,587.1
Average annual share (1992/3–2002/3)	0.0	11.3	1.9	8.4	86.3	13.3	75.4	100.0	72.8

Source: Commercial Bank of Ethiopia (CBE) *Annual Reports* (various years).

Table 8.5 Commercial Bank of Ethiopia: loan collection by sector (per cent, unless otherwise stated)

	1985/6	1986/7	1987/8	1988/9	1989/90	1990/1	1985-91 (avg.)	1992-3 (avg.)
Before reform								
Central government	0.0	0.0	0.0	0.0	0.0	0.0	0.0	0.0
Agriculture	4.8	3.6	15.4	10.1	5.2	1.5	6.8	14.6
Industry	19.7	12.2	10.9	10.6	16.7	17.7	14.6	12.1
Domestic trade	27.4	33.4	21.2	36.6	26.5	39.5	30.8	35.1
International trade	30.2	30.1	37.0	24.3	31.6	20.2	28.9	14.4
Exports	19.3	17.7	12.1	8.6	23.8	8.3	15.0	7.0
Imports	10.9	12.4	24.8	15.7	7.8	11.8	13.9	7.5
Housing & construction	2.0	2.8	4.5	3.4	2.9	1.8	2.9	2.6
Transport & communication	8.7	11.3	5.0	9.5	9.2	7.9	8.6	9.9
Hotels and tourism	2.3	2.8	2.0	2.2	2.6	3.8	2.6	4.0
Mines, power & water resources	0.0	0.0	0.0	0.0	0.0	0.0	0.0	0.0
Personal	3.8	2.4	2.9	1.8	3.6	5.4	3.3	1.5
Others	1.1	1.2	1.1	1.5	1.7	2.3	1.5	5.8
Grand total (millions of Birr)	324.3	274.1	403.9	383.1	400.6	334.9		
Inter-bank lending	0.9	0.0	0.9	0.9	0.9	1.8	0.9	45.0
Total (millions of Birr)	325.2	274.1	404.8	384.0	401.5	336.7		

After reform	1992/3	1993/4	1994/5	1995/6	1996/7	1997/8	1998/9	1999/2000	2000/1	2001/2	2002/3
Central government	0.0	0.0	0.0	0.0	0.0	0.0	0.0	0.0	0.0	0.0	0.0
Agriculture	0.7	2.4	10.5	12.8	9.6	14.0	17.6	22.3	26.3	24.6	19.7
Industry	25.0	26.7	12.5	8.1	6.9	6.7	8.5	11.6	10.2	9.7	7.3
Domestic trade	40.8	39.2	47.8	35.6	42.2	36.2	35.2	33.2	27.0	25.6	23.9
International trade	15.1	14.5	12.5	17.6	16.8	17.3	11.9	4.6	11.3	17.3	19.8
Exports	8.8	9.5	4.4	9.1	6.6	6.2	6.5	1.6	4.3	6.2	13.4
Imports	6.3	5.1	8.1	8.5	10.2	11.0	5.4	2.9	6.9	11.1	6.4
Housing & construction	1.6	1.4	0.7	0.3	0.8	2.0	2.2	2.7	2.1	4.5	10.1
Transport & communication	4.6	5.1	4.8	7.8	12.5	11.9	13.4	14.7	13.0	11.0	9.9
Hotels and tourism	5.8	4.8	5.0	6.2	3.8	3.8	3.4	3.3	2.7	2.8	2.2
Mines, power & water resources	0.0	0.0	0.0	0.0	0.0	0.0	0.0	0.0	0.0	0.0	0.0
Personal	2.9	2.2	1.6	0.9	1.2	1.4	1.3	1.5	1.3	1.2	1.5
Others	3.6	3.7	4.6	10.7	6.2	6.7	6.6	5.2	6.1	3.3	5.8
Grand total (millions of Birr)	532.4	1334.1	2038.5	2702.9	2684.9	2625	2693	2070.5	2393.9	2112.5	2225.86
Inter-bank lending	1.7	1.4	1.2	0.1	71.9	44.2	69.7	102.4	121.1	27.8	56.7
Total (millions of Birr)	534.1	1335.5	2039.7	2703	2756.8	2669.2	2762.7	2172.9	2515	2140.3	2282.56

Source: Commercial Bank of Ethiopia (CBE) *Annual Reports* (various years).

Table 8.6 Commercial Bank of Ethiopia: asset quality, end of the fiscal period, June of each year, 1988–98 (millions of Birr)

Year[4]	Liquid assets to net deposits ratio[1]	Excess liquidity (over the 20% requirement)	Liquidity ratio (%)[2]	Loan to deposit ratio	Loan to deposit ratio (including loans to government) (%)	Non-performing assets to total assets	Credit quality (%)[3]	Total assets (millions of Birr)	Annual growth of assets
1988	0.407	723.9	63.87	0.7927	37.51		18.2	4825.72	0.041
1989	0.348	539.9	60.26	0.8388	34.65		20.7	5021.4	0.036
1990	0.331	540.0	63.56	0.8212	29.08	0.04*	23.9	5199.98	0.031
1991	0.298	428.3	50.79	0.8533	26.08	0.39*	27.4	5363.6	
After reform									
1992	0.372	854.3	68.42	0.7846	26.29	0.039	26.1	6090.29	0.135
1993	0.423	1334.9	86.37	0.8362	42.07	0.026	15.8	9060.84	0.488
1994	0.534	2319.7	87.86	0.7857	43.75	0.018	14.2	11217.4	0.238
1995	0.514	2842.6	79.68	0.7881	52.15	0.015	25.4	14273.1	0.272
1996	0.358	1668.9	57.59	0.8590	61.92		8.4	15858.0	0.11
1997	0.4	2938.0	59.09	0.7982	63.46		12.1	16549.4	0.044
1998	0.44	4286.9	63.11	0.7113	57.14		10.9		

Sources: Commercial Bank of Ethiopia, *Annual Reports* (various years); and Statistical Review of the CBE.

Notes: [1] Liquid assets are {cash (local or foreign) + reserves with NBE + demand balance with other domestic banks + deposits with Eritrea Bank + treasury bills + demand balance with foreign banks}/net deposit balance which is {total deposits − uncleared cheques paid (local) − uncleared effects (foreign)}.
[2] Liquidity ratio is [reserves with NBE + cash on hand in local currency + net foreign assets [foreign assets − short term liabilities]]/net demand deposit [total demand deposit − uncleared cheques], expressed in per cent.
[3] Provision for bad and doubtful debts to total deposits ratio.
[4] The fiscal year is the preceding year followed by /. For example, 1988 on this table is fiscal year 1987/8 and 1997 is fiscal year 1996/7.
* Figures taken from the graphs given in the *Annual Reports*.

the increase in credit), which in turn shows that the bank had a strong resource base. By 1998, the loan-to-deposit ratio had the lowest figure, of 71 per cent. (Note however, that this analysis is based on official figures.) Observations and discussions with other researchers showed that non-performing loan figures, which are usually modest in government reports, need to be viewed with caution.[3] However, the main conclusion that may be made from the analysis of the bank's asset quality (as reported) is that the CBE has quite an impressive record. This may be contrasted with the IMF's and the World Bank's recommendation to either privatize or divide the CBE. On asset quality grounds there is no justification for such a policy proposal. The IMF and World Bank argument may stand on competition grounds: I shall return to this at the end of the chapter.

As can be seen from Table 8.6, the CBE's total assets showed a modest growth rate before reform, and in the post-reform period, the bank's assets grew annually by double-digit figures. In particular, the unprecedented growth of nearly 50 per cent in 1993 is clearly associated with the reform process. According to the CBE's *Annual Report*, this high growth is attributed to the growth in net loans and advances, customers' liability for letters of credit (LC), cash with foreign banks, and deposits with NBE (in order of importance). In particular, loans and advances in 1992/3 increased by nearly 125 percentage points (constituting nearly 25 per cent of the bank's total assets, for the first time in two decades). This is attributed to the growing demand for credit (and hence the effort to satisfy that demand) resulting from liberalization. The availability of foreign exchange and the devaluation that took place during this period (a devaluation of 240 per cent in 1992) also contributed to the growth of this figure. Throughout the subsequent years, loans and advances to the private sector have shown sustained increments.

In sum, the CBE is the dominant bank in the country. Both the quality and the structure of assets and various performance indicators show that the bank is generally in good shape. There are certain areas, such as non-performing loans and a failure to adopt new technology to improve the efficiency of its services, where the CBE is weak. The relevant policy prescription would seem to be to intensify the ongoing restructuring, and accompany that with prudential regulation. It seems extremely difficult to arrive at a policy prescription of privatization from an examination of the existing data, as the World Bank and IMF have done.

The Development Bank of Ethiopia (DBE)

The mobilization of deposits by the DBE was fairly stagnant in the five years before reform. However, it fell sharply just before the reform period and during the first two years of the post-reform period. At the time of writing, the DBE's level is picking up again, approaching the level registered in the pre-reform period (see Geda 1999 for detail).

Table 8.7 shows the DBE's loan disbursement by sector. In both the post- and pre-reform periods, the highest share of loans disbursed went to the agricultural sector. This was followed by loans disbursed to the industrial sector. In terms of the magnitude of the loans advanced, recent years have seen a marked decline, with total loans advanced by DBE declining from 155 million Birr in 1992/3 to about 57 million Birr in 2002/3 (see Table 8.7). In terms of loan by type of ownership, the bias against the private sector witnessed during the pre-reform period has been reversed in the post-reform period. This reversal shows the success of redirecting the emphasis from the public to the private sector.

Outstanding loans were a serious problem in the pre-reform period. This problem has eased in the post-reform period, although in 2001/2 their value was estimated to have been some 4.4 billion Birr (see Tables 8.8 and 8.9). In terms of sector, the agricultural sector was the most indebted in the pre-reform period. The industrial sector has taken over from the agricultural sector in the post-reform period, however. In terms of institutional disaggregation, outstanding loans were mainly with the public sector in the pre-reform period. Again, the private sector took over from the public sector in this respect in the post-reform period.

The relatively recent phenomenon of high levels of outstanding loans with the private sector needs closer attention. Although complete data on arrears was not available, the level of arrears in the pre-reform period (in particular in the agricultural sector – where the role of state farms was crucial) had reached an alarming level. The arrears in the pre-reform period, on average more than 75 per cent of the total principal outstanding, declined sharply to about 40 per cent in the first two years of the post-reform period because of the rescue (bailing out) effort by the government (Geda 1999).

In terms of loan collection, the performance of the DBE is not impressive (see Table 8.10). However, in the post-reform period, the DBE has made a good effort to collect its outstanding loans, particularly from the co-operative and private sectors.

Other performance indicators of the DBE were not impressive either. For a good part of the period under analysis the DBE was operating at a loss and was in bad financial shape, as can be seen from the change in working capital. The DBE's total assets were, by and large, stagnant in the pre-reform period and declined thereafter. In general, since the DBE was operating under the auspices of the central planning organ of the

Table 8.7 Development Bank of Ethiopia: loan disbursement by sector, 1985/6–2002/3 (millions of Birr)

Before reform	1985/6	1986/7	1987/8	1988/9	1989/90	1990/1
Agriculture	267.1	132.3	305.1	238.8	214.2	81.0
Industry	25.9	38.0	35.9	110.9	78.9	43.3
Domestic trade	0	0	0	0	0	0
International trade						
Exports	0	0	0	0	0	0
Imports	0	0	0	0	0	0
Housing & construction	2.5	0.4	1.4	1.6	1.0	2.2
Transport & communication	0.4	0	0	2.9	0.7	0
Hotels and tourism	0.5	0	1.0	1.7	4.7	12.7
Mines, power & water resources	3.9	18.0	19.8	18.1	19.9	0
Personal	0	0	0	0	0	0
Others	0.2	0.2	0	0	0	0
Total	300.5	188.9	363.2	374	319.4	139.2

After reform	1992/3	1993/4	1994/5	1995/6	1996/7	1997/8	1998/9	1999/2000	2000/1	2001/2	2002/3
Agriculture	117.6	27.8	162.5	266.3	275.4	417.5	284.9	223.9	108.5	60.1	31.7
Industry	24.3	118.9	134.2	153.2	172.9	426.0	190.8	146.4	124.3	37.9	14.9
Domestic trade	0	0	1.1	0	0	0	0	0	0	0	0
International trade											
Exports	0	0	0	0	0	0	0	0	0	0	0
Imports	0	0	0	0	0	0	0	0	0	0	0
Housing & construction	0.8	0.3	1.6	0.6	32.6	17.7	20.9	41.9	8.9	3.8	1.0

(*Continued*)

Table 8.7 Continued

After reform	1992/3	1993/4	1994/5	1995/6	1996/7	1997/8	1998/9	1999/2000	2000/1	2001/2	2002/3
Transport & communication	0	0	0	1.8	2.4	0.2	0	0.8	0.5	0.1	0.1
Hotels and tourism	12.3	17.8	22.1	16.1	43.9	32.5	38.6	16.4	6.5	4.2	1.9
Mines, power & water resources	0	0	0.2	0	0	0	0	0	0	0	0
Personal	0	0	0.3	0.2	0	104.7	0	0	0	0	0
Others	0	1.2	14.3	64.3	30.6	138.7	247.4	115.5	83.1	22	7.2
Total	155.0	166.0	336.3	502.5	557.8	1137.3	782.6	544.9	331.8	128.1	56.8

Source: Development Bank of Ethiopia (DBE) Annual Reports (various years).

Table 8.8 Development Bank of Ethiopia: outstanding balances of loans and advances by sector, 1985/6–2001/2 (millions of Birr)

Before reform	1985/6	1986/7	1987/8	1988/9	1989/90	1990/1
Agriculture	1200.2	1358.3	1582.2	1685.1	1835.2	1887.1
Industry	168.5	170.2	181.2	259.7	328.5	359.2
Housing & construction	23.1	18.8	19.1	19.3	19.7	20.9
Transport & communication	42.7	39.3	39.3	25.5	20.3	17.5
Hotels and tourism	5.8	4.9	5.6	7.2	10.8	20.7
Mines, power & water resources	19.0	36.9	55.3	75.4	90.2	86.6
Personal	0	0	0	0	0	0
Others	2	0	0	0	0	0
Total	1461.3	1628.4	1882.7	2072.2	2304.7	2392

After reform	1992/3	1993/4	1994/5	1995/6	1996/7	1997/8	1998/9	1999/2000	2000/1	2001/2
Agriculture	1966.8	235.2	234.4	475.9	565.9	712.3	897.1	999.0	1029.8	1052.5
Industry	437.8	530.7	619.7	852.3	959.6	948.1	1126.6	1228.5	1314.4	1358.9
Housing & construction	18.7	18.5	17.8	0	84.7	103.7	130.0	181.9	204.0	221.8
Transport & communication	17.5	17.5	15.1	22.9	27.7	26.7	27.5	31.4	33.0	18.6
Hotels and tourism	38.3	53.1	73.4	111.4	164.9	212	271	179.1	268.4	259.8
Mines, power & water resources	74.8	51.0	42.0	36.8	29.9	31.5	23.4	24.5	25.6	26.7
Personal	0	0	2.5	2.5	0	94.6	0	0	0	0
Others	0	2.1	10.4	234.4	104.1	681.1	1020.9	1376.9	1389.7	1503.8
Total	2553.9	908.1	1015.3	1736.2	1936.8	2810	3496.5	4021.3	4264.9	4442.1

Source: Development Bank of Ethiopia (DBE) *Annual Reports* (various years); DBE (1996).

Table 8.9 Development Bank of Ethiopia: outstanding balances of loans and advances by institutional disaggregation, 1985/6–2001/2 (millions of Birr)

Before reform	1985/6	1986/7	1987/8	1988/9	1989/90	1990/1
State enterprises	1414.3	1577.3	1811.1	1972.4	2125.2	0
Financial sector	0	0	0	0	0	0
Non-financial sector	1414.3	1577.3	1811.1	1972.4	2125.2	0
Private sector	47.0	51.1	71.6	99.8	179.5	0
Co-operatives	27.1	29.0	46.3	69.7	137.2	0
Private enterprises and agencies	19.9	22.1	25.3	30.1	42.3	0
Total	1461.3	1628.4	1882.7	2072.2	2304.7	0

After reform	1992/3	1993/4	1994/5	1995/6	1996/7	1997/8	1998/9	1999/2000	2000/1	2001/2
State enterprises	2,286.0	478.8	477.6	595.7	464.9	405.8	371.8	336.0	321.4	322.7
Financial sector	0.0	0.0	0.0	0.0	0.0	0.0	0.0	0.0	0.0	0.0
Non-financial sector	2,286.0	478.8	477.6	595.7	464.9	405.8	371.8	336.0	321.4	0.0
Private sector	267.9	429.3	0.0	1,140.5	1,471.9	2,404.2	3,124.7	3,685.3	3,943.4	4,118.5
Co-operatives	180.2	210.7	181.5	332.4	322.4	305.7	341.1	368.1	379.5	395.9
Private enterprises and agencies	87.7	218.6	356.2	808.1	1,149.5	2,098.5	2,783.6	3,317.3	3,563.9	3,722.6
Total	2,553.9	908.1	1,015.3	1,736.2	1,936.8	2,810.0	3,496.5	4,021.4	4,264.8	4,441.2

Source: Development Bank of Ethiopia (DBE) *Annual Reports* (various years).

Table 8.10 Development Bank of Ethiopia: loan collection by sector, 1985/6–2002/3 (millions of Birr)

Before reform	1985/6	1986/7	1987/8	1988/9	1989/90	1990/1
Agriculture	92.9	64.3	81.2	92.0	129.4	61.5
Industry	11.7	28.8	28.5	20.8	8.9	17.6
Domestic trade	0	0	0	0	0	0
International trade	0	0	0	0	0	0
Exports	0	0	0	0	0	0
Imports	0	0	0	0	0	0
Housing & construction	0.4	2.3	1.1	1.1	0.7	1.7
Transport & communication	2.7	3.4	0	16.7	6.4	2.8
Hotels and tourism	0.7	0.6	0.9	0.8	0.8	4.2
Mines, power & water resources	0.5	2.5	1.9	2.0	3.1	3.6
Personal	0	0	0	0	0	0
Others	0.1	0.2	0	0	0	0
Total	109.0	102.1	113.6	133.4	149.3	91.4

After reform	1992/3	1993/4	1994/5	1995/6	1996/7	1997/8	1998/9	1999/2000	2000/1	2001/2	2002/3
Central government	0	0	0	0	0	0	0	0	0	0	0
Agriculture	39.3	19.6	108.5	162.6	281.3	318.7	200.0	221.6	162.9	112.6	99.0
Industry	14.9	31.5	31.6	104.0	105.3	112.0	134.1	151.0	149.2	89.6	114.3
Domestic trade	0	0	0	0	0	0	0	0	0	0	0
International trade	0	0	0	0	0	0	0	0	0	0	0
Exports	0	0	0	0	0	0	0	0	0	0	0
Imports	0	0	0	0	0	0	0	0	0	0	0

(Continued)

Table 8.10 Continued

After reform	1992/3	1993/4	1994/5	1995/6	1996/7	1997/8	1998/9	1999/2000	2000/1	2001/2	2002/3
Housing & construction	0.5	0.6	0.5	0.3	0.9	4.9	3.7	5.1	6.8	5.7	6.4
Transport & communication	0	0.7	0	2.1	1.0	0.7	0.9	2.0	1.9	16.1	0.9
Hotels and tourism	1.7	3.6	3.8	5.7	12.4	15.8	18.9	19.7	23.4	19.0	15.9
Mines, power & water resources	3.9	4.0	3.1	13.9	9.3	0	9.3	0	0	0	0
Personal	0	0	0.2	0.2	0	73.2	0	0	0	0	0
Others	0	0	0.4	6.3	14.5	15.2	94.4	58.7	66.2	24.2	54.5
Total	60.3	60.0	148.1	295.1	424.7	540.5	461.3	458.1	410.4	267.2	291.0

Source: Development Bank of Ethiopia (DBE) Annual Reports (various years).

government and exposed to loss-making sectors (such as state farms), its performance epitomized the inefficiency in the public-sector (Geda 1999). This should be contrasted with the CBE, a public sector entity, yet it performed relatively well – even in financial terms. Thus the interesting conclusion is that what matters most is probably not ownership but rather exposure (or not) to loss-making clients and having (or not) management autonomy.

The policy regime in the pre-reform period: financial sector and ideology

The Derg may be characterized as a controlled regime, where all economic activities were based on the directives that came from the central (national) planning organ. To facilitate this, the 1976 reorganization proclamation redefined the role of the NBE as a developmental organ, as is clearly emphasized by the infamous Article 6 in the proclamation, which states that the objective of NBE is 'to foster balanced and accelerated development'.

In this period, the NBE was actively involved in the direct control of all financial institutions by (i) fixing both deposit and lending interest rates, (ii) controlling directly foreign exchange and credit allocation, which was done in a discriminatory manner by favouring the public sector; and (iii) financing the government deficit directly (NBE 1998). Bank supervision and regulation was largely limited to the sporadic inspection of a few branches.

The Derg regime is also characterized by an economic policy largely informed by socialist ideology. The sine qua non of such a set-up is the prominent role accorded to the socialized (public and co-operative) sectors by discriminating against the private sector. During this time, indirect ways of regulating the financial sector were not important because it was directly controlled. The most important financial instruments used to control the sector were (i) the interest rate; and (ii) the discriminatory allocation of foreign exchange and credit.

The interest rate was set deliberately at a very low level (repressed). Depending on the degree of socialization, different sectors faced different interest rates. The ruling interest rates for each sector in both (pre- and post-reform) periods are given in Table 8.11. The socialized sectors were accorded priority in credit as well as foreign exchange allocation. All foreign exchange earnings were surrendered to the NBE, and the NBE rationed this limited supply of foreign exchange to the sectors that were accorded priority in the national plan. In general, the socialized sectors were prioritized – with the private sector being the least preferred.

Table 8.11 Interest rate developments in Ethiopia post-1991 (per cent)

Deposit rates		Lending rates	
1 October 1992–31 August 1994		**1 October 1992–31 August 1994**	
Time deposits		Agriculture	11.0–12.0
		Industry	13.0–14.0
		Domestic trade	14.0–15.0
30 days' notice	10.5	Transport and communication	13.0–14.0
3 months to less than 6 months	10.5	Export trade	13.0–14.0
6 months to less than 12 months	11.0	Import trade (agricultural inputs)	14.0–15.0
1 year to less than 2 years	11.5	Import trade (others)	14.0–15.0
2 years and above	12.0	Hotels and tourism	14.0–15.0
		Construction	14.0–15.0
Savings deposits	10.0	House: 1. Purchase	11.0–12.0
		2. Construction	11.0–13.0
		Central government	10.0
		Banks and financial institutions	14.0–15.0
		Personal loans	–
1 September 1994–1 January 1995		**1 September 1994–1 January 1995**	
The same structure as that of		Lending to all sectors	14.0–15.0
1 October 1992–31 August 1994		Lending to central government	12.0–13.0
		NBE lending to	
		CBs	10.5
		Other financial institutions	10.5
		International bank lending	10.0

Later developments	2 Jan. 1995–30 Nov. 1995	1 Dec. 1995–30 May 1996	1 June 1996–15 Sept. 1996	16 Sept. 1996 to time of writing*	2002/3 (%)
Minimum interest rate on time and savings deposits	10.0	11.0	10.0	7.0	3.56 & 3.00
Maximum (and average) lending rate by commercial banks and other institutions, except for central government	15.0	16.0	15.0	10.5	13.00 (10.25)
Central government loans	12.0	12.0	12.0	12.0	

Note: * Since January 1998 the lending rate has been fully liberalized, while the deposit rate floor has been set at 6 per cent.

Sources: National Bank of Ethiopia (NBE), *Quarterly Bulletin*, 13(1), 1997/8; NBE *Annual Report 2002/3*.

Similarly, credit allocation was informed by the same ideological considerations. In consultation with the Ministry of Finance and Planning, the NBE projected the financial planning of the economy. It identified the financial needs of different sectors through surveys and data obtained from credit institutions. Based on such information, it determined the distribution of credit, favouring priority investments and aiming to keep the internal and external purchasing power of the national currency unaltered. In credit allocation, financial institutions used credit policy as a factor to strengthen and expand the socialized sector and encourage the socialization of others (Di Antonio 1988: 71–2). This favouring of the socialized sector is shown by the fact that a good part of bank resources were directed to the socialized sector (for example, 68 per cent of ADB resources were allocated to state farms), and that collateral was not required from the state farms and co-operatives when they were granted loans (Di Antonio 1988: 74). As noted by Di Antonio, this restrictive policy resulted in excess liquidity in the banking sector in the 1980s, chiefly because of (i) the biased credit policy; (ii) the collateral requirement on the private sector; (iii) seasonal trends and the economic conditions prevailing at the time; and (iv) the CBE's inefficiency. The latter two factors were identified by the 'Liquidity Appraisal Committee' set up by the CBE to understand the excess liquidity problem (Di Antonio 1988: 80).

The structure of the financial system in the post-reform period

Proclamation No. 84/1994, which allowed the private sector (owners have to be Ethiopian nationals, however) to engage in banking and insurance business marked the beginning of a new era in Ethiopia's financial sector. Following this proclamation, the country witnessed a proliferation of private banking and insurance companies. At the time of writing, there were six new private banks (with 115 branches) and eight insurance companies (with 79 branches) in operation. The new private banks account for about a quarter of the total banking capital in the country. This change took place over a matter of ten years. Table 8.12 gives a list of these financial institutions.

Performance of the new private banks

Despite the proliferation of privately-owned companies, their relative market share was still extremely small. This can be seen from the Figures in this section: Figures 8.2 and 8.3 show a summary picture of the share

Table 8.12 Private banks and insurance companies

Private banks	Date of licence	Number of branches (2002/3)	Capital (2002/3)* (millions of Birr)
1. Awash International Bank	10 November 1994	26	132 (4.9%)
2. Dashen Bank S.C.	20 September 1995	28	122 (4.6%)
3. Bank of Abyssinia	15 February 1996	14	141 (5.3%)
4. Wegagen Bank	30 April 1997	23	83 (3.1%)
5. United Bank S.C.	10 September 1998	13	91 (3.4%)
6. Nib International	26 May 1999	11	111 (4.2%)
Private insurance companies			
1. Africa Insurance Co.	22 December 1994	9	
2. Awash Insurance Co.	1 October 1994	13	
3. Global Insurance	14 January 1997	4	
4. Nib Insurance	2001/2	4	
5. National Insurance Co.	23 September 1994	8	
6. Nile Insurance Co.	11 April 1995	16	
7. Nyala Insurance	27 September 1995	11	
8. United Insurance Co.	9 November 1994	14	

Note: * For comparison, the total capital of CBE, DBE and CBB was 1277 (47.7%), 75 (2.8%) and 643 (24%) million Birr, respectively. Ethiopian Insurance (the only publicly-owned company) has 27 branch networks.
Source: National Bank of Ethiopia, *Annual Report* 2002/3 (and various years).

of banks in deposit mobilization (and loan disbursement) in the pre- and post-reform periods. As can be seen from these charts, the dominant position in terms of savings mobilization was held by the public sector in general, and the CBE in particular. The public sector's share did, however, fall from 96 per cent in 1996/7 to 80 per cent in 2002/3, while the share of the private banks rose from 4 per cent to 20 per cent over the two periods. This private sector share was highest for time deposits, followed by savings and demand deposits.

A similar pattern is observed in terms of disbursement of loans, loans outstanding, and loan collection. In general, in terms of loan disbursement, the share of the public sector (the CBE being the dominant bank, accounting for more than 95 per cent of the public banking sector in the figures analysed in this section, followed by the DBE) declined from 93 per cent in 1996/7 to 44 per cent in 2002/3, while the share of the private banking sector increased, from 7 per cent to 56 per cent. In terms of loan collection the public banks' share declined from 94 per cent to 60 per cent during the two periods, while the share of the private sector increased from 6

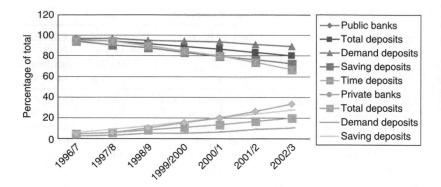

Figure 8.2 Share of deposit mobilization by type of deposit, and by private and public banks (per cent)
Sources: Commercial Bank of Ethiopia (CBE) *Annual Reports* (various years); and Statistical Review of the CBE.

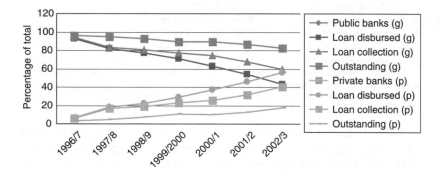

Figure 8.3 Share of loan disbursed, collected and outstanding by public (g) and private (p) banks (per cent)
Sources: Commercial Bank of Ethiopia (CBE) *Annual Reports* (various years); and Statistical Review of the CBE.

per cent to 40 per cent. Outstanding loans were highest in the public sector, being 96 per cent in 1996/7 and declining a little to 82 per cent in 2002/3 (the corresponding figure for the private banks increased from 4 per cent to 18 per cent). In sum, the private banks are catching up relatively quickly with the public banks in almost all banking activities. The disaggregation of disbursed credit by institutional category also shows the increasing role of the private sector, which can be attributed chiefly to ongoing liberalization.

A detailed account of each bank reveals that, using the data for the year 2002/3, the most important private banks in terms of deposit mobilization, loan disbursement, and loans outstanding were Dashen Bank, followed by Awash International Bank, placing Abyssinian Bank in third place (the only exception being that Wegagan Bank is in second place, (making Abyssinia third), in terms of loan collection and disbursement). Clearly, the trend of the existing data shows that the share of the private banks – both in terms of deposit mobilization and lending – could increase significantly in the years ahead. It is also worth noting that the share of credit extended to the private sector increased sharply in the recent past, while the public sector's share declined (the share of co-operatives remained fairly stable) (Geda 1999).

Other financial liberalization schemes pursued

Two other important liberalization schemes pursued by the Ethiopian government in the post-reform period were (i) the exchange rate policy; and (ii) the introduction of an inter-bank money market. As discussed earlier, the pre-reform period was characterized by discriminatory interest rates and foreign exchange as well as credit allocation policies. At the time of writing, the interest rate is fairly liberalized and the NBE has set a floor only for the deposit rate, leaving all other rates to be determined by the market. Banks are now allowed to set any rate within a range. Moreover, pursuing a strategy of gradualism, the NBE implemented this policy step by step. Interest-rate policy and actual rates at the time of writing, as well as their evolution, are given in Table 8.11.

The exchange rate policy

A related policy of liberalization carried out by the government was the introduction of the 'auction-based exchange rate' determination scheme, and the introduction of the inter-bank money market. Again, the principle of gradualism (in liberalization) is at the heart of this policy development.

The exchange rate reform began by devaluing by 140 per cent, the currency that had been fixed for nearly two decades at 2.07 Birr per US$1, to 5 Birr per US$1 in October 1992. Such a massive devaluation was partly justified by the premium on the parallel market that was close to 238 per cent. In 1993, the NBE introduced an auction-based exchange-rate system. This used to be conducted on a fortnightly basis and took the form of a 'Dutch auction' system (discriminatory price), where the marginal rate, which clears the market, is taken as the ruling rate for the coming two weeks. The supply of funds for this market came from export earnings, and loans and grants. The auction-based exchange rate system initially worked side by side with the official exchange rate. The system was overseen by a committee composed of the NBE, Ministry of Finance, Ministry of

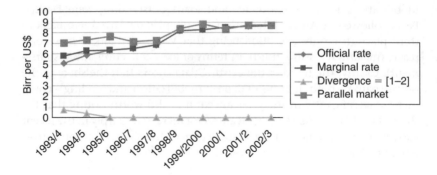

Figure 8.4 Exchange rate, Ethiopia, 1993–2003 (annual average, Birr/US$)
Sources: Commercial Bank of Ethiopia (CBE) *Annual Reports* (various years); and Statistical Review of the CBE.

Economic Development and External Co-operation (MEDaC), and two representatives from the private sector.

In the course of its implementation, an intensification of the liberalization effort – including reducing the bid cover requirement, the abolition of the negative import list, and a reduction of the ceiling on demand for foreign exchange – was made. Moreover, after the 86th auction (in July 1996), the NBE introduced a weekly auction replacing the previous system. By August 1995, the official or fixed exchange rate (used for the import of fertilizer, petroleum and pharmaceutical products as well as Ethiopia's contribution to international organizations and external debt service payments) was also unified with the auction rate. The NBE replaced the retail auction system with a wholesale auction system, where banks are seen as wholesale bidders (discussed below). Figure 8.4 shows the evolution of the official, the parallel and the auction rates in the recent past.

The inter-bank foreign exchange and money markets

The NBE issued directives aimed at establishing inter-bank foreign exchange and money markets in 1998 (Directives No. IBM/01/1998 and IBM/02/1998). The establishment of this market was motivated primarily by the recognition that the foreign exchange supply by NBE through the auction system is not sufficient to satisfy the demand of banks. The interbank foreign exchange market (IBFEM) is a wholesale market, where the amount traded is large and the spread between buying and selling rates is narrower than the norm for commercial transactions. It is an exclusive market for banks to trade foreign exchange with each other (NBE Directive No. IBM/01/1998).

The directive sets various guidelines for the market. For example, the minimum amount to be traded is US$50,000, banks do not charge each other any fees, and all transactions are conducted with the strictest confidentiality. Banks are also required to report their foreign exchange operations to the NBE. Thus the NBE uses this as one instrument of regulation. It is also gradually liberalizing the market, because all these functions used to be handled by the NBE itself. This market is very active, with a volume of daily inter-bank foreign exchange transactions of around US$160 million in 2002/3.

A related liberalization policy pursued was the establishment of the inter-bank money market (IBMM). The IBMM describes the borrowing and lending of funds between banks, microfinance institutions and non-bank financial institutions at interest rates that are freely determined by the borrowers and lenders themselves (NBE Directive No. IBM/02/98). The directive specifies how this market should function. For example, transactions should be for a minimum of 300,000 Birr, there are specific times at which deals and requests for deals should be made, and the nature of collateral required. The directive also requires banks to report all their activities in this market on a daily basis to NBE. The NBE uses this information to regulate and monitor banking activity. Moreover, the NBE has also issued a code of conduct, which has extensive regulatory content (NBE Code of Conduct for IBMM). Between its establishment in 1998 and the time of writing, only eleven transactions, involving 142 million Birr, were traded in this market. During this period, the average inter-bank rate stood at 7.8 per cent. According to the NBE *Annual Report* (2002/3), persistent excess liquidity, lack of collateral and weak economic activity are given as possible reasons for the poor performance of this market.

Concluding remarks

Since 1992, Ethiopia has gradually been liberalizing its financial sector, as discussed in this chapter. The hallmark of the strategy is gradualism. This approach, however, is not without problems. The international institutions that sponsor and support the liberalization process financially, in particular the IMF, are not satisfied with the pace of liberalization. This has, at times, reached a point where the IMF has suspended its support temporarily.

The various policy framework papers jointly authored by the Ethiopian government and the staff of the two Bretton Woods institutions are quite comprehensive, embracing almost all major polices. Thus it is difficult to relate any disagreement between Ethiopia and the IMF and the World Bank solely to the financial sector.

Examination of such a policy framework papers reveals that: (i) since the start of the SAP in Ethiopia, the performance has by and large been in line with the target set in the document (there have been occasional years where the performance has been either above or below the target); and (ii) when the time schedule set in the policy framework papers and the actual implementation of policies are compared, the Ethiopian government has been behind schedule on many occasions. However, it is interesting to note that this has not usually led to disagreement between the IMF and Ethiopia.

There have been occasions when the IMF has suspended its help. However, an examination of the time schedule set in the policy matrix of the various policy framework papers, and the performance of Ethiopia with respect to these targets, reveals that if this is the sole cause of disagreement, the IMF should have suspended the programme long ago. This obviously points to the possibility of there being other explanations that are not apparent in the financial data. An informed guess points to at least the following areas of disagreement. First, the World Bank and the IMF might disagree with the Ethiopian government's strategy of gradualism in its reform programme in general, and in reforming the financial sector in particular. Second, the Ethiopian government's implicit belief in a pragmatic mix between the public and private sectors might have been unacceptable to the IMF and World Bank. Third, the insistence of the IMF and World Bank on the need for competition by addressing the alleged monopoly position of the CBE has been resisted by Ethiopia. This last point is quite sensitive, because the Ethiopian banking system may be weakened by any intervention to address the CBE's supposed monopoly power (such as breaking it up or privatization). This would reduce the Ethiopian banking system's capacity to compete with foreign banks should they be allowed to enter the market at the same time. Moreover, the CBE's strong performance does not signal the need for privatization, even assuming unrealistically that privatization is a panacea for such problems (Geda and Addison 2003).

In general, given the nascent level of development in using market mechanisms in Ethiopia, the challenge of transition from the pre-reform to the post-reform period outlined in this chapter, the relatively good shape in which the existing financial institutions find themselves, and the weak supervision and regulation department of the NBE (which is new and lacks skilled human resources), the government's strategy of gradualism and its overall reform direction need to be appreciated and be supported by World Bank, IMF and other relevant institutions. The only concession the government should make is to lay out clearly a time schedule for its financial sector liberalization programme, and explore the possibility of joint venture schemes with foreign banks. Obviously, the government cannot rationally protect the sector for ever, and it is time to recognize this and act accordingly.

Acknowledgements

I thank my former students, Seife Dender and Abera Sebeta, and the editor of this volume for their help in the course of writing this chapter.

Notes

1 An Amharic term meaning 'the committee' (of soldiers).
2 The commercial banks were Addis Ababa Bank, Banco di Napoli and Banco di Roma. The insurance companies were African Solidarity, Ethio-American life, Blue Nile, Ethiopian General, Imperial, Afro-Continental, Pan-African, Union, Ras, and Ethiopian Life and Rasi. The non-bank financial intermediaries were the Imperial Saving and Home Ownership Public Association and the Mortgage Corporation (Degefe 1995: 273).
3 There are unconfirmed reports that put this figure as high as 40 per cent since 2000, but now (at the time of writing) falling closer to 15 per cent.

References

Degefe, B. (1995) 'The Development of Money, Monetary Institutions and Monetary Policy (in Ethiopia), 1941–75', in S. Bekele (ed.), *An Economic History of Ethiopia: Volume 1: The Imperial Era 1941–74* (Dakar: CODESERIA).
Development Bank of Ethiopia (1996) 'Credit Operation and Other Activities of DBE: 1970/71–1993/94, Condensed Statistics', Mimeo, Research and Planning Department, Research Division, DBE, Addis Ababa.
Di Antonio, M. (1988) 'The Excess Liquidity of Commercial Banking in Ethiopia', *African Review of Money, Finance and Banking*, 1/1988: 71–101.
Geda, A. (1999) 'The Structure and Performance of Ethiopia's Financial Sector in the Pre and Post Reform Period: With Special Focus on Banking', in A. Geda and B. Nega (eds), *The Ethiopian Economy: Problems and Prospects* (Addis Ababa: Addis Ababa University and Ethiopian Economic Associations).
Geda, A. and T. Addison (2003) 'The New Financial Sector and Its Regulation: The Case of Ethiopia', in T. Addison (ed.), *From Conflict to Recovery in Africa* (Oxford: Oxford University Press for UNU-WIDER).
Geda, A. and S. Dendir (2001) 'Banking Sector Regulation and Performance in Post-Reform Ethiopia', Paper presented at the International Conference on Finance and Development: Evidence and Policy Issues, 10–11 July, Nairobi, Kenya.
Gedey, B. (1990) *Money, Banking and Insurance in Ethiopia* (Addis Ababa: Berhanena Selam Printing Press) (in Amharic).
McKinnon, R. I. (1973) *Money and Capital in Economic Development* (Washington, DC: Brookings Institution).
National Bank of Ethiopia (1996) 'Manual for Bank Licensing and Supervision', Unpublished document, April.
National Bank of Ethiopia (1998) 'Review of the Evolution and Functions of Financial Institutions in Ethiopia', Mimeo, Economic Research Department, Money and Banking Division.

National Bank of Ethiopia (various years) *Annual Report* (Addis Ababa: National Bank of Ethiopia).

Shaw, E. S. (1973) *Financial Deepening in Economic Development* (New York: Oxford University Press).

Vos, R. (1993) 'Financial Liberalization, Growth and Adjustment: Some Lessons for Developing Countries', in S. Griffith-Jones (ed.), *Financial Policies and Macroeconomic Policies in Transition Economies* (London: Macmillan).

Appendix

Table 8.A1 Deposit mobilization by the banking system before reform (millions of Birr)

	1979/80	1980/1	1981/2	1982/3	1983/4	1984/5	1985/6	1986/7	1987/8	1988/9	1989/90	1990/1	1991/2
Commercial Bank of Ethiopia	1,321.0	289.5	170.5	292.5	2,311.4	2,684.2	3,048.7	3,264.8	3,570.9	3,778.2	4,201.3	4,414.4	5,021.9
Demand deposits	692.8	199.3	91.9	169.4	1,258.2	1,531.3	1,784.7	2,029.3	2,251.1	2,255.8	2,496.0	2,602.9	2,869.9
Savings deposits	442.2	47.8	58.3	108.6	761.1	812.8	939.2	1,053.2	1,208.0	1,367.1	1,574.5	1,676.7	1,999.1
Time deposits	186.0	42.4	20.3	14.5	292.1	340.1	324.8	182.3	111.8	155.3	130.8	134.8	152.9
Development Bank of Ethiopia	31.7	15.4	−0.4	0.1	48.2	49.3	47.9	132.1	135.9	136.7	183.6	185.9	164.1
Demand deposits													
Savings deposits	0.2	15.4	0.1	0.2	0.6	0.5	0.5						
Time deposits	31.5	0.0	−0.5	−0.1	47.6	48.8	47.4	132.1	135.9	136.7	183.6	185.9	164.1
Construction and Business Bank	154.7	16.5	10.4	22.1	218.7	222.9	235.5	320.4	375.3	440.1	469.3	520.7	484.6
Demand deposits													
Savings deposits	10.3	3.4	5.7	8.8	38.2	35.7	33.5	32.4	58.8	65.7	64.1	76.0	86.6
Time deposits	144.4	13.1	4.7	13.3	180.5	187.2	202.0	288.0	316.5	374.4	405.2	444.7	398.0
Awash International Bank	0.0	0.0	0.0	0.0	0.0	0.0	0.0	0.0	0.0	0.0	0.0	0.0	0.0
Demand deposits													
Savings deposits													
Time deposits													
Dashen Bank	0.0	0.0	0.0	0.0	0.0	0.0	0.0	0.0	0.0	0.0	0.0	0.0	0.0
Demand Deposits													
Savings deposits													
Time deposits													

(Continued)

200

Table 8.A1   Continued

	1979/80	1980/1	1981/2	1982/3	1983/4	1984/5	1985/6	1986/7	1987/8	1988/9	1989/90	1990/1	1991/2
Bank of Abyssinia													
Demand deposits	0.0	0.0	0.0	0.0	0.0	0.0	0.0	0.0	0.0	0.0	0.0	0.0	0.0
Savings deposits													
Time deposits													
Wegagen Bank													
Demand deposits	0.0	0.0	0.0	0.0	0.0	0.0	0.0	0.0	0.0	0.0	0.0	0.0	0.0
Savings deposits													
Time deposits													
United Bank													
Demand deposits	0.0	0.0	0.0	0.0	0.0	0.0	0.0	0.0	0.0	0.0	0.0	0.0	0.0
Savings deposits													
Time deposits													
Nib International Bank													
Demand deposits	0.0	0.0	0.0	0.0	0.0	0.0	0.0	0.0	0.0	0.0	0.0	0.0	0.0
Savings deposits													
Time deposits													
All banks	1,507.4	321.4	180.5	314.7	2,578.3	2,956.4	3,332.1	3,717.3	4,082.1	4,355.0	4,854.2	5,121.0	5,670.6
Demand deposits	692.8	199.3	91.9	169.4	1,258.2	1,531.3	1,784.7	2,029.3	2,251.1	2,255.8	2,496.0	2,602.9	2,869.9
Savings deposits	452.7	66.6	64.1	117.6	799.9	849.0	973.2	1,085.6	1,266.8	1,432.8	1,638.6	1,752.7	2,085.7
Time deposits	361.9	55.5	24.5	27.7	520.2	576.1	574.2	602.4	564.2	666.4	719.6	765.4	715.0

Source: National Bank of Ethiopia, *Annual Report* (various years).

Table 8.A2 Deposit mobilization by the banking system after reform (millions of Birr)

	1992/3	1993/4	1994/5	1995/6	1996/7	1997/8	1998/9	1999/2000	2000/1	2001/2	2002/3
Commercial Bank of Ethiopia	6,226.8	7,436.9	9,598.3	11,193.6	12,704.3	15,518.1	15,016.9	16,917.0	18,822.5	19,588.8	21,133.8
Demand deposits	3,460.7	4,211.4	5,503.5	6,038.2	7,067.9	9,197.5	8,579.5	9,862.0	10,857.6	11,055.8	12,070.1
Savings deposits	2,450.5	2,844.3	3,649.3	4,584.8	5,090.2	5,623.1	6,000.1	6,648.8	7,474.5	8,087.5	8,685.4
Time deposits	315.6	381.2	445.5	570.6	546.7	697.5	437.3	406.2	490.4	445.5	378.3
Development Bank of Ethiopia	162.8	169.9	85.6	8.7	37.7	632.0	776.0	726.7	729.1	688.8	743.6
Demand deposits				8.7	35.5	29.6	15.0	11.5	6.3	4.5	2.7
Savings deposits					2.1	2.0	2.1	2.6	2.6	3.0	2.5
Time deposits	162.8	169.9	85.6		0.1	600.4	758.9	712.6	720.2	681.3	738.4
Construction and Business Bank	358.4	386.4	392.6	438.5	556.6	568.1	554.4	503.3	519.2	603.5	615.1
Demand deposits			10.5	37.8	36.7	26.8	39.9	55.6	41.7	63.9	84.8
Savings deposits	125.5	161.1	201.1	218.5	260.8	256.0	265.3	285.4	311.7	355.0	387.1
Time deposits	232.9	225.3	181.0	182.2	259.1	285.3	249.2	162.3	165.8	184.6	143.2
Awash International Bank	0.0	0.0	0.0	0.0	273.1	350.3	431.7	591.0	752.3	930.0	1,163.8
Demand deposits					64.3	82.1	108.0	132.0	136.6	165.8	245.4
Savings deposits					185.8	242.7	289.5	408.7	552.3	713.3	874.2
Time deposits					23.0	25.5	34.2	50.3	63.4	50.9	44.2
Dashen Bank	0.0	0.0	0.0	0.0	263.0	374.6	489.3	631.4	885.3	1,191.2	1,621.3
Demand deposits					133.5	153.6	206.0	209.6	260.2	393.3	466.3
Savings deposits					118.5	186.5	245.2	370.6	532.9	737.3	1,056.3
Time deposits					11.0	34.5	38.1	51.2	92.2	60.6	98.7

(*Continued*)

Table 8.A2 Continued

	1992/3	1993/4	1994/5	1995/6	1996/7	1997/8	1998/9	1999/2000	2000/1	2001/2	2002/3
Bank of Abyssinia	0.0	0.0	0.0	0.0	44.6	143.6	294.2	485.2	651.7	909.3	1,076.2
Demand deposits					7.7	26.0	52.4	84.1	94.3	133.5	207.0
Savings deposits					30.0	93.8	180.8	330.3	468.1	631.3	719.0
Time deposits					6.9	23.8	61.0	70.8	89.3	144.5	150.2
Wegagen Bank	0.0	0.0	0.0	0.0	1.8	118.3	273.2	372.7	443.8	578.2	704.1
Demand deposits					1.4	30.6	76.1	119.1	154.1	238.9	253.4
Savings deposits					0.4	79.6	164.0	200.3	232.1	201.9	271.9
Time deposits					0.0	8.1	33.1	53.3	57.6	137.4	178.8
United Bank	0.0	0.0	0.0	0.0	0.0	0.0	0.0	75.4	135.8	195.5	331.3
Demand deposits								20.5	34.7	48.5	103.7
Savings deposits								43.7	89.2	113.8	172.3
Time deposits								11.2	11.9	33.2	55.3
Nib International Bank	0.0	0.0	0.0	0.0	0.0	0.0	0.0	0.0	208.4	345.6	588.1
Demand deposits									61.4	95.1	151.8
Savings deposits									121.6	203.4	336.4
Time deposits									25.4	47.1	99.9
All banks	6,748.0	7,993.2	10,076.5	11,640.8	13,881.6	17,705.0	17,835.7	20,302.7	23,148.1	25,030.9	27,977.3
Demand deposits	3,460.7	4,211.4	5,514.0	6,084.7	7,347.0	9,546.2	9,076.9	10,494.4	11,646.9	12,199.3	13,585.2
Savings deposits	2,576.0	3,005.4	3,850.4	4,803.3	5,687.8	6,483.7	7,147.0	8,290.4	9,785.0	11,046.5	12,505.1
Time deposits	711.3	776.4	712.1	752.8	846.8	1,675.1	1,611.8	1,517.9	1,716.2	1,785.1	1,887.0

Source: National Bank of Ethiopia, Annual Report (various years).

9
Financial Sector Development in Zambia: Implications for Domestic Resource Mobilization

Samuel Munzele Maimbo and George Mavrotas

Introduction

Many Sub-Saharan African (SSA) countries introduced financial-sector reforms to improve the performance of the financial sector in general, and financial savings levels in particular, in the 1980s and 1990s. Yet, despite these reforms, for many countries, the expected increase in financial savings levels was short-lived. Compared to East Asian economies, SSA countries such as Zambia continue to register very low levels of savings mobilization, which is of great concern for policy-makers working on the country's poverty reduction strategy. Along these lines, this chapter examines the linkages between the financial reforms of the early 1990s and savings mobilization efforts in Zambia. It considers the characteristics of banks and non-bank financial institutions (NBFIs), in particular, micro finance institutions (MFIs), and identifies problems associated with the relatively poor performance of savings in recent years.

The low savings phenomenon is multi-dimensional and has a complex causality structure. Understanding the nature and causes of this phenomenon is therefore multi-faceted and methodologically diverse, but inclusive of both qualitative and quantitative measures. The absence of consistent and reliable data complicates the study of Zambia's low savings rates, resulting in a dearth of literature on the subject. Nevertheless, this chapter identifies a number of key factors affecting savings mobilization in Zambia, which include the poor state of the economy; the 1995 and 1997/8 bank closures; increased investment in property for private and commercial purposes; foreign exchange liberalization; the absence of rural financial savings institutions; the parastatal sector reforms; and the HIV/AIDS epidemic.[1]

Financial sector development and savings mobilization: theoretical linkages

Low-income countries often lack an appropriate financial sector that provides incentives for individuals to save, and acts as an efficient intermediary to convert these savings into credit for borrowers. In what follows, we discuss briefly the theoretical linkages between financial-sector development and savings mobilization.[2]

Traditional theoretical linkages and the life-cycle model of saving

Traditionally, the models that look at the interface between savings and development are based around the life-cycle or permanent income theory of consumption, and it will be useful to review these hypotheses briefly, and then discuss the relevance of financial-sector development to these models. The model described below draws on Gersovitz (1988), but is typical of the style used by most authors.

We consider an individual who lives for T periods and receives income payments of y_i and consumes c_i. S/he neither receives nor leaves bequests. The only constraint on the individual's consumption is that the present value of lifetime consumption (C) cannot exceed the present value of lifetime income (Y):

$$C \equiv \sum_{i=0}^{T-1} \left[\frac{c_i}{(1+r)^i} \right] \le \sum_{i=0}^{T-1} \left[\frac{y_i}{(1+r)^i} \right] \equiv Y \qquad (9.1)$$

However, s/he is able to borrow or lend at interest rate r in period i if his/her objective, namely to maximize his/her discounted lifetime utility, V, does not require that $y_i = c_i$. and V is defined as follows:

$$V \equiv \sum_{i=0}^{T-1} \delta^i U[c_i] \qquad (9.2)$$

The decision-maker's problem is solved for the two-period model by the first-order condition:

$$U'[c_0] = (1+r)\delta U'[c_1] \qquad (9.3)$$

which, along with the condition in Equation (9.1) holding as an equality, yields optimal values of consumption, c_0^* and c_1^*. Current savings are then treated as a residual, which is why most models examining savings are formulated in terms of consumption rather than saving.

Bayoumi (1993), using an overlapping-generations model, describes the effects of financial deregulation on household saving in the life-cycle model. It is assumed that consumers live for a fixed number of periods and wish to smooth their consumption path. It is also assumed that the endowments available to individuals when they are young are small, so they would like to borrow when young in order to smooth consumption over their life-cycle. Prior to financial liberalization, consumers have limited access to financial intermediation; they are unable to finance their desired level of consumption when young, as they have no financial assets and are unable to go into debt, so they are in a corner solution.

After the initial period, consumers are able to use capital markets to smooth consumption over middle to old age. Because consumption was lower than desired when young, consumption is higher in middle and old age than it would have been had individuals been able to follow an optimal consumption path over their entire lifetime. Financial liberalization increases competition between providers of financial intermediation, thereby eliminating the constraint on going into debt. This means that the young can now borrow in order to attain their optimal lifetime consumption path.

This produces two effects:

- Initially, there is a temporary effect. In the short term, there will be an increase in aggregate consumption, which will wane over time. The immediate increase reflects the fact that consumption by the young increases as soon as financial deregulation occurs. There is no immediate effect on the borrowing of older consumers, as they are still affected by their inability to borrow while young. The effect dwindles as previously credit constrained consumers drop out of the economy and overall consumption tends back to its original level.

- There is also a permanent effect. As young consumers are no longer credit-constrained, they smooth their consumption. As a result, young consumers' saving becomes sensitive to wealth, real income, demographics and interest rates. This means that aggregate saving in the economy becomes more sensitive to these factors. Thus, during youth and old age, an individual will dissave, and saving will occur when an individual is productive.

Obviously, such a model relies on a number of strong assumptions. There must be a system of financial intermediation that permits saving and dissaving to a degree that it is hard to envisage the saving taking place in a non-monetary form. Therefore, a major element of the process of financial liberalization is the reform of the financial sector, in order to generate institutions that provide more efficient financial intermediation. The intertemporal elasticity of substitution in consumption determines the extent to which individuals are prepared to defer consumption into the future, and therefore their propensity to save. This, in turn, will depend on the real rate of interest, which will both determine the preparedness of individuals to save in the financial sector, and influence their consumption decision depending on whether it is above or below the individuals' subjective discount rate.

Theoretical linkages derived from models of financial-sector development and endogenous growth

Apart from models of savings behaviour rooted in the popular life-cycle hypothesis, there is a quite interesting strand of theoretical literature that focuses on the role of savings in the context of models of endogenous growth and financial-sector development.[3] Most of these models appear to emphasize the relationship between the banking system and economic growth. The spirit of these models can be represented by the model of Pagano (1993), who considers the simplest endogenous growth model (known as the AK model) where the aggregate output is a linear function of the aggregate capital stock, to capture the potential effects of financial development on growth.

The steady growth rate in Pagano's model can be written as:[4]

$$g = A\left(\frac{I}{Y}\right) - \delta = A\phi s - \delta \tag{9.4}$$

where g is the growth rate; A is the social marginal productivity of capital; I is investment; Y is income; ϕ is the proportion of saving channelled to investment; s is the private saving rate; and δ is the depreciation rate.

Along these lines, financial-sector development can affect growth by:

- Raising ϕ; that is, under the assumption that financial-sector development reduces the leakage of resources (the X-inefficiency of the intermediaries and their market power) this will raise ϕ and therefore raise the growth rate g in the above model.
- Increasing A; that is, allocate funds to those projects with the highest marginal product. The productivity of capital will be improved by

collecting information to evaluate alternative investment projects and by inducing individuals to invest in riskier but more productive technologies by providing risk management.

- Affecting the private saving rate s; Bencivenga and Smith (1991, 1993) show that the emergence of banks may reduce the savings rate but also identify conditions under which the growth-enhancing effect of financial intermediation (higher A) outweighs the lower savings rate (lower s) – situations of credit rationing. Capital markets also channel funds from households that save to households that dissave, in the form of consumption credit and mortgage loans. Clearly, the possible shortage of loan supply can raise the issue of liquidity constraints on households.[5]

Finally, another strand of the literature (not related directly to savings mobilization) stresses the importance of stock market development for economic growth by acquiring information on investment opportunities, facilitating risk amelioration, monitoring managers and exerting corporate control.[6]

Savings institutions and savings mobilization activities

Financial savings institutions before financial-sector reforms

Before the 1990s financial reforms, the banking sector in Zambia consisted of four distinct groups – pre-independence foreign banks; government banks; post-independence foreign banks; and local banks. The government perceived the pre-independence foreign banks – namely, Barclays Bank (1918), Standard Chartered Bank (1906) and Grindlays Bank (1956) – as not serving the interests of the local population in need of small- and medium-scale financial services and created a number of banks, principally the Zambia National Commercial Bank (ZNCB) (1969) and the National Savings and Credit Bank (NSCB) (1972). During the 1980s, the government also established Lima Bank (1987) and the Co-operative Bank (1989) (Brownbridge 1996: 7; Musokotwane 1997: 1; Muke 1998a: 2; Simatele and Ndulo 1998: 6; Maimbo 2000b: 290).

The government also established a number of monopoly NBFIs, notably the Zambia National Building Society (ZNBS) and the Zambia National Provident Fund (ZNPF). Because the ZNBS restricted its loan portfolio to the total amount of its deposits and shares, it actively engaged in savings mobilization to sustain its operations. Despite its deposit rates being below market rates, it offered easy account opening procedures; it was accessible, with several branches nationwide, and therefore managed to attract public deposits through the 1970s and 1980s. The ZNPF, on the other hand, attracted compulsory contributions, which never resulted in meaningful benefits to its contributors, since the government used the funds as a cheap source of financing for its own activities.

Until the 1990s, the government also took the lead in providing micro, small and medium-scale financial services. In the early 1980s, for example, the Bank of Zambia (BoZ) set up the Credit Guarantee Scheme as a means of encouraging banks to extend credit to small-scale industries. Other important organizations included the Small Industries Development Organization, Village Industries Service, and the Small Enterprise Promotion Unit. Policy-makers thought that banks did not extend credit to this group of entrepreneurs because of their inability to raise adequate collateral. These schemes, like many others before them, relied on government and donor funds for their operations, which precluded the need to raise funds directly from the public.

Overall, government involvement in the financial sector resulted in an inefficient and non-competitive market, which inhibited the development of the private sector financial institutions and discourage private savings. Interest rate controls, which, together with high reserve requirements, deteriorating macroeconomic conditions, political interference, negative interest rate policies and directed credit policies, depressed profit margins for banks (Brownbridge 1996: 3–4) and reduced returns on financial assets for savers. Furthermore, an inefficient payments system, an inadequate legal framework and weak accounting standards reduced the banking system's efficiency, especially its ability to perform its financial intermediation function (Muke 1998a: 3; Mbalashi 1999: 1). For the above reasons, few private banks entered the sector between 1970 and 1990. However, when the financial liberalization programme began in the late 1980s, the prospects for profitability improved, and the banking sector attracted more bank licence applications. Further, the low capital requirements required by the Bank of Zambia permitted easy access for the new banks, and by 1990 there were twelve banks in operation (compared to five in 1980).

Financial-sector reforms

The BoZ began to implement its financial liberalization programme as part of the World Bank/IMF economic reforms. The reforms started with the partial liberalization of interest rates and the removal of sectoral credit ceilings in the late 1980s. However, the most significant reforms took place during 1992/3 with the restructuring of government banks, prudential supervision reforms and foreign-exchange and interest-rate liberalization.

Restructuring of government-owned banks

By the late 1980s, the ZNBS, ZNPF, NSCB, Lima Bank and Co-operative Bank were either financially distressed, illiquid or insolvent. Though initially successful in providing savings facilities, they all faced severe financial problems because of high transaction costs, mismanagement, political interference and the withdrawal of government subsidies that had previously sustained their high overheads.

By 1992/3, the NSCB was insolvent and only saved from collapse by government reorganization. As part of a K400 million (US$100,000) investment programme, the government separated it from the national post office and restructured it to manage external financing intended for micro and small enterprises. Lima Bank and Co-operative Bank, however, failed to attract government resources and went into liquidation. Lima Bank, which handled agricultural loan disbursements, had incurred long-running financial losses, a negative capital position, and a large, non-performing loan portfolio. Mismanagement, severe drought, low loan recovery rates and erratic government funding accelerated its closure. Co-operative Bank too, failed primarily because of mismanagement and weaknesses in the agriculture-based co-operative movement.

Reforms to the prudential system

Prudential reforms involved a revision of the 1972 Banking Act and the enactment of the 1994 Banking and Financial Services Act (BFSA 1994), the introduction of new reporting and accounting procedures, and the strengthening of the BoZ's supervisory capacity. The BFSA 1994 granted the BoZ new legal powers to license, regulate and supervise banks. All decisions concerning licensing and other banking activities became subject to the BoZ's approval (Muke 1996: 1). Banks were required to submit additional, and more frequent, financial reports. Further, statutory instruments were issued for capital adequacy, insider loans, large loans, fixed assets, interest disclosure, classification and provisioning of loans (Mwape 1997a: 6–10; Mwape 1997b: 4–8). The reforms were part of the BoZ's overall capacity-building programme, which involved the recruitment of professionally qualified people, and provision of specialized training (Kani 1996: 21). The number of off-site bank inspectors also increased, from four in 1994 to thirteen in 1995 (Maimbo 2000a).

Liberalization of foreign exchange and interest rates

In 1992, the BoZ ceased the direct determination of interest rates and introduced weekly auctions of treasury bills. It progressively reduced the commercial bank statutory and core liquid assets ratios, and began open-market operations through the sale of deposits of banks and repurchase agreements. By 1993, the BoZ had removed all restrictions on commercial bank lending and deposit rates (Kani 1996: 21).

It also started to adjust the foreign exchange rate in order to reflect the true value of the local currency, the Kwacha. Weekly auctions of foreign exchange began in 1993 (Muke 1996: 2; 1998b: 3). By January 1994, the government-controlled official exchange rate and the market rate had merged, and all remaining foreign exchange regulations were suspended. Also suspended were the need to obtain import and export licences, and the need for exporters, including ZCCM, to surrender a portion of their foreign exchange earnings to the central bank (Kani 1996: 21).

Financial savings mobilization performance

Foreign exchange and interest rate liberalization had a profound effect on banking sector profitability. The interest rate rise from 40 per cent (1992) to 192 per cent (June 1993), shown in Figure 9.1, led to a sharp rise in interest rates on loans and government securities (Muke 1996: 2).

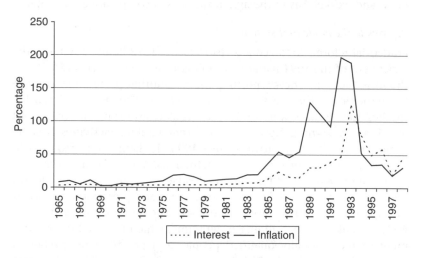

Figure 9.1   Interest and inflation rates, Zambia, 1965–98
Source: Bank of Zambia.

Because deposit interest rates did not increase proportionately, the interest rate spread resulted in higher nominal banking profits. By December 1994, there were twenty-five registered banks, nineteen of which were operational, with 188 branches (Muke 1996: 2).

There was also a rise in the number of NBFIs. By 1996, there were more than twenty-six NBFIs registered with the BoZ – leasing companies, building societies, deposit-taking NBFIs, and development finance institutions. Compared to banks, their relative size remained small. Deposits, and deposit-like instruments, amounted to K28.5 billion in 1996, almost half of which was accounted for by the ZNBS, which represented 4.5 per cent of the total deposits of banks.

There was also a marked increase in the number of MFIs after liberalization of the financial services industry in 1992/3. By September 1999, there were around thirty organizations engaged in MFI activities (Maimbo 2000c: 10; 2003). Two organizations now exist that foster the interests of MFIs – the Micro Banks Trust (MBT) and the Association of Micro-finance Institutions in Zambia (AMIZ). The MBT, established in 1996 at the initiative of the government and the European Union, provides wholesale funds, as well as limited training, to micro-financing institutions. The AMIZ, established by micro-finance practitioners, has taken a leading role in advocating new legislation, the setting of standards, and training the staff of new institutions (BoZ 1999: 6). Table 9.1 shows that, with a few exceptions, the majority of MFIs emerged between 1996 and 1998.

Although the financial reforms resulted in the emergence of new forms and types of financial institutions, they did not boost savings mobilization. The relatively stationary level of GDS in absolute terms means that Zambia has suffered a declining rate of GDS, as depicted in Figure 9.2. The impact of the collapse of copper prices is clear; after a high rate of GDS in the early 1970s, there is a structural break in the series around 1974, when a decline set in that has continued, with the rate reaching around 4 per cent by 1994. Figure 9.2 documents the trends in GNS and GDS over the period 1968–94. It is clear that the GNS rate is lower than the GDS rate, and that both rates follow a downward trend over the same period. The GNS rate was around 15 per cent lower than GDS until 1988, at which time the two series converged somewhat, reflecting the fact that Zambia had negative net transfers from abroad during the period to 1988. IMF measures imposed in 1988, and a devaluation of the currency helped to correct the problems to some degree; since 1988, the two series have been at a similar level.

212

Table 9.1 The growth of micro finance institutions, Zambia

Institution	Year	Legal status	Target group
CARE-PULSE	1994	NGO	Entrepreneurs in peri-urban Lusaka
CMS	1992	Company	Small and medium-scale enterprises
Country Services	1997	Company	Small-scale farmers and businesses
C.P.G. Castor Oils	1996	Company	Peasants
ECLF	1993	NGO	Women, youth and church groups
Irish Aid	1996	NGO	Small-scale entrepreneurs
ISBDA	1997	NGO	Marketers, vendors, small businesses
Keepers Foundation	1997	NGO	Enterprises in livestock development
MBT	1996	Trust	MFIs
Mukungwila Village Bank	1998	NGO	Rural poor people
PPF	1996	Company	The rural disadvantaged
Pride (Zambia)	1999	NGO	Small-scale manufacturers
Progress Financing Ltd	1988	Company	Women and youth
Women Finance Co-operative	1995	Co-operative	Low-income women entrepreneurs
ZFAWIB	1998	NGO	Farm workers

Source: Maimbo (2000c).

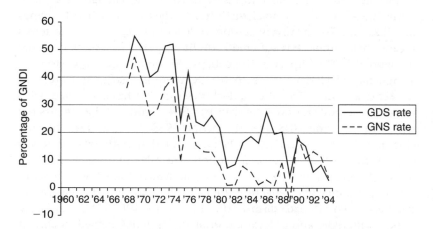

Figure 9.2 Gross domestic savings and gross national savings, Zambia, 1968–94
Notes: GNDI = gross national disposable income; GDS = gross domestic savings; GNS = gross national savings.
Source: World Bank (1998).

Explaining Zambia's poor savings mobilization performance

Data is not available on private enterprises, so aggregate savings can only be disaggregated into private and government savings. However, it is immediately clear that the driving force behind the decline in the aggregate savings figure over the period is private savings, which have decreased from a peak of almost 40 per cent in 1975 to dissaving of around 3 per cent in 1994 (see Figure 9.3). It is interesting to note that private savings showed a recovery to around 16 per cent following the implementation of financial liberalization measures in 1991. However, this recovery was short-lived, lasting until the onset of the financial crisis in 1995. At the same time, for most of the period, the government was dissaving, partly as a result of the country's crippling external debt, although matters seemed to improve somewhat in the 1990s.

The low savings phenomenon is multi-dimensional and has a complex causality structure. In what follows we discuss a number of factors that appear to have influenced the level and rate of private savings in Zambia. They include the poor state of the economy; increased levels of poverty and unemployment; the 1995 and 1997/8 bank closures; increased investment in property for private and commercial purposes; foreign exchange liberalization; the absence of rural financial savings institutions; the parastatal sector reforms; and the HIV/AIDS epidemic.

The state of the economy

Following independence in 1964, mining revenues provided Zambia with steady economic growth and one of the highest levels of per capita

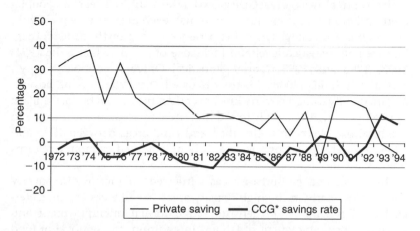

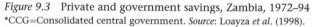

Figure 9.3 Private and government savings, Zambia, 1972–94
*CCG=Consolidated central government. *Source*: Loayza *et al.* (1998).

income in SSA. However, subsequent to the 1973 copper prices collapse, Zambia faced what has become an almost permanent adverse shift in its terms of trade. The over-dependence on copper revenues, and weaknesses in other areas of the economy, such as the high degree of protection afforded to the manufacturing sector, which made exports non-competitive, meant that the economy has deteriorated significantly.[7] Zambia faced problems of a kind typical in an inflexible, poorly diversified economy: rapid money supply growth, rocketing inflation, large and unsustainable fiscal and balance of payments deficits, low real incomes, and declining private investment (BoZ 1999). Zambia's problems were compounded by the world interest rate and oil shocks of the 1970s and 1980s: the high level of external debt in relation to exports and GDP meant that by 1987 the per capita debt burden was the highest in the developing world (Jones 1994). To date, despite a number of IMF and World Bank adjustment programmes undertaken in the 1980s and 1990s, Zambia has not succeeded in reversing the declining investment and per capita income trends, nor has it been able to bring about fiscal and monetary stability. From being one of the strongest economies in SSA at independence, Zambia is now one of the world's poorest countries, with a per capita income of about US$300 (1964: US$1,200). Zambia's impoverishment resulting from these problems has had an adverse effect on savings.

In 1991, 67.7 per cent of Zambia's population – nearly eight million people – were poor, with 58.2 per cent in the extremely poor category; by 1998, 73 per cent of the population were considered to be poor (GRZ 2001: 4). Despite economic reforms between 1991 and 1998, Zambia, with an annual average real GDP growth rate of only 0.2 per cent, double-digit inflation and continuous nominal exchange rate depreciation and high indebtedness, has not experienced real growth. Instead, there has been an increased level and incidence of poverty. Using the 1991, 1993, 1996 and 1998 Central Statistical Office Household Surveys, McCulloch *et al.* (2000: 15–16) discussed the evolution of poverty and inequality using a poverty line lower than the international standard of US$1 per day. Their study found that there was a dramatic increase in the level of poverty in both urban and rural areas between 1991 and 1996, induced in part by the recently implemented economic reforms (ibid.: 27).

The urban and peri-urban areas witnessed an increase in poverty levels, particularly in the high-density areas. These areas are characterized by high population densities, high formal unemployment and general underemployment of labour. In addition, the removal of food subsidies, the privatization of overstaffed government institutions, and trade liberalization also contributed to the higher levels of poverty. The formal sector employed only 17 per cent of the labour force in 1991. Despite a 46 per cent increase in the labour force, formal-sector employment has declined by 15 per cent and now constitutes less than 10 per cent of total employment. The declining performance of the mining and manufacturing sectors is primarily responsible for the decline in employment demand. Mining and quarrying, which employed 64,800 workers in 1991, only employed 34,434 workers by 1998. Formal manufacturing sector employment declined from 75,400 in 1991 to 43,320 in 1998 (ibid.: 6) Information on informal sector employment is largely unavailable, but was estimated at 2.3 million in 1993 and subsequently increased by at least 35 per cent in the agricultural sector and 15 per cent in non-agricultural activities between 1995 and 1998 (ibid.: 7). In the rural areas, drought devastated rural livelihoods over the same period. The economic reforms, such as the maize marketing reforms, mainly benefited those near major urban centres, but hurt more remote rural farmers. Poor rural infrastructure and thin to non-existent markets for key agricultural inputs and services, notably fertilizer, credit and transport, reduced the ability of rural farmers to benefit from the reforms and exploit their agricultural potential (ibid.: 27). Finally, a lack of food, safety nets and poor access to social services accelerated the rate and growth of poverty (GRZ 2001: 4).

The 1995 and 1997/8 bank closures

As inflation and the exchange rate began to stabilize, in the last quarter of 1993 and early 1994, it became more difficult to maintain earlier levels of profitability. Instead of curtailing activities in line with declining profit margins, some banks took greater risks to match previous results (Mwape 1997b: 3; Mbalashi 1999: 7). In the third quarter of 1994, and early 1995, adverse developments were taking place. Reckless lending left banks with unrecoverable loans and, in the quest to attract and retain customers, banks were disregarding prudent loan procedures and security arrangements. This was compounded by a rise in the cost of funds, the erosion of earnings from treasury bills and foreign exchange operations, and shortages of capital and liquidity (Brownbridge 1996: 11; Muke 1996: 2). These developments culminated in the closure of three banks in 1995. Meridien BIAO Bank, then the fourth-largest bank, with 25 per cent of the total industry deposits, collapsed on 19 May, African Commercial Bank on 17 November and Commerce Bank later in the same month (Maimbo 2000a: 2).

The crisis affected the remaining banks in different ways. There was a general loss of confidence in the banking system, which favoured foreign banks at the expense of local ones. The latter experienced unprecedented deposit withdrawals, and, consequently, some faced severe liquidity problems. There was a general 'flight to quality' as customers moved accounts to foreign banks, which they perceived as being more stable and better managed. The declining financial performance of the local banks was made worse by the managerial deficiencies exhibited over the following two years. Despite the efforts of the BoZ to redress the situation, the last quarter of 1997 saw yet another crisis emerge. Prudence Bank collapsed on 17 October, followed by Credit Africa Bank on 2 December, Manifold Investment Bank on 5 December, and First Merchant Bank on 2 February 1998.

After the 1995 bank failures, the pre-independence foreign banks continued to dominate the banking sector with respect to deposit size. Figure 9.4 shows that, in the period 1994 to 1999, the total deposit market share of pre-independence foreign banks grew from 35 per cent to well over 50 per cent. Local banks, on the other hand, lost the largest proportion of the market, with a decline from 25 per cent of total deposit market share in December 1994 to just below 10 per cent in December 1999.

The 1995 and 1997/8 bank failures dissipated public confidence in the banking system. Although there was a general 'flight to quality' from local banks to foreign banks, there was also a 'flight to non-financial assets'. First, the foreign banks required higher minimum bank balances and therefore excluded a large proportion of private savings. Second, they offered much lower interest rates on deposits, which discouraged

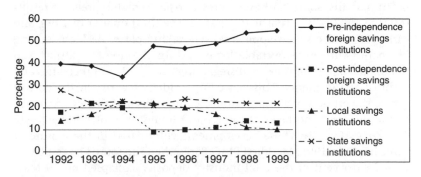

Figure 9.4   Total deposit trends, Zambia, 1992–9
Source: Bank of Zambia.

savers. Third, they were generally reluctant to open accounts for individuals who were not in formal employment, and therefore a proportion of the informal-sector labour force must have been dissuaded from applying for savings accounts. Last, and perhaps most importantly, the fear of losing one's deposits was probably highest among those who had recently been retrenched or declared redundant and had received lump-sum separation financial packages. In the absence of a deposit insurance scheme and a working social security system, people were understandably wary of the risk of losing their money in failing banks. In the event of a bank failure, the BFSA 1994 only provided for a fixed compensation amount of K500,000 (US$150). As a result, would-be financial savers turned to investments in non-financial assets, especially real estate, to secure their personal livelihoods.

Investment into real estate for private and commercial purposes

There has been a substantial increase in the level of investment into real estate for both private and commercial purposes since 1995. In a study of the property market, Chikolwa (1996) found that the rise had been funded primarily by private savings, retirement benefits and, for a very small proportion of the formal sector, through employers offering mortgages with low interest loans of less than 5 per cent to their employees. The mortgage market is still in its infancy, with only three building societies in existence. The funds at these building societies are expensive as the interest rates are high (at the time of writing, on average 35–40 per cent) and the conditions are generally not flexible. Funds from commercial banks are no better, as they cost more than building society loans. Chikolwa (1996: 3) further noted that, while the 1996 National Housing Policy and the 1999 Budget Speech allocated 15 per cent of the gross national product (GNP) for housing development (GRZ 2001: 15), these public pronouncements have not been implemented. Public investment in housing development dropped from 3 per cent of GNP in 1969 to less than 0.5 per cent by 1992: far below the World Bank recommended minimum of 5 per cent (GRZ 2001: 6). Consequently, the use of personal savings to build or acquire land and housing continues to grow at the expense of investment in financial assets.

The growth in private property investment has been further encouraged by the recent privatization of state enterprises and the central and local government divestment from public provision of housing for employees and residents. Of approximately 15,000 central government housing units in 1996, about 14,000 have been offered to sitting tenants, and nearly 2,000 people have paid a total of almost

K15 billion (US$3 million). The entire local government housing stock of 25,000 local units has been offered to sitting tenants, and nearly 65 per cent people have paid in full. The housing stock of privatized firms has also been made available for private purchase. Because of the rising interest in property as an alternative form of investment, property prices in Lusaka have been rising at an annual rate of approximately 30 per cent. The value of vacant urban land for development, already in short supply, has also been rising at a very higher rate of around 70 per cent per annum (Chikolwa 1996: 5).

Foreign exchange liberalization

One of the reasons why the financial reforms failed to encourage domestic financial savings is that foreign-exchange liberalization, which allowed individuals and companies to legally hold foreign-currency-denominated financial assets, coincided with the negative real interest rates period. Individuals and corporate entities transformed (and continue to do so) their savings into foreign currency. Zambia has now been listed as one of the countries whose citizens are making huge anonymous deposits in secret Swiss accounts. According to a recent study by an organization called Swissmoney Research, Zambia was among the six 'least affluent' countries that were identified as having the 'largest percentage growth' of deposits last year. Other countries in this group of 'least affluent' countries include Albania, Benin, Eritrea, Sierra Leone and Vietnam. Using publicly available data, the report traced the flow of funds from more than 180 countries and territories to Switzerland between 1990 and 1999, examined where the money was reinvested, and showed which banks were most active in gathering these funds. The study examined so-called fiduciary transactions, which consist mainly of large, short-term cash deposits placed with Swiss banks by foreigners. Unlike conventional deposits, they are then transferred to banks outside Switzerland in order to avoid the 35 per cent Swiss withholding tax on interest. Moreover, by placing the funds abroad in the name of the Swiss bank, clients are able to maintain anonymity (*Financial Times*, 4 January 2000).

Absence of informal and rural financial savings institutions

However, for the majority of Zambians, in particular the peri-urban and rural poor, who cannot afford to externalize their savings, let alone meet the minimum savings balance required by banks, there are few informal and rural financial savings institutions that offer viable alternatives. Rural areas are characterized by poverty, isolation and marginalization from the mainstream economy, and women, who play a leading role in economic activity, are involved in small economic activities, which typically yield insignificant (for financial institutions) marginal returns.

Initial expectations that the new NBFIs would foster financial deepening and encourage financial savings mobilization were short-lived. First, the new NBFIs did not target the general population as a primary source of their funds. Leasing companies generally focused on loans from their parent banks, other NBFIs and foreign parent organizations. Second, while it would have been less expensive to mobilize deposits from the general public, the low level of customer confidence following the 1995 banking failures made it difficult for new institutions to solicit public deposits.

Third, the financial condition of the NBFIs did not inspire confidence. A study commissioned by the BoZ in 1996 revealed that at least half of the NBFIs were in a weak or financially distressed condition. Most of the government institutions and some of the private institutions faced severe financial constraints. Two of the leasing companies and the ZNBS were practically insolvent. Several of the other insolvent financial institutions had suspended lending, either on instructions from BoZ or because of illiquidity. Despite opening the building society market to competition, at the time of writing it remains underdeveloped, with only three institutions in the market – ZNBS, the Finance Building Society (FBS) and the Pan African Building Society (PABS). As of December 1996, the ZNBS was insolvent. Both FBS and PABS are were undercapitalized with capital of only K200 million and K88 million, respectively, with the latter holding non-performing loans amounting to 94 per cent of its total loan portfolio (Simatele and Ndulo 1998: 15). Although not yet insolvent, a significant number of the other leasing companies were under-capitalized, had low earnings or impaired loan portfolios.

This financial distress was a result of several factors. Most significant, however, was that many of the NBFIs served risky segments of the credit market – small businesses (especially in transport, trade and agriculture) at very high interest rates. Nominal lending rates were between 60 per cent and 120 per cent per annum, and real lending rates were between 30 per cent and 60 per cent. The combination of high interest rates and a risky clientele resulted in high default rates. In addition, the BoZ revealed that poor management, deficient credit procedures, weak internal controls and a general failure to comply with basic prudential management affected the financial performance of the NBFIs.

With respect to MFIs, while their number has grown significantly in recent years, their size, in terms of loans made, remains relatively small compared to the rest of the financial sector (see Table 9.2). In a country where 70 per cent of the population (estimated at 10 million) is said to be living in poverty, with 54 per cent of these classified as being part of the 'core poor' – living on an income of less than US$1 per day (Musona and Mbozi 1998: 5) – the potential for MFI growth remains high.

There are several contributing factors responsible for the slower than expected growth in loan portfolios and outreach levels by MFIs. Two factors, in particular, contribute to the lower-than-expected perform-ance of MFIs. First, demographically and geographically, low population density in rural areas, the practice of barter and the rural culture of self-sufficiency does not augur well for MFIs (BoZ 1999: 5). Therefore, MFIs are concentrated in the urban areas, which are more familiar with cash transactions, while their rural counterparts traditionally depend on once-yearly maize sales, or remittances from urban relatives. Second, the

Table 9.2   The acceptance of deposits by micro finance institutions in Zambia

Micro finance institution	No. of savers	Value of savings held K(millions) (US$)	Interest on deposits
CARE PULSE	3,007	460 (141,538)	Bank rates
Country Services	0	0	0
C.P.G. Castor Oils Zambia Ltd	250	2.5 (769)	Market rates
Ecumenical Church Loan Fund	0	0	0
Irish Aid	0	0	0
Informal Sector Business Development Association	500	5 (1,538)	0
Keepers	0	0	0
Micro Bankers Trust	0	0	0
Mukungwila Village Bank	0	0	0
People's Participation Fund	407[a]	10	0
Pride Africa	0	0	0
Progress Financing	570	31 (9,538)[b]	n.a.
Women Finance Co-operative	4,300	151 (46,461)	8%
Zambia Federation of Associations of Women in Business	0	0	0

Notes: [a] Groups; [b] Approximately – exchange rate: US$1 = K3,250.
Source: Maimbo (2000c).

unfavourable legislative and regulatory environment has not been conducive to MFI growth. The licensing requirements for NBFIs were too stringent for the establishment of MFIs.

For example, the minimum capital requirement of K25 million (US$6,000) was considered to be too high. Thus MFIs they preferred to continue operating as non-governmental organizations (NGOs), as registration did not require such a high capital requirement. However, without BoZ registration, MFIs are not allowed to collect deposits from the public. Two of the countries largest MFIs – CARE Peri-Urban Lusaka Small Enterprise (CARE PULSE) and Project and Credit Management Services – do not collect savings because they are not registered as NBFIs with the BoZ (Musona and Mbozi 1998: 19; Maimbo 2000a; Muntemba 1999: 2).

Parastatal sector reforms

The recovery to around 16 per cent following the implementation of financial liberalization measures in 1991 is partly explained by the huge redundancy payments employees received in the wake of the parastatal and public-sector reforms, either invested in treasury bills or in long-term deposit accounts. The Meridien Investment Bonds, for example, attracted investments in excess of K39 billion within less than nine months of appearing on the market. However, by 1995, the financing to fund the redundancy packages was either exhausted or redirected towards other activities. Meanwhile, recipients of the funds either invested the funds into real estate or ventured into business, with the encouragement of government-funded programmes.

HIV and AIDS

The impact of the HIV/AIDS epidemic on the economy as a whole, and savings in particular, is not hard to recognize, despite not yet being formally calculated. About 650,000 people died from HIV/AIDS between 1996 and 1999, and a survey conducted between 1996 and 1999 estimated that a million people are infected. The survey estimated that 20 per cent of 15–49-year-old Zambians were HIV positive (Gondwe 2000). The most distressing trend has been the drop in life expectancy, from 54 years in the mid-1980s to an estimated 37 years in 1998 (Mulenga 2000; GRZ 2001: 5). The Health Ministry projects that the number of HIV-infected people will increase to 1.1 million by 2010 (Mulenga 2000).

Bloom *et al.* (2000) note that Zambia has suffered one of the worst declines in health status over the 1980s and 1990s, and that the loss of production by sick individuals, the increased direct financial cost of health care, and the opportunity cost of caring for the sick in SSA have increased significantly in recent years. The financial costs to families of looking after orphans have increased, and so have the medical costs of looking after infected relatives. Further, the high-risk group includes young men and women, in both the formal and informal sector, those most capable of generating incomes that ought to be leading to higher savings portfolios.

Conclusions and tentative policy recommendations

In addition to the specific constraints that banks and NBFIs face in mobilizing public deposits, this study considered the poor state of the economy, increased levels of poverty and unemployment, the 1995 and 1997/8 bank closures, increased investment in property for private and commercial purposes, foreign exchange liberalization, the absence of rural financial savings institutions, the parastatal sector reforms, and the HIV/AIDS epidemic. These factors have contributed significantly to the poor level and rate of private-sector savings in Zambia. The consequent increase in purchases of foreign-currency-denominated financial assets, and increased investments in domestic non-financial assets, such as real estate, are the possible key explanatory variables for the decline in private-sector domestic savings. To redress the above trends, it is important that both government initiatives to improve the rate and level of savings mobilization are targeted in particular at micro, small and medium-sized individual and enterprise deposits; increasing the incentives to invest in local financial assets, as opposed to foreign currency assets or non-financial domestic assets, is equally important.

Some of the immediate requirements include the improvement of macroeconomic stability; improving the regulation and supervision of local banks; improving the regulatory environment for MFIs; and encouraging the provision of savings facilities to individuals and micro, small and medium-sized enterprises in the way the NSCB has been attempting to do recently. The government must also be supportive of private-sector programmes such as the Financial Deepening Challenge Fund, which is aimed at developing the financial sector.

Improving macroeconomic stability

Efforts to improve the level and rate of savings mobilization must be made within the overall context of improving the state of the economy. Investments in domestic financial assets will only increase if the domestic currency is stable, interest rates are positive, and local banks and NBFIs are managed prudently and safely. Worried about the continued investment in foreign financial assets (especially by corporate entities), on 18 January 2000 the government announced foreign-exchange measures aimed at easing pressure on the local currency. Some of the key measures included the overall foreign-exchange exposure limit for all banks and financial institutions was reduced from 25 per cent to 15 per cent of regulatory capital; limiting total foreign-exchange placements and deposits in internationally recognized off-shore banking centres whose laws (for example, secrecy laws) may impede supervision of foreign-exchange activities of the bank or financial institution by the BoZ to 5 per cent of its total foreign exchange placements or deposits; and requiring all business entities and members of the public wishing to make external payments in excess of US$5,000 to do so through banks. Members of the public will be allowed to continue to hold foreign currency deposits in the form of demand, savings and time deposits. However, the foreign currency demand deposits of each commercial bank or financial institution must not exceed 25 per cent of its foreign currency deposit liabilities (BoZ 2001). The efficacy of these reforms must be evaluated within the overall long-term reforms aimed at restoring and maintaining macroeconomic stability.

Strengthening the regulation and supervision of local banks

Despite the recent failure of local banks, it is important that the BoZ does not discourage their registration. Brownbridge (1996, 16) rightly argues that local banks can provide services that foreign and government banks are either unwilling or unable to supply, and can also inject much-needed financial competition into the financial sector. They extend access to individuals and small businesses experiencing difficulty in relating to the formal banking sector. Private-sector deposit growth in the early 1990s occurred the most among local banks, especially Meridien Bank. They provided longer opening hours, shorter queues, higher deposit rates and/or lower minimum balances shorter and quicker bank account opening procedures, and provided speedier and more personalized services (Brownbridge 1996: 11).

Furthermore, unlike foreign banks, they invested in the rural sectors, where the foreign banks were either divesting themselves of that market altogether, or maintaining a presence but concentrating on corporate clients. Brownbridge (1996: 17) points out that, while local banks will face a higher level of non-performing loans than foreign banks because of the markets they serve, that need not result in financial distress. The key to ensuring that local bank failures are avoided, however, is not in discouraging their registration, but rather in ensuring that they are run prudently and honestly.

Improving the regulatory framework for MFIs

In the aftermath of the 1995 and 1997/8 bank failures, the BoZ continues with the process of reforming the regulatory and supervisory framework for banks and NBFIs. The BoZ completely revised the BFSA 1994, and the Zambian Parliament approved the new Act in December 2000. The most significant revision with respect to financial-sector mobilization is the recognition of NBFIs as a key component of the financial system. The revised Act now covers all institutions providing financial services, and the BoZ now has ultimate responsibility of all providers of financial services, regardless of whether they are the product of other Acts of Parliament. However, despite the strengthening of the Zambian banking sector and the introduction of numerous financial institutions (such as the stock market, a venture capital company and business assistance funds), access to institutional credit for working capital and equipment continues to be a major constraint for micro, small and medium-scale enterprises. Most individuals and small and medium enterprises continue to depend on informal and non-financial assets for their savings facilities and arrangements. Policy-makers need to encourage the part played by MFIs, which, with a relatively smaller cost base, as a more viable option in the effective delivery of financial savings facilities to low-income individuals and small and medium-scale enterprises, especially in rural areas. MFIs help to bridge the financing gap between large banks and small savings and credit unions (Maimbo 2000). The challenge for MFIs is to create structures that facilitate successful MFI clients to access larger, more diverse and longer-term sources of finance. Because MFI funds are typically of a short-term nature (to ensure repayment), they do not encourage long-term investments. MFIs need to create linkages between themselves and other financing institutions, such as venture capital firms and leasing companies, for some of their clients, with the potential to reach the export market (Maimbo 2000b).

Encouraging the provision of savings facilities to micro, small and medium-sized enterprises: the NSCB and ZNCB

The potential for the NSCB to play an important role in the development of the rural areas is great. As banks continue to pull out of rural areas because of low profitability, and to concentrate their activities in more developed centres and urban areas of the country, the availability of vital banking and financial services to rural communities has been declining.

NSCB has been given a fresh mandate to help and develop small, medium, rural and emerging private-sector enterprises through the provision of innovative and credit savings institutions. The bank is expected to play an active role in stimulating economic activity among the poorest sectors of the economy. It has also been structured to act as a financial intermediary for donor funds and external financing intended for micro and small enterprise development, and in some cases for bringing previously marginalized populations into the money economy through the implementation of poverty alleviation programmes. It is expected that the bank will act as a major catalyst for the mobilization of savings among ordinary Zambians in both rural and urban areas by offering banking services to meet the special needs of low-income customers, whether personal, organizational or corporate.

Of the remaining government institutions, ZNCB remains the largest despite ongoing financial difficulties. It retains 25 per cent of the industry's deposits, though its loan portfolio remains poor. At least 70 per cent of the loan portfolio is non-performing, resulting in significant cash flow problems. The government, BoZ and ZNCB accept that the only way of solving ZNCB's problems is through privatization of the institution, and in September 2000 the government made a commitment that the privatization of the government-owned ZNCB could begin by December of that year. The challenge will be finding a suitable partner willing and able to take on the challenge of restructuring ZNCB. With its large branch network, ZNCB remains in an advantageous position in the provision of savings facilities to individuals and micro, small and medium-sized enterprises.

Encouraging international and private sector initiatives

The government should also encourage international and private-sector initiatives such as the fund Deloitte and Touche (Zambia) manages on behalf of, and in conjunction with, the UK Department for International Development (DFID). The Financial Deepening Challenge Fund initiative provides funding in the form of grants from UK£50,000–£1,000,000 per proposal and works with the private sector to invest in commercial financial services in emerging markets. It aims to improve the access of poor and middle-income groups (including micro, small and medium-sized companies) to services such as credit, savings, insurance and investment capital. Sponsored by DFID, the scheme offers assistance to organizations wishing to mobilize, invest in and develop the capacity of financial services and catalyse the financial services sector, and to widen the range of products available, improve the efficiency of financial intermediation and extended services to the poor (Deloitte & Touche 2000).

Notes

1 This study was conducted before the recent sharp increases in copper prices (driven mainly by the high demand for copper from China and India), which have had a significant impact on the Zambian economy and have been responsible for the relatively high growth rates since 2004. At the same time, however, this resource boom has been associated with the expected 'Dutch disease'-type effects (that is, an appreciation of the real exchange rate, and a negative effect on non-traditional tradable sectors) as a recent study has documented – see Cali and te Velde (2007).

2 Clearly, there are causality issues related to the direction of causation between growth and savings; see Mavrotas and Kelly (2001) for recent evidence on this in the context of a new econometric approach. This departs substantially from traditional Granger causality tests.

3 See Levine (1997) for a comprehensive review of the theoretical literature, Arestis and Demetriades (1997) for a critical discussion of the empirical literature, and Mavrotas and Santillana (1999) for a brief discussion.

4 It is notable that the production function on which this model is based has been influenced by theoretical developments on the endogenous-growth theory, as presented in Romer (1989) and Lucas (1988) among others.

5 Liquidity constraints issues are considered in depth in Jappelli and Pagano (1994). Financial deregulation on national savings rates will reduce savings and growth rates in countries where households currently have limited access to credit; along these lines, the increase in financial savings does not necessarily yield an increase in effective post-savings, but rather helps to finance consumer credit, commercial construction and housing.

6 See Demirgüç-Kunt and Levine (1996) as well as Levine and Zervos (1996) for an excellent discussion.

7 Needless to say, the above situation has changed dramatically in recent years in view of the large increases in copper prices that have had a beneficial impact on the economy (at least as far as growth rates are concerned), although at the same time some negative 'Dutch disease'-type effects have also been present (Cali and te Velde 2007).

References

Arestis P. and P. Demetriades (1997) 'Financial Development and Economic Growth: Assessing the Evidence', *Economic Journal*, 107: 783–99.

Bank of Zambia (BoZ) (1999) *Proceedings*, International Conference on 'Economic Liberalisation: Experiences and the Way Forward', Lusaka.

Bank of Zambia (BoZ) (2001) *Annual Report*, Lusaka.

Bayoumi, T. (1993) 'Financial Saving and Household Saving', *Economic Journal*, 103(November): 1432–43.

Bencivenga, V. R. and Smith, B. D. (1991) 'Financial Intermediation and Endogenous Growth', *Review of Economic Studies*, 58(April): 195–209.

Bencivenga, V. R. and Smith, B. D. (1993) 'Some Consequences of Credit Rationing in an Endogenous Growth Model', *Journal of Economic Dynamics and Control*, 17: 97–122.

Bloom, G., Lucas, H., Edun, A., Lenneiye, M. and Milimo, J. (2000) 'Health and Poverty in Sub-Saharan Africa', IDS Working Paper 103, Institute for Development Studies; University of Sussex, Brighton.

Brownbridge, M. (1996) 'Financial Policies and the Banking System in Zambia', IDS Working Paper 32, Institute for Development Studies, University of Sussex, Brighton.

Cali, M. and te Velde, D. Willem (2007) 'Is Zambia Contracting Dutch Disease?', Working Paper 279, Overseas Development Institute, London.

Chikolwa, B. (1996) *An Integrated Housing Development System as a Tool for Housing Delivery in Zambia* (Rotterdam: Institute of Housing and Urban Development).

Deloitte & Touche (2000) *The Financial Deepening Challenge Fund*, Lusaka.

Demirgüç-Kunt, A. and Levine, R. (1996) 'Stocks Markets, Corporate Finance and Economic Growth: An Overview', *The World Bank Economic Review*, 10(2): 223–39.

Gersovitz, M. (1988) 'Savings and Development', in H. Chenery and T. Srinivasan (eds), *Handbook of Development Economics* (Elsevier, North-Holland).

Gondwe, K. (2000) 'AIDS Claims 650,000 in Zambia between 1996–99', *The Post*. Available at: http://www.medguide.org.zm/aids/aidszam28.htm#claims (2 October 2000).

Government of the Republic of Zambia (GRZ) (2001) 'Interim Poverty Reduction Strategy Paper', Ministry of Finance, Lusaka, 20 February.

Jappelli, T. and M. Pagano (1994) 'Saving, Growth and Liquidity Constraints', *Quarterly Journal of Economics*, CIX: 436.

Jones, S. (1994) 'Structural Adjustment in Zambia', in van der Geest (ed.) *Negotiating Structural Adjustment in Africa* (London: James Currey for UNDP).

Kani, F. (1996) 'Central Banking and Macroeconomic Stability', Paper presented at the Bank of Zambia International Conference on 'Economic Liberalization: Experiences and the Way Forward', Geneva, 21–23 August.

Levine, R. (1997) 'Financial Development and Economic Growth: Views and Agenda', *Journal of Economic Literature*, XXXV(June), 688–726.

Levine, R. and S. Zervos (1996) 'Stock Market Development and Long-Run Growth', *The World Bank Economic Review*, 10(2): 323–39.

Loayza, N., Lopez, H., Schmidt-Hebbel, K. and Serven, L. (1998) 'The World Saving Data Base', Mimeo, World Bank.

Lucas, R. (1988) 'On the Mechanics of Development', *Journal of Monetary Economics*, 22(1): 3–42.

Maimbo, S. (1999) 'The Regulation and Supervision of Commercial Banks in Zambia: A Study of the Design, Development and Implementation of Prudential Regulations by the BoZ between 1990 and 1999', Mimeo, Bank of Zambia.

Maimbo, S. (2000a) 'The Diagnosis and Prediction of Bank Failures in Zambia', Finance and Development Programme Working Paper 13, University of Manchester.

Maimbo, S. (2000b) 'The Regulation and Supervision of Banks in Tanzania, Uganda and Zambia', *Journal of Financial Regulation and Compliance*, 8(4).

Maimbo, S. (2000c) 'The Regulation and Supervision of Micro Finance Institutions in Zambia', Paper presented at the Development Studies International Conference, SOAS, University of London, 4 November.

Maimbo, S. (2003) 'The Design, Development and Implementation of Bank Licensing Policies and Procedures in Zambia', *Journal of African Business*, 4(2): 21–45.

Mavrotas, G. and Kelly, R. (2001) 'Old Wine in New Bottles: Testing Causality between Savings and Growth', *The Manchester School*, 69: 97–105.

Mavrotas, G. and Santillana, M. (1999) 'Savings and Financial Sector Development: Key Issues', Paper presented at the International Conference on Finance and Development, University of Manchester, 9–10 July.

Mbalashi, C. (1999) 'Development of the Financial Services Industry in Zambia', Paper presented at a Dow Jones Conference, African Business and Development Forum, Marrakech, 10–11 May.

McCulloch, N., Baulch, B. and Cherel-Robson, M. (2000) 'Poverty, Inequality and Growth in Zambia during the 1990s', IDS Working Paper 114 (August).

Muke, J. (1996) 'The State of Banks in Zambia', Paper presented at a Senior Auditors Seminar in Siavonga, Bank of Zambia, Lusaka.

Muke, J. (1998a) 'Investment Opportunities in the Banking Sector and the Effects of Bank Closures', Paper presented at the Zambia Investment Promotion Mission in South Africa, Bank of Zambia, Lusaka, 8–23 February.

Muke, J. (1998b) 'The Zambian Experience with Reforming the Banking System', Paper presented at the Graduate Institute of International Studies, Geneva, October.

Mulenga, M. (2000) 'Zambian Activists Urge Men to Fight AIDS', Panafrican News Agency. Available at: http://www.medguide.org.zm/aids/aidszam28.htm#-claims (30 November).

Muntemba, S. (1999) 'CARE Peri-Urban Lusaka Small Enterprise (CARE PULSE) Project – Zambia', *Findings*, 147 (November), World Bank.

Musokotwane, S. (1997) 'Bank Competitiveness, Restructuring and Privatisation in Zambia', Paper presented at the first Commonwealth Policy Seminar on Bank Competitiveness, Restructuring and Privatisation, Mombassa, 1–4 July.

Musona, D.T. and Mbozi, D.M. (1998) 'Credit Management Services Limited Zambia: A Case Study of a Micro Finance Scheme', *Studies in Rural and Micro Finance*, 5, World Bank.

Mwape, A. (1997a) 'Effectiveness of Bank of Zambia Supervision of Commercial Banks', Paper presented at the Economics Association of Zambia Meetings, Pamodzi Hotel, Lusaka, 11 February.

Mwape, A. (1997b) 'The Regulation of Banks in Zambia', Paper presented at the British Council Management Centre, Lusaka, 27 November.

Pagano, M. (1993) 'Financial Markets and Growth', *European Economic Review*, 37: 613–22.

Romer, P. (1989) 'Capital Accumulation in the Theory of Long Run Growth', in R. Barro (ed.), *Modern Business Cycle Theory* (Cambridge, Mass.: Harvard University Press).

Simatele, M. and Ndulo, M. (1998), 'Financial Services Sector in Zambia', Mimeo, Bank of Zambia, Lusaka.

World Bank (1998) *World Bank Savings Database* (Washington, DC: World Bank).

10
The Determinants of Loan Contracts to Business Firms: Empirical Evidence from a Private Bank in Vietnam

Pham Thi Thu Trà and Robert Lensink

Introduction

This chapter deals with loan contracting from a private bank in Vietnam – the Asia Commercial Bank (ACB). Loan contracting forms part of the broader financial contaracting literature. The financial contracting literature has been developed from two influential papers by Grossman and Hart (1986), and Hart and Moore (1990). These papers discuss agency problems in situations where contracting is incomplete in the sense that some important future variables are difficult or impossible to describe initially and therefore must be left out of the contract. These variables are *ex-post* observable for the parties in a given contract, but are not verifiable for any third party. Financial contracting can be seen as an instrument to avoid or reduce agency problems of all kinds. The financial contracting literature deals with the optimal financial structure of firms, focusing on the entire set of characteristics of the different financial contracts that the firm is linked to.

In this chapter we deal with only one aspect of financial contracting – the lender–borrower relationship that concerns banking, ignoring other issues related to the financial structure of the firm. We call this loan contracting. In general, loan contracting deals with the toolbox of contracting devices the borrower and the lender have to avoid informational problems between the two parties. A loan contract is a complex relationship between a borrower and a bank. Ideally, a loan contract should stipulate all obligations of the two parties for all possible contingencies in the future. This would imply that, for each possible future situation – for example, the amount of repayment, or the interest rate on remaining debt– possible adjustments in required collateral and actions undertaken by the borrower should be specified (Freixas and

Rochet 1997: 91). Writing a complete contingent contract, however, would be prohibitively expensive. In practice, therefore, loan contracts are much less complex. In most cases, loan contracts specify only the interest rate on debt, the repayment amount, the duration of the loan, and possible collateral requirements. Sometimes covenants, fees and default declarations are also specified.

So, a commercial bank has a toolbox of contracting devices that can be used in setting up a loan contract, such as collateral, guarantees, covenants, fees and the loan interest rate. This chapter focuses on the loan contracting of the ACB, the largest private bank in Vietnam. The main loan contract features that the ACB uses – namely, maturity, collateral and the loan interest rate – will be analysed. The ACB offers a range of debt contracts, with varying values for these three loan contract items. Borrowers then have the possibility of choosing a preferred debt contract, by trading-off different loan items. This implies that the loan contracts of the ACB are multi-dimensional, and suggests that the contract terms are inter-dependent.

There is a growing theoretical literature on loan contract design, focusing on the interdependencies of the loan terms (Merton 1974; Myers 1977; Smith and Warner 1979; Bester 1985; Flannery 1986; Chan and Thakor 1987; Midle and Riley 1988; Boot *et al.* 1991; Diamond 1993; Pozzolo 2002). The various theories used to explain the debt contract design, however, do not give unambiguous answers regarding the relationships between the different loan terms specified in a debt contract. For example, the Bester (1985) signalling model points towards a negative relationship between collateral and the interest rate, whereas Pozzolo (2002) argues that banks both require collateral and charge higher interest rates to *ex-ante* riskier borrowers. Another example refers to the relationship between lending rates and maturity. According to the so-called trade-off hypothesis, loans of a longer maturity bear higher interest rates to offset the higher risk premium. So this view predicts a positive relationship between lending rates and the period to maturity. On the other hand, Merton's (1974) option pricing model predicts an uncertain relationship between the lending rate and the maturity date. Empirical studies need to show under which circumstances certain theories hold or fail.

Empirical studies on loan contract design should allow for the interdependencies of the different loan contracting tools, and consider that different contracting items are related to a common set of exogenous variables. However, most empirical studies on loan contracting focus on a single contract feature, ignoring the possible interdependencies between different contract terms. The standard approach is to set up an equation for one of the loan contract items and to estimate this equation by assuming that all the explanatory variables are exogenous. If the right-hand-side variables are truly exogenous, and hence do not contain proxies for one of the contracting tools, this approach will result in unbiased estimates. However, in many cases, one of the right-hand-side variables is related to a contracting tool. As the contracting tools are interdependent, estimates of such an equation using the ordinary least squares (OLS) technique, as is generally done, will lead to biased estimates. The study by Dennis *et al.* (2000) is an exception. They account for the possible inter-dependencies between different contract terms by estimating a system of equations.

This chapter contributes to the small empirical literature on loan contract design. The aim is to provide an empirical analysis of loan contracting determinants of the largest private bank in Vietnam, the ACB. We focus on ACB bank lending to small and medium-sized enterprises (SMEs) in Vietnam. A special feature of the analysis is that, in line with Dennis *et al.* (2000), we focus on the possible interdependency of different loan contracting tools, and hence estimate a simultaneous equation model. We also try to determine the relevant firm character-istics for the loan contracts, and how they affect the different contract features. In this way we hope to provide some additional evidence on the different, often conflicting, theories of loan contract design. Another novelty of this chapter is that the empirical analysis relates to a private bank in a developing country, Vietnam, which has just begun a process of economic liberalization. The prior empirical work on loan contract design deals almost exclusively with developed economies (Berger and Udell 1995; Strahan 1999; Degryse and Cayseele 2000; Dennis *et al.* 2000; Pozzolo 2002). Given a more-or-less adequate infrastructure for financial contracting and financial information, the setting of a developed econ-omy ensures that banks are profit-seeking and loans are commercially orientated. In the absence of such an adequate setting, the relevance and applicability of loan contract design for transition economies remains unclear. A reason for this gap in the literature of loan contract design seems straightforward: there is simply no data available on loan contracts in developing countries. We are in the fortunate position that the largest private bank in Vietnam, the ACB, is currently devel-oping a database on loan contracts, and were willing to provide us with this dataset. The focus on contracts from a private bank in Vietnam is particularly interesting from the applied perspective. With the financial reform on the move, the Vietnamese (private) banking sector has strengthened its position considerably in mobilizing resources and allocating them to investments. Despite the fact that state-owned commercial banks still dominate the credit market, non-state-owned commercial banks are gaining a market share through their more customer-orientated approach and distinct profit motive.

The Vietnamese banking sector

The Vietnamese banking sector has experienced significant changes since the early 1990s, in line with a variety of imperative financial reforms. The banking reform process began with the establishment of a two-tier banking system during 1988–9 to include the State Bank of Vietnam and a system of commercial banks. The four state-owned commercial banks (SOCBs) still account for 78 per cent of the total assets of the banking system (Fitch Ratings 2002). However, they coexist with several new players, including thirty-six joint stock banks (JSBs), eighty branches and representative offices of foreign banks, and four joint venture banks (JVBs) (World Bank 2002).

Notably, banking regulations have been improved in both form and content to facilitate the more distant supervision and inspection. With the main focus on recapitalization and resolving the multitude of non-performing loans, the restructuring of the commercial banks has progressed considerably. Most commercial banks have greatly increased their chartered capital and considerably reduced non-performing loans. The ratio of non-performing loans to total outstanding loans decreased from 12.7 per cent on 31 December 2000 to 5 per cent on 31 December 2002 (World Bank 2003). According to the State Bank of Vietnam, over 80 per cent of commercial banks will have chartered capital of VND 1,000 billion upwards by 2007. In addition, the autonomy of banks has been enhanced. The commercial banks have the right to decide the deposit and lending interest rate, and to select the method of loan security and have in practise diversified depositary services and applied flexible credit policies for specific groups of clients. Gradually, policy-orientated lending has been separated from commercial credit in SOCBs and banking products and services have become more diverse.

Firms in transition economies need finance for their investment and growth. Since July 2000, Vietnam has had a stock exchange, but it is still in its infancy, with less than 200 firms listed as of the end of 2006. So, the Vietnamese banking sector is the main source of financial resources for firms. However, both state and non-state commercial banks are still facing great difficulties in fulfilling their role as credit providers. These difficulties can be attributed to several factors. First, the legal framework and market conditions are not yet well defined to facilitate credit operations. Second, the banking sector is insufficient, both in terms of finances and operational capability (World Bank 2002). As a result, the outreach of the formal banking sector is limited to meeting only 30 per cent of credit needs (McCarty 2001). The remainder of this section examines the interactions between the banking sector and business borrowers with respect to credit access and allocation to different types of business borrowers.

State-owned commercial banks (SOCBs)

The four main SOCBs in Vietnam are the Foreign Trade Bank of Vietnam (Vietcombank – VCB), the Industry and Commerce Bank of Vietnam (Incomebank – ICB), the Bank for Investment and Development of Vietnam (BIDV), and the Vietnam Bank for Agriculture and Rural Development (VBARD). Capturing 78 per cent of the total assets of the banking system in 2002, SOCBs dominate the credit market with 75 per cent of total lending to the economy and 76 per cent of resources mobilized through formal institutions (ADB 2003). In addition, SOCBs have advantages in providing banking services and credit for customers, given their nationwide networks, better technical conditions, more qualified staff, and better means of communication compared to the joint stock banks. SOCBs also play a major part in serving large investment projects, in particular infrastructure projects financed by the government. The main customers of SOCBs are the state-owned enterprises (SOEs), which contribute 75 per cent of the economic output and hold 53 per cent of the banks' loans (Vietnam Investment Review 2003). The intimate relationship between SOEs and the banking sector, which characterizes all transition economies, results in a weak banking sector in several ways. First, given the absence of profit-taking incentives, the low profitability of the SOEs reduces the profitability of the banking sector. Second, credit concentration on SOEs exposes SOCBs to high credit risk because of high volumes of bad loans. Third, assuming the government guarantees credits to SOEs, SOCBs do not exert much effort in screening and monitoring borrowers, distorting the fundamental role of commercial banks and weakening the soundness of the banking sector. Last, but not least, the government-directed lending crowds out private-sector access to formal credit, within which SMEs account for over 97 per cent of the total number of enterprises.

SMEs are considered to be high-risk borrowers mainly because of insufficient assets and low capitalization, vulnerability to market fluctuations, and high mortality rates. Furthermore, high administrative costs and the transaction costs of lending do not make SME financing a profitable, and hence attractive, business for SOCBs.

Additionally, the banks in general lack skills in credit evaluation and risk management – for example, to evaluate creditworthiness and the value of collateral – while SMEs fail to provide adequate information as a result of deficient accounting practices and weak corporate governance. Given the failures in acquiring information for lending to SMEs, SOCBs maintain difficult borrowing procedures and a heavy requirement for collateral. As a result, the lengthy loan process and excessive documentation impose a burden on firms, reducing their incentive to apply for bank credit (Ninh 2003). Moreover, laws on property rights, collateral and bankruptcy are not yet well defined and their enforcement is still ineffective, making it very difficult for the banks to value the pledged assets and recover loan losses in case of default. Access to SOCB credit is very challenging for private SMEs.

Joint-venture banks and other foreign banking operations

There are four JVBs, twenty-seven branches of foreign banks and fifty-three representative offices from twenty foreign banks operating in Vietnam. Since their establishment, the market share of foreign branches has increased, both in the deposit and the credit market. Nevertheless, the current regulatory framework still prevents foreign banks from participating fully in the Vietnamese financial system. Operations are on a small scale because of market size and operating restrictions. Foreign banks are mainly engaged in lending to foreign-owned enterprises rather than competing to lend to domestic firms, whether state-owned or private.

Joint stock banks

JSBs are private banks established using money pooled by shareholders. The majority of the thirty-six JSBs were founded rapidly in the mid-1990s following the initial liberalization of the financial sector, and accompanied the increasing demand for credit. Many JSBs were set up out of the ailing credit co-operatives. The collapse of credit co-operatives because of unpaid deposits left these JSBs with large amounts of bad debt from the outset (Ninh 2003). Some other JSBs were established through capital supplied by a mix of SOCBs, SOEs, private businesses and individuals. Foreign investors also have minority stakes in some of the larger JSBs.

Generally, JSBs are undercapitalized. Out of the thirty-six existing JSBs as at September 2002, 34 met the minimal chartered capital requirement. Together, they accounted for only 15.4 per cent of the total assets within the banking system (Fitch Ratings 2002). Despite their considerable growth in number, JSBs are exposed to intense competition and high risk because of their characteristics: low capital base, having to focus on higher-risk private companies; a lack of scale economies because of the small number of branches; inadequate banking services, and concentration in two business centres (Hanoi and Ho Chi Minh City). In addition, a lack of banking expertise and managerial skills has led many JSBs into problems. Some JSBs faced serious problems with regard to loans to real estate and troublesome companies, and were severely affected by the crash of the property market in Hanoi and Ho Chi Minh City, and the collapse of many trading companies in 1996 (Soo-Nam 1999). In addition, the management of some JSBs also undertook fraudulent activities in credit evaluation and extension. For example, in the late 1990s, some JSBs defaulted on importers' letters of credit (LCs), with approximately US$65 million of LCs reported to be outstanding (Ninh 2003).

The State Bank of Vietnam (SBV) implemented a JSB restructuring programme by raising the minimum capital level. As a result, the consolidation of JSBs saw twelve licences being revoked as of September 2002. Under an agreement with the IMF, the SBV further reduced the number of JSBs to twenty-five by the end of 2003. As of the end of August 2007, thirteen applications to establish new JSBs were being considered, all surpassing the minimum capital requirement.

With regard to credit allocation, JSBs primarily serve the private sector, particularly local businesses and small enterprises, comprising some 15 per cent of the business credit market. Whereas loans to the private sector represented 40 per cent of the SOCBs' total outstanding loans, 70 per cent of the JSBs' loan portfolio was channelled to the private sector (IMF 2002). However, loans to the private sector by SOCBs were about three times those by JSBs at the end 1998. Rapid loan growth and weak capacity to assess credit risk could result in non-performing loan problems, as noted earlier, and JSBs might not have adequate access to external sources of capital. The focus on lending to the private sector requires JSBs to establish larger branch networks as distribution channels. Unlike SOCBs, JSBs are not, however, permitted to open an extensive branch network. This regulatory discrimination constrains the operations of JSBs.

As economic development in Vietnam has progressed, JSBs have enhanced their role considerably in serving the country's economy. The portion of credit provided by private banks has increased steadily over time, as can be seen from Table 10.1, which also shows that the credit

Table 10.1   Bank credit in Vietnam, 1994–2002

Year	Total bank credit		Credit extended by SOCBs		Credit extended by non-SOCBs	
	Amount (VND billions)	Per cent	Amount (VND billions)	Per cent	Amount (VND billions)	Per cent
1994	33,345	100	27,610	82.8	5,735	17.2
1995	42,277	100	33,647	79.6	8,630	20.4
1996	50,751	100	38,320	75.5	12,431	24.5
1997	62,201	100	48,042	77.2	14,159	22.8
1998	72,597	100	59,087	81.4	13,510	18.6
1999	112,730	100	76,559	67.9	36,171	32.1
2000	155,720	100	114,193	73.3	41,527	26.7
2001	189,103	100	143,355	75.8	45,748	24.2
2002	231,078	100	175,489	75.9	55,589	24.1

Notes: VND – Vietnam dong; SOCB – State-owned commercial banks.

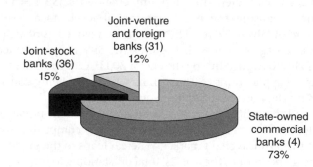

Figure 10.1   Lending market shares, Vietnam, 2000
Sources: IMF (2003); Asian Development Bank (2003).

extension by non-SOCBs has increased by a greater degree than by SOCBs. Figure 10.1 shows the lending market shares of the different banks.

In sum, the position of commercial banks in credit allocation has improved. It is characterized by the gradual growth of private banks, despite SOCBs still holding the dominant position. Whereas SOCBs are not meeting the needs of the country's economy adequately, given their lack of exposure to the rigours of competition, the country's better JSBs are gaining market share. Remarkably, the distinct motive for profit on the part of the JSBs will ensure that they continue to grow in the future.

For our study, we focus on one of the most successful joint stock banks – Asia Commercial Bank (ACB) – with the aim of examining its lending practice empirically, especially the determinants of its loan contracting.[1]

The specification of the model

The previous section showed that private banks in Vietnam in general, and the ACB in particular, have become increasingly important. This section focuses on the loan contracting of the ACB. In particular, we explain how we model this loan contracting of the ACB. After the model specification is given in general terms, we are more specific about the signs of the relationships and the set of exogenous variables we take into account. This is done by surveying the literature on loan contract design.

The structure of the model in general terms

In order to allow for the potential interdependencies between different contract terms, we follow Dennis *et al.* (2000) by specifying a system of equations that simultaneously explains a set of contract features. We focus on three contract terms: the loan maturity; collateral requirements; and the loan interest rate. Our model takes the following form:

$$collat = \alpha_1 lmat + \alpha_2 loanr + \beta_1 X_1 + \varepsilon_2 \tag{10.1}$$

$$lmat = \alpha_3 collat + \alpha_4 loanr + \beta_2 X_2 + \varepsilon_2 \tag{10.2}$$

$$loanr = \alpha_5 lmat + \alpha_6 collat + \beta_3 X_3 + \varepsilon_3 \tag{10.3}$$

where *collat* is a zero–one dummy, with a one if collateral is asked, and a zero if not; *lmat* refers to the loan maturity; and *loanr* refers to the interest rate of loans denominated in Vietnamese currency, Vietnam dong (VND). X_k for $k = 1$ to 3 are vectors of other explanatory variables (to be explained below); ε_k are the residuals.

The structure of the system of equations assumes that there are bi directional relationships between the three contract terms taken into account. Note that this differs from Dennis *et al.* (2000), who assume that there is a bi-directional relationship between *lmat* and collat, but a uni-directional relationship from both *lmat* and *collat* to *loanr* (in their case, the spread). We allow for a bi-directional relationship between *loanr* and *lmat* and *collat* because there is no reason to assume why one of these relations should be uni-directional. At the least, the bi-directional relationships between all of the contract terms are a testable assumption.

Interdependencies between the loan interest rate, collateral requirement and maturity

The model emphasizes the possible interdependencies between the loan rate, the loan maturity, and the collateral requirement. An important question is whether these contract features are related positively or negatively to each other. The existing theories on loan contract design may shed some light on this. However, it should be noted that an obvious problem of a description of the interdependencies of the loan contracting tools is that the different loan contract items are endogenous – and are, therefore, equilibrium outcomes. Theories on loan contracting show that the equilibrium outcomes depend on bank policies as well as firm strategies. It may well be that, for banks, the contract items are positively related, whereas for firms they have a negative relationship. In that case, the ultimate positive or negative co-movement depends on the origin of the shock.[2] In addition, the existing theories, as we show below, are conflicting with respect to the interdependencies between the various loan contract terms, so it is very difficult to provide unambiguous signs. We show that these interdependencies are theoretically indeterminate and depend ultimately on the relative strength of one or other theory. Empirical studies are needed to weigh the importance of the different possible theoretical outcomes.

There is also a question of normalization. Equation (10.1) is normalized with respect to *collat*, Equation (10.2) is normalized with respect to *lmat*, and Equation (10.3) is normalized with respect to *loanr*. In other words, in Equation (10.1) *collat* is the dependent variable, whereas *lmat* and *loanr* are the dependent variables in Equations (10.2) and (10.3), respectively. By definition *collat, lmat* and *loanr* are jointly determined, so that, strictly speaking, we cannot talk about dependent variables in one or another equation. The way of normalization is important, though, because in over-identified systems the estimators are different for different normalizations.[3]

The system of normalization we have chosen is based on the loan policies of the ACB. In personal conversations with ACB managers, it has been made clear to us that the ACB primarily sets collateral requirements and the loan rate, based on the maturity time of the loan that is requested by the firm. The loan maturity demanded by the firm is taken as given by the ACB. On the other hand, the loan maturity demanded by the firm is, of course, affected by the loan rate and the collateral requirements set by the ACB. The equilibrium values for *collat, lmat* and *loanr* are determined by the three equations together. However, based on the ACB loan policies, we see Equations (10.1) and (10.3) as primarily being determined by the loan policies of the ACB, whereas equation (10.2) mainly reflects the demand policies of the firm. In what follows, it will become clear that this affects our choice of exogenous variables; that is, the modelling of X_1, X_2 and X_3.

Collateral or the secured status of a loan *vis-à-vis* the loan interest rate

Signalling theory argues that collateral can be used as a screening device to identify credit applicants (Bester 1985). One presumes that the interest rate is designed as a function of collateral, creating pairs of different credit contracts that act as a self-selection mechanism in that it reveals information about the default risk of loan applicants. The model implies that high-risk borrowers can be identified because they prefer loan contracts with lower collateral and a higher interest rate. Similarly, high-quality borrowers tend to post more collateral to reveal their true type and thereby enjoy a lower loan interest rate. Therefore, according to this theory, a negative relationship between collateral and the loan rate is expected.

The contrasting view by Pozzolo (2002) predicts that banks simultaneously require collateral and charge higher interest rates to *ex-ante* riskier borrowers. This result is derived from two major assumptions. First, collateral is more valuable to borrowers than to the banks. Second, borrowers maximize their profits by choosing the level of effort to put in to the project. Probability of success is jointly determined by the level of borrower riskiness and the level of effort. The model shows that, for a given probability of success, banks face a trade-off between higher interest rates and lower collateral. However, when the probability of success decreases, banks cover the higher credit risk both by augmenting the degree of loan security and by charging higher interest rates.

Most empirical studies provide evidence on a positive relationship between collateral and the loan rate. Pozzolo (2002), for example, finds that interest rates on secured loans are on average higher than those on unsecured loans. Furthermore, small firms, perceived to be high-risk, borrow on a secured basis and have to pay higher interest rates (Strahan 1999). Positive empirical relations between collateral and the loan rate have also been found by Berger and Udell (1990) and Dennis *et al.* (2000).

Collateral or the secured status of a loan *vis-à-vis* the loan maturity

The agency cost of debt theory (Myers 1977; Smith and Warner 1979; Chan and Thakor 1987) predicts that collateral and loan maturity are positively related. The reason is that both collateral and loan maturity are tools for coping with asset substitution and under-investment problems. These problems refer to the situation where a firm with risky debt has an incentive to undertake relatively more risky projects and/or to under-invest in low-risk, positive net present value projects. These incentives may be reduced by shortening the debt maturity or requiring collateral. As substitutes, loan maturity and collateral are positively related. According to trade-off theory, this positive relationship is also expected if the loan contracting choice is determined primarily by borrowers' actions. An increase in loan maturity has a positive effect on a borrower's utility, whereas collateral requirements have a negative effect. If borrowers try to trade-off the decrease in utility resulting from the collateral requirements by trying to increase the maturity, a positive relationship is expected.

On the other hand, Boot *et al.* (1991) derive a theoretical model in which collateral and maturity are negatively related. Assuming that banks incur a dissipative cost in taking possession of and liquidating collateral, they argue that the dissipative costs of collateral are lower for longer maturity loans. The reason is that, for a longer maturity loan, a bank has more timing flexibility in terms of when to force default on the loan and take possession of collateral. In such a situation the bank can make use of its flexibility and then cut its collateral costs by lowering collateral for longer maturity loans.

The empirical literature is also not conclusive with regard to the sign of the collateral–loan maturity relationship. Harhoff and Korting (1998) and Dennis *et al.* (2000) provide empirical evidence for a positive relationship between collateral and loan maturity. However, Boot *et al.* (1991) find evidence for a negative relationship between collateral and maturity in their empirical estimates.

Loan maturity *vis-à-vis* the loan rate

The relationship between the interest rate and loan maturity is also ambiguous. Some authors rely on the trade-off hypothesis. According to this view, loans with a longer maturity carry higher interest rates to offset the higher risk premium that results from such loans. So, the loan maturity and the loan rate are positively related.

Other authors, however, argue that there may be a negative relationship. High-risk borrowers may be forced to accept higher interest rates and low maturity if credit risk is very high. Also Merton's (1974) option pricing model predicts a negative relationship conditional on a certain range of the debt-to-firm value ratios, with debt valued at the riskless rate.

Empirical studies provide evidence for both possibilities. Gottesman and Roberts (2004) find a positive relationship between loan maturity and the loan interest rate. Alternatively, the empirical analyses of Strahan (1999) and Dennis *et al.* (2000) suggest a negative relationship.

Effects of exogenous variables on the endogenous loan contract items

The model specified above shows that the three loan contract terms are also affected by different sets of exogenous variables. The literature on loan contracting points to a long list of theories that affect the pricing of the loan, and consequently the explanatory variables that may influence the different contract features. Very often, authors refer to, for example, the importance of tax rates, firm quality, growth opportunities, agency costs, the relationship between the bank and the borrower, and the impact of the signalling hypothesis. Based on the existing theories, and the variables that are available in our dataset, we come up with the following set of exogenous variables that may affect the different contract terms, and consequently would appear in a reduced form specification of our system

$$X = \begin{bmatrix} liquidr, \ debta, \ inventc, \ profitbt, \ areceive, \ turno, \ taxa, \\ amat, \ fsize, \ lsize, \ numberlc, \ loanc, \ debte, \ dummyus, \ c \end{bmatrix}$$

Where: *liquidr* = current assets/current liabilities; *debta* = debt/total assets; *inventc* = inventories/cost of goods sold; *profitbt* = profit before tax/total assets; *areceive* = accounts receivable/net sales; *turno* = net sales/total assets; *taxa* = taxes/total assets; *amat* = (fixed assets/total assets) (fixed assets/depreciation); *fsize* = ln(total assets); *lsize* = ln(loan size); *numberlc* = number of loan contracts a firm had with the ACB on July 2003; *loanc* = cumulative loan outstanding of a firm/the sum of total debt of the firm plus the cumulative loan outstanding; *debte* = debt/ equity; *dummyus* = dummy with a one if the loan contract originally referred to a loan denominated in US dollars (US$), and a zero if the loan contract was originally denominated in VND; and *c* = constant.

Below, we categorize these exogenous factors in light of several hypotheses, so as to capture the impact of firm quality, agency cost of debt, taxes and relationship lending on the endogenous contract terms. In our estimation, firm quality is assumed to be proxied by *fsize, turno, areceive* and *inventc*. In addition, firm credit quality is proxied by *debta*, *debte* and *liquidr*. The effect of the agency cost of debts is examined through the growth potential of a firm, as proxied by *profitbt*, firm asset maturity (*amat*) and firm leverage (*debta* and *debte*). Taxes/total asset ratio (*taxa*) is for the tax considerations. Finally, the number of loan contracts a firm has with ACB (*numberlc*) and the degree of loan concentration (*loanc*) aim to measure the relationship lending effect. These hypotheses will be analysed below.

Firm quality hypothesis

According to conventional wisdom, firms that are as perceived as a high risk have to face higher lending rates and collateral requirements. However, in certain circumstances, because of lender policies that may result in decisions not to lend to risky firms, the effects are different. From a theoretical viewpoint, the effect of firm quality is also complex. The signalling theory predicts that firm quality influences the loan contract terms – for example, collateral and loan interest rates – through the self-selection mechanism. Under this mechanism, high-quality firms are inclined to post more collateral to reveal their true type and thereby enjoy the lower loan interest rate (Bester 1985), implying that firm quality has a positive effect on collateral and a negative effect on the loan interest rate. Alternatively, the Merton (1974) option-pricing model suggests a positive relationship between loan interest rate and firm credit quality, as proxied by firm leverage. In addition, another theory predicts an inverse relationship between collateral and firm quality. In particular, a high level of collateral is associated with low-quality projects because of difficulties in project valuation (Chan and Kanatas 1985). Besides, a high level of collateral causes default to be more costly, and hence failure avoidance to be more attractive (Chan and Thakor 1987), suggesting a positive relation between collateral, firm risk and credit quality. These implications find strong empirical support (Berger and Udell 1990; Pozzolo 2002; Gonas *et al.* 2002).

The choice of maturity is also affected by firm quality and firm credit risk. Diamond (1993) predicts that loan maturity relates directly to firm size and firm quality, and relates inversely to credit risk given that small firms with high informational opacity are significantly limited in their access to long-term debt. By contrast, Flannery (1986) and Diamond (1991a) expect a negative relationship between loan maturity and firm quality as viable firms choose and repay shorter maturity loans, thereby separating themselves from low-quality firms.

In our estimation, firm quality is represented by *fsize, turno, areceive* and *inventc*, with the following justifications. First, measured by the book value of total assets, because the market value is lacking, size of firm (*fsize*) may influence contract terms through risk diversification and reputation effects (Diamond 1989, 1991b). A larger firm is considered to be well-established and hence less risky than its smaller counterparts. Second, a high asset turnover (*turno*) indicates that the firm is efficient in generating revenues, which are a source of debt service. Third, a low inventory period (*inventc*) and a low accounts receivable period (*areceive*) reflect the firm's efficiency in asset management. Given that credit quality is considered as one aspect of firm quality, in our analysis we proxy firm credit quality by firm leverage and firm liquidity. First, firm leverage is measured by the debt-to-total-assets ratio (*debta*) and the debt-to-equity ratio (*debte*). Quite reasonably, a high-leverage firm may face a higher likelihood of a future insolvency. Second, firm liquidity (*liquidr*) measures the extent to which a firm can liquidate assets and cover short-term debts, implying that a highly liquid firm is less prone to default risk.

Agency cost hypothesis

Agency costs of debt may influence the design of loan contract terms (Myers 1977; Smith and Warner 1979; Chan and Thakor 1987). These costs may be potentially high for risky firms and for firms with growth options. We pick up the effect of agency costs through four variables. First, firm profitability (*profitbt*) suggests that a profitable firm is strong and therefore more likely to expand. Second, asset maturity (*amat*) reflects the time pattern of cash flows generated from a firm's fixed assets. The last term in this variable aims to support the idea that longer maturity assets will be depreciated at a slower rate (Guedes and Opler 1996). Firms match the maturity of debt payments with the maturity of assets. Firms with longer-lived assets in place are able to have longer maturity debt without increasing the agency costs of debt (Myers 1977). Agency costs may be mitigated by matching debt maturity with asset maturity, suggesting a direct relationship between asset maturity *amat* and loan maturity. Third, firm leverage is admittedly relevant, based on the argument that agency costs may be limited by reducing leverage as well as shortening maturity or requiring collateral. Accordingly, the debt-to-total-assets ratio (*debta*) and the debt-to-total-equity ratio (*debte*) are also taken into account to reflect an inverse relationship between firm leverage and loan maturity, and a positive relationship between firm leverage and collateral.

Tax hypothesis

We also include tax considerations in our analysis, measured by *taxa*. Several hypotheses exist with respect to the relationship between loan maturity and the marginal tax rate. Dennis *et al.* (2000) hypothesize a negative relationship between the marginal effective tax rate and duration of borrowing. However, Guedes and Opler argue that duration is positively related to the marginal tax rate. Borrowers try to accelerate interest payments to maximize the present value of interest tax shields. A maturity structure that accelerates tax payments is more costly to borrowers than a maturity structure that lowers tax payments, because an additional premium has to be paid to the lender (see Guedes and Opler 1996: 1814).

Relationship lending hypothesis

For the effect of relationship lending, we proxy relationship strength by two variables: the number of loan contracts a firm has with the ACB (*numberlc*) and the cumulative value of loans outstanding over the sum of total debt and the cumulative value of loan outstanding (*loanc*). In most relationship lending studies, relationship strength is measured by the duration of the relationship (the number of years a firm stays with the bank) or the scope of the relationship (the number of services a firm purchases from the bank). Firms that have a stronger relationship with a bank may obtain better contract terms: for example, less collateral (Boot and Thakor 1994; Berger and Udell 1995; Harhoff and Korting 1998; Degryse and Van Cayseeke 2000) and lower loan interest rates (Diamond 1989; Boot and Thakor 1994; Berger and Udell 1995; Petersen and Rajan 1995; Repetto *et al.* 2002). However, firms with a close relationship with a bank may also face a lock-in situation and rarely switch to other banks. This results in worse loan contract terms; for example, loan interest rates increase over the course of the relationship (Greenbaum *et al.* 1989; Sharpe 1990; Degryse and Van Cayseele 2000). In our analysis, we use two relationship proxies, frequency of the relationship (*numberlc*) and loan concentration (*loanc*). Interestingly, Bodenhorn (2003) proves that the frequency of the relationship is valuable in that it lowers loan interest rates. For loan concentration, Dennis *et al.* (2000) provide empirical support for a positive association with loan interest rates. In short, we hypothesize that *numberlc* and *loanc* both have a negative relationship with collateral and the sign of the relationship with loan interest rate is uncertain.

The size of the loan is also taken into consideration, because many studies stress the importance of the loan size in explaining the other contract terms of the deal. Here it should be noted that the size of the loan may also be considered as an endogenous variable in line with the theoretical implication by Midle and Riley (1988). In their model, loan size can play a signalling role and banks screen by offering larger loans at higher interest rates. However, we follow Berger and Udell (1990), Boot *et al.* (1991), Harhoff and Korting (1998), Elsas and Kranen (2000) and Gonas *et al.* (2002) by considering loan size (*lsize*) as an exogenous variable in the system. We could have considered *lsize* as an endogenous variable, but that would have complicated the identification of the system considerably. Relating collateral to loan size, Harhoff and Korting (1998) and Elsas and Kranen (2000) find a higher incidence of securitization on larger loans, but Boot *et al.* (1991) and Gonas *et al.* (2002) discover that loan size is inversely related to the probability that a loan is secured. Concerning the loan size–loan interest rate relationship, it is commonly argued that loans of a larger size carry lower interest rates, given that larger loans incur lower transaction costs in lending. In contrast, Midle and Riley (1988) predict a positive relationship between loan size and loan interest rates.

The final exogenous variable we have to explain is *dummyus*. This variable is added because some of the contracts were originally denominated in US dollars (US$). We wanted to take these contracts into account because the sample could then be increased considerably. In order to make these contracts comparable with the contracts denominated in Vietnamese dong (VND), we have to convert the loan contracts denominated in US dollars into loan contracts denominated in Vietnamese dong. The conversion of the loan size is simple. We could do that by using the actual US$–VND exchange rate. However, the conversion of the lending rate is more complicated because we need a proxy for the expected depreciation of the VND *vis-à-vis* the US dollar. As the expected depreciation is an unobservable variable, we have to use a proxy for this. We used the following approach. We searched for two loan contracts in our dataset that had similar loan sizes, the same loan maturity, and where both had collateral requirements and were provided to the same firm. These contracts therefore differ only in that one of them is denominated in US$ (and consequently have a dollar lending rate) and the other is denominated in VND (and has a dong lending rate). The difference between the two lending rates of these two contracts is used as a proxy for the expected depreciation (this comparison gave an expected depreciation of 7.4 per cent). To pick up the remaining differences, we added a binary zero-one dummy variable with a one if the loan contract was originally denominated in US$.

As explained above, existing empirical studies point to a list of variables that may affect the contract terms. However, they do not give much guidance with respect to the variables that are most important for one or the other of the contract terms. In other words, it is not clear whether, for example, variables that are meant to proxy for firm quality have a direct relationship with the loan maturity, collateral requirements or with the loan rate, or whether these variables have a direct effect on the three contract features simultaneously. In fact, it seems that the same set of explanatory variables appear in studies on collateral requirements, the loan rate, and the loan maturity. Therefore, it could be argued that most of the variables mentioned above may have a direct relationship with the endogenous variables identified. However, the identification of the system does not allow for this. In order to identify the three equations, we need to make some assumptions regarding the variables that directly (or only indirectly) affect the different contract features. In other words, the X_k vectors cannot contain the same set of exogenous variables. We base our choice on our assumption (see above) that the collateral and loan rate equations primarily reflect bank policies, whereas the maturity equation primarily reflects the policies of the firm. However, we admit that this choice is still somewhat ad hoc. We specified the X_k vectors of the relationship between the exogenous variables and the endogenous variables as follows:

$$X_1 = \begin{bmatrix} liquidr, \ debta, \ inventc, \ profitbt, \ areceive, \ turno, \\ numberlc, \ loanc, \ debte, \ fsize, \ lsize, \ c \end{bmatrix} \quad (10.4)$$

$$X_2 = \begin{bmatrix} liquidr, \ debta, \ inventc, \ profitbt, \ areceive, \ turno, \\ taxa, \ amat, \ fsize, \ lsize, \ c \end{bmatrix} \quad (10.5)$$

$$X_3 = \begin{bmatrix} liquidr, \ debta, \ inventc, \ profitbt, \ areceive, \ turno, \\ numberlc, \ loanc, \ dummyus, \ fsize, \ lsize, \ c \end{bmatrix} \quad (10.6)$$

Regarding the exogenous variables that do not appear in all equations, some explanation is needed. The two proxies for relationship lending are included in the Collateral equation (X_1; see Equation (10.4)) and in the loan interest rate equation (X_3; see Equation (10.6)) and excluded from the loan maturity equation (X_2; see Equation (10.5)) because the relationship lending literature provides little evidence on the effect of relationship banking on loan maturity. The choice is also based on our assumption that the collateral and the loan rate equations primarily reflect bank behaviour, whereas the maturity equation reflects firm behaviour. This also explains why asset maturity only appears in the loan maturity equation. Asset maturity is brought only into the X_2 equation because of the unique association between asset maturity and loan maturity in mitigating agency costs of debt. It is obvious why the dummy for loans originally denominated in US$ only appears in the loan rate equation (X_3).

By using the rank condition, it can be seen that all equations are now identified.[4] The order condition shows that the three equations are over-identified.[5]

The dataset

We use information on 277 ACB loan contracts as of July 2003, the dataset being retrieved from the bank's database system. This is an ongoing process. Accordingly, many relevant types of data are unavailable: for example, the value of collateral, the purpose of the loan, and the deposit rate. In addition, some contracts lack information on one or more of the contract terms. After leaving out all contracts with missing data on any contract terms, in the end we had a smaller dataset of 152 contracts with complete information on all the variables we use in our equations.

It should be noted that some firms have several loan contracts with the ACB at the same time. The 152 contracts refer to forty-seven ACB relationships with different firms in different industries and regions in Vietnam. This also implies that some variables are at a contract level, and others are at the firm level. More specifically, the three contract features: *lmat*, *collat* and *loanr* as well as the loan size, *lsize*, and the dummy indicating whether the contract was originally in VND or in US$ are measured at a loan contract level, whereas all other variables are measured at the firm level. Table 10.2 gives descriptive statistics for the three contract items.

As can be seen from Table 10.2, most of the ACB loans – nearly 90 per cent – are provided on a secured basis. Loan maturity varies considerably from one contract to another, ranging from one month to ten years with a mean (median) of 15.7 (six) months. Unlike loan maturity, loan interest rates remain rather smooth across the sample with a mean (median) of 10 per cent/year (10.2 per cent/year). It should be noted that

248   *Loan Contracts to Business: Vietnam*

Table 10.2   Descriptive statistics of three key contract features

	Loan maturity (months)	Loan interest rate (% per year)	Collateral (dummy 0,1)
Mean	15.71	10.00	0.88
Median	6.00	10.20	1.00
Max	120.00	11.40	1.00
Min	1.00	6.00	0
Std dev.	20.45	0.53	0.32
Jarque–Bera	349.66	2831.71	222.44
Observations	152	152	152

Source: see text, p. 247; calculated from the loan sample by the authors.

the loan contract variables are far from normally distributed, as can be seen from the Jarque–Bera statistic. This is not unusual in these types of studies, but obviously might affect our results.

Table 10A.1 in Appendix A on page 260 presents descriptive statistics of all exogenous variables used in the analysis. Table 10.A2 in Appendix A on page 261 gives a correlation matrix of these variables.

The estimation results

Our model contains three simultaneous equations of contract terms. The variables *lmat* and *loanr* are continuous variables, whereas *collat* is a discrete choice variable. This requires a specific estimation technique that allows for estimating a simultaneous equation model, including continuous and discrete choice variables. We use Nelson and Olson's (1978) two-stage estimation procedure of a simultaneous equation model with limited dependent variables. This approach consists of first regressing the endogenous regressors from the structural equations on their reduced forms. Then we estimate the structural equations in which we replace the endogenous regressors by the fitted values of the first stage. So the method is essentially comparable to a two-stage least squares regression. The difference is that one of the equations is estimated by logit and not by OLS, because one of the dependent variables is a dichotomous variable. The reduced form equations are specified as:

$$collat = \Pi_1 X + \varepsilon_4 \tag{10.7}$$

$$lmat = \Pi_2 X + \varepsilon_5 \tag{10.8}$$

$$loanr = \Pi_3 X + \varepsilon_6 \tag{10.9}$$

where X is the set of exogenous variables in the X_k vectors and ε_4, ε_5, ε_6 are reduced form residuals. Equations (10.8) and (10.9) are estimated with OLS and Equation (10.7) with logit. These estimates are presented in Table 10B.1 in Appendix B on page 262.

Note that the significance of the reduced form estimates does not necessarily imply that the structural coefficients in the second step are significant. Moreover, the reduced form parameters cannot be used to estimate the structural parameters, because all equations are over-identified. The goodness of fit of the reduced form estimates, however, can give some useful information on the results. Table 10B.1 shows that the adjusted R^2 of the *lmat* and the *loanr* equations are acceptable. The same holds for the McFadden R^2 of the *collat* equation. For *collat*, we also present a cross-tabulation of actual and predicted results (see Table 10B.2 in Appendix B). Here we have generated predictions of *collat* (*collatf*) on the basis of the estimated logit probabilities by predicting one if the estimated probability is above 0.5 and zero otherwise. The off-diagonal elements in this table indicate the number of observations for which the model's prediction is incorrect. Note that there is a predominance of ones in our sample, with a proportion of $134/152 = 0.88$. This may imply that a high number of correct predictions would occur even if the model were bad. This implies that purely by chance the proportion of correct predictions equals $0.88^2 + (1 - 0.88)^2 = 0.79$. The proportion of correct predictions for our model equals $(132 + 11)/152 = 0.94$, indicating that the model performs well. All in all, the reduced form regressions suggest that the endogenous regressors are reasonably well explained by the variables in their reduced form. Thus the fitted values from the first-stage regression seem to be reasonable proxies for the actual values. This provides some confidence in the appropriateness of our set of exogenous variables; that is, the set of instruments.

The reduced form results are used to obtain fitted values for all endogenous variables:

$$collat^f = \Pi_1^f X \tag{10.10}$$

$$lmat^f = \Pi_2^f X \tag{10.11}$$

$$loanr^f = \Pi_3^f X \tag{10.12}$$

where the superscript f denotes fitted value.

The second step consists of substituting the fitted values in the underlying structural models:

$$collat = \alpha_1 lmat^f + \alpha_2 loanr^f + \beta_1 X_1 + \varepsilon_1 \tag{10.13}$$

$$lmat = \alpha_3 collat^f + \alpha_4 loanr^f + \beta_2 X_2 + \varepsilon_2 \tag{10.14}$$

$$loanr = \alpha_5 lmat^f + \alpha_6 collat^f + \beta_3 X_3 + \varepsilon_3 \tag{10.15}$$

These equations are estimated with logit, OLS and OLS, respectively. Note that the standard errors reported in the second stage are not correct, but can be used as approximations (Nelson and Olson 1978: 702), and that is what we do.

Table 10.3 gives the second-stage results. In Table 10B.3 in Appendix B we present estimates of our structural model in which we ignore the endogeneity of *lmat, collat* and *loanr*. A comparison between Table 10.3 and Table 10B.3 shows the degrees at which the assumption of endogeneity affects the results. In Table 10.3, columns marked with '*' indicate the results from the regression in which we have ignored the highly insignificant exogenous variables.[6] In Table 10.4 we present a cross-tabulation of actual and predicted results of *collat* (based on a cut-off value of 0.5). Table 10.4 shows that, in almost all cases, our model predicts collateral requirements correctly. However, in seven of the eighteen cases, the model predicts collateral requirements whereas collateral was not requested. Of the seven – wrongly – predicted cases, three cases entail the predicted probabilities in excess of 0.6. Generally speaking, the resulting collateral equation seems appropriate in explaining whether a loan is securitized or not.

Interdependencies between the endogenous contract terms

The coefficients of the contract term interdependence are of great interest, as can be seen from Table 10.3. Specifically, we find significant bi-directional relationships between collateral (*collat*) and loan maturity (*lmat*), and between loan rate (*loanr*) and loan maturity (*lmat*); and a uni-directional relationship between loan rate (*loanr*) and collateral (*collat*). These results provide support for the underlying premise of our study that these three key contract terms are interrelated and determined simultaneously in the loan contract design process.

Table 10.3 Second-step estimation results of the structural equation of the endogenous contract terms

	collat	collat (*)	lmat	lmat (*)	loanr	loanr (*)
collat^f			16.99697 (0.018)	16.56602 (0.0245)	0.02746 (0.8879)	0.04854 (0.7805)
lmat^f	-0.21212 (0.0324)	-0.103011 (0.0172)			0.01181 (0.1749)	0.011209 (0.0414)
loanr^f	-9.82386 (0.0179)	-4.914005 (0.0003)	-13.3016 (0.0085)	-14.73545 (0.0039)		
C	175.4094 (0.0269)	125.8468 (0)	22.12017 (0.7161)	44.31400 (0.4332)	15.25876 (0)	15.2418 (0)
liquidr	1.447864 (0.2891)		-0.07102 (0.0137)	-0.069087 (0.0147)	0.000862 (0.1124)	0.001114 (0.0282)
debta	-47.6954 (0.0123)	-72.82207 (0.0299)	2.884085 (0.7584)		-1.53134 (0.0032)	-1.610594 (0.0003)
inventc	-1.71867 (0.7464)		23.40218 (0.0387)	23.735 (0.012)	0.143124 (0.5502)	
profitbt	106.4617 (0.0083)	83.57097 (0.0082)	-29.2934 (0.0323)	-31.18835 (0.0058)	-0.15156 (0.6354)	
areceive	-3.46357 (0.4769)	1.560710 (0.4997)	7.543622 (0.5493)		-0.07013 (0.7898)	
turno	-0.28098 (0.5309)		0.170446 (0.7157)		-0.01084 (0.3498)	-0.01164 (0.2676)
taxa			338.4387 (0.1221)	331.4889 (0.1103)		

(Continued)

Table 10.3 Continued

	collat	collat (*)	lmat	lmat (*)	loanr	loanr (*)
amat			1.215238	1.10871		
			(0.0019)	(0.0013)		
fsize	-3.28246	-2.630631	1.7729	1.334046	-0.23794	-0.257795
	(0.0952)	(0.001)	(0.1304)	(0.0454)	(0.0009)	(0.0002)
lsize	0.122768		4.944255	5.206386	-0.03242	
	(0.8592)		(0.0237)	(0.0083)	(0.5528)	
numberlc	0.728943	0.555345			0.028413	0.032996
	(0)	(0.0113)			(0.0052)	(0.0007)
loanc	-35.3062	-30.38032			-2.33478	-2.541453
	(0.0236)	(0.0008)			(0.0011)	(0)
debte	6.796181	9.866333				
	(0.0435)	(0.0730)				
dummyus					0.696508	0.692249
					(0)	(0)
R^2	0.569652	0.496667	0.334786	0.332477	0.397488	0.392604
Adjusted R^2	0.222143	0.220819	0.277358	0.290170	0.34073	0.354107
McFadden R^2	0.496667				0.430117	0.425731
S.E. of regression	6.809966	6.924088	17.38711	17.23230	25.53007	25.73503
Sum squared resid.			42021.33	42167.19		
Log likelihood	-23.7951	-27.83060	-642.955	-643.2180	-80.0929	-80.70647
Mean dependent var.	0.881579	0.881579	15.70395	15.70395	10.00638	10.00638
S.D. dependent var.	0.324174	0.324174	20.45342	20.45342	0.52973	0.529730
Restr. log likelihood	-55.2926	-55.29261				
LR statistic (13 df)	62.99512	54.92402				
Probability (LR stat)	1.52E-08	1.26E-08				

Notes: The number of observations in all equations is 152. The figures in parentheses are P-values. * indicates results from the regression in which we have ignored the highly insignificant exogenous variables.

Table 10.4   Cross-tabulation of actual and predicted outcomes for the logit model
(based on estimates where insignificant variables are ignored)

		collat (predicted)		
		0	1	Total
	0	11	7	18
collat (actual)	1	2	132	134
	Total	13	139	152

Turning to specific interdependence effects, we find bi-directional relationships between collateral and loan maturity. The collateral equation
suggests that longer maturity loans lead to requirements for less collateral.
This corresponds to the findings of Boot *et al.* (1991), who argue that the
costs for banks of seizing collateral are smaller for longer maturity loans. At
the same time, the loan maturity equation shows a positive relationship
between the two contract terms. This is in line with the agency costs
theory, in which shortening maturity and requiring collateral are
substitutes. The conflicting signs between collateral and loan maturity
in the two equations seem to suggest that the collateral equation primarily
represents bank behaviour, and the loan maturity equation represents
borrower behaviour. This provides some evidence for our assumption with
respect to the normalization of the equations (see above).

As for the interrelation between loan rate and loan maturity, there is
evidence of a bi-directional relationship between these two terms,
although this only appears in the set of equations where we ignore the
insignificant exogenous variables. Again, the signs of the relationships
are conflicting. In the loan maturity equation, loan rate and loan
maturity are negatively related, whereas these variables are positively
related in the loan rate equation. The negative relationship can be
explained by the option pricing approach of Merton (1974). The positive
sign is in line with the trade-off theory. Again, these results suggest that
the loan maturity equation does not reflect bank behaviour and is more
in line with borrower behaviour.

Finally, the relationship between the loan rate and collateral appears
to be uni-directional. The loan rate has a negative effect on collateral
requirements in the collateral equation, whereas in the loan rate
equation collateral is insignificant. The negative significant sign of the
loan rate in the collateral equation is in line with the Bester (1985)
signalling model, and with trade-off theory, in which high-quality firms
are inclined to enjoy lower loan rates by pledging more security.

Effects of exogenous variables

Also from Table 10.3, we find evidence of the effects of exogenous variables on the three endogenous contract terms, as previously formulated. The collateral equation shows significant positive direct effects of *numberlc*, *debte* and *profitbt* and significant negative effects of *debta*, *loanc*, *fsize*. The loan maturity equation proves that *inventc*, *amat*, *fsize* and *lsize* have a positive impact, while *liquidr* and *profitbt* have a negative impact on loan maturity. Finally, the loan rate equation brings us a positive effect of *liquidr*, *numberlc* and *dummyus* and a negative effect of *debta*, *fsize* and *loanc* on loan interest rate.

The agency cost theory receives support from both the collateral and loan maturity equations. Firms with substantial growth opportunities, as proxied by *profitbt*, mitigate agency problems by borrowing from banks short-term and on a secured basis. This corresponds with the positive sign of *profitbt* in the collateral equation and its negative sign in the loan maturity equation. Another support for the agency cost theory is provided by the positive sign of the asset maturity (*amat*)–loan maturity relationship. However, concerning the effect of firm leverage, as proxied by the debt–total asset ratio (*debta*) and the debt–equity ratio (*debte*), the result remained mixed in the collateral equation because of the conflicting signs of impact on collateral.

The hypotheses on the impact of firm quality are strongly supported by our result. All three equations confirm the effect of firm size (*fsize*) as a proxy for firm quality on contract terms. In line with the empirical studies of Berger and Udell (1990), Strahan (1999), Dennis *et al.* (2000), Gonas *et al.* (2002) and Pozzolo (2002), we find that larger firms borrow longer-term, at lower interest rates and provide less collateral, given the negative effect of *fsize* on collateral and loan rate but the positive effect on loan maturity. Turning to the significant effects of other proxies for firm quality, which are firm liquidity (*liquidr*) and firm inventory period (*inventc*), it appears in the loan rate equation that highly liquid firms should obtain loans at lower cost, and in the loan maturity equation that efficiently operating firms prefer shorter-term loans. Additionally, a positive effect of *inventc* and a negative effect of *liquidr* on loan maturity are also consistent with the signalling hypothesis, which implies that viable firms choose shorter-term loans to distinguish themselves from risky firms. All in all, these results support the theoretical implications on the effects of firm quality on debt contract terms (Chan and Kanatas 1985; Flannery 1986; Chan and Thakor 1987; Diamond 1991a, 1991b; Diamond 1993).

From our results, the impact of relationship lending looks interesting. In the loan rate equation, the positive sign for number of loan contracts (*numberlc*) contrasts with the relationship-lending literature. This finding may be explained by the fact that this variable is a very poor proxy for relationship lending. It could be argued that a firm with many contracts with ACB also has the potential to have close relations with other banks, and could borrow under many contracts. Whereas *numberlc* cannot capture relationship lending effects, loan concentration (*loanc*) has a negative effect on both collateral and loan rates, suggesting the benefits of relationship banking as predicted by Diamond (1989), Boot and Thakor (1994), Berger and Udell (1995), Petersen and Rajan (1995), Harhoff and Korting (1998), Degryse and Van Cayseele (2000), Repetto *et al.* (2002).

The effect of loan size is observed in the loan maturity equation with its positive sign, which reflects our expectation that large investments may require loans of a larger size and of longer maturity. Concerning the effect on collateral, we find a similar result as in the studies of Harhoff and Korting (1998) and Elsas and Krahnen (2000): loan size imposes a positive influence on collateral.

Finally, the indicator variable *dummyus* shows a strong significance in the loan rate equation. As we expected, this variable is closely related to the loan rate.

It should be noted that our results support most of above-mentioned hypotheses on the loan contract design (agency cost and relationship lending, and firm quality). However, there is little support for the tax hypothesis. This differs from the study of Dennis *et al.* (2000), which finds no evidence for the relationship-lending hypothesis, but strong evidence of the influence of tax considerations.

Conclusions

By investigating the loan contract design of the Vietnamese private bank ACB, our study addresses a gap in the empirical literature of loan contract design with regard to developing economies. Based on the loan contracting policies of the ACB we specify a three-equation system to determine collateral requirements, loan maturity, and the loan interest rates. Following Dennis *et al.* (2000) we explicitly consider the endogeneity of three loan contract terms: collateral, loan maturity, and the loan interest rate. We hypothesize that the ACB determines collateral requirements and the loan rate, given the loan maturity, which is primarily determined by the borrowing firms. The loan maturity, on the other hand, is chosen by firms, given the collateral requirements and the loan rate set by banks. The equilibrium values for loan maturity, collateral requirements and the loan interest rate are determined by the three equations together.

Our results provide additional support for interdependencies between the three contract terms identified. More specifically, we find significant bi-directional relationships between collateral and loan maturity, loan rate and loan maturity, and a uni-directional relationship between loan rate and collateral. Each relationship is consistent with certain well-known theories of financial contracting (Merton 1974; Bester 1985; Boot *et al.* 1991; Diamond 1991a). We find conflicting signs between loan maturity and collateral in the loan maturity and collateral equations, respectively. The same holds for loan maturity and the loan interest rate in the loan maturity and the loan rate equations, respectively. These results can be explained by our hypothesis that the choice for certain loan maturities is determined primarily by borrower behaviour, whereas the loan rate and collateral requirements are determined primarily by bank policies. However, more studies are needed to provide additional evidence for this hypothesis. Future studies of loan contract design should be conducted using a theoretical framework that takes into account simultaneously the behaviour of banks and borrowers. We expect further research to focus on the theoretical aspect of this preliminary proposition to examine under which conditions, and to what extent, bank behaviour and borrower behaviour determine final outcomes.

Like Dennis *et al.* (2000), who argue that the interrelated nature of loan contract features has econometric implications for testing hypotheses related to their underlying determinants, we also find that some exogenous factors are relevant determinants of the three contract terms. Our results are in line with the agency cost theory which predicts that firms with high growth opportunities (measured by firm profitability) are more likely to borrow shorter-term and on a secured basis, and firms with higher asset maturity take longer maturity loans. In addition, our findings on the effects of firm quality, as proxied by firm size, inventory period and firm liquidity are consistent with related theories (Chan and Kanatas 1985; Flannery 1986; Chan and Thakor 1987; Diamond 1991a, 1993). Finally, the benefits of relationship lending are reflected in our study by the inverse influence of loan concentration on collateral and loan interest rates.

A final remark refers to the limits of our study. As mentioned earlier, our final dataset comprises only 152 loan contracts covering 47 different firms that borrowed from the ACB as of July 2003. This may induce small sample problems that bias our interpretations. These issues suggest the need for future empirical studies based on a more comprehensive database.

Notes

1 More general information on the ACB can be found at www.acb.com.vn.
2 A comparison with a simple demand–supply system may explain this. The relationship between the endogenous variables price and quantity depend on whether the shock originates from the demand or supply side. Shifts in the supply curve lead to negative co-movements between price and quantity, whereas shifts in the demand curve imply positive co-movements.
3 This does not hold for all estimation methods, but holds for our estimation technique, which is comparable to a 2SLS method.
4 The rank condition states that an equation is identified if it is possible to construct at least one $(M-1) \times (M-1)$ matrix with a non-zero determinant from the coefficients of those variables excluded from that equation but included in other equations of the model, where M is the number of endogenous variables in the system. The rank condition is necessary and sufficient for identification.
5 The order condition is as follows: if $K-k < m-1$ the equation is under-identified; if $K-k=m-1$, the equation is just identified; if $K-k>m-1$ the equation is over-identified. Here K refers to the total amount of exogenous variables (including the constant), k the number of exogenous variables in the equation under consideration, and m the number of endogenous variables in the equation under consideration.
6 In order to still have the same set of exogenous variables in our structural equations as in our reduced form equations (step 1), we decided to keep *turno* and *areceive* in one of the equations, although they are insignificant.

References

Asia Commercial Bank website. Available at: www.acb.com.vn.
Asian Development Bank (ADB) (2002, 2003) *Key Indicators*.
Berger, A. and Udell, G. F. (1990) 'Collateral, Loan Quality, and Bank Risk', *Journal of Money, Credit and Banking*, 8: 839–56.
Berger, A. and Udell, G. F. (1995) 'Relationship Lending and Lines of Credit in Small Firm Finance', *Journal of Business*, 68: 351–81.
Bester, H. (1985) 'Screening vs. Rationing in Credit Markets with Imperfect Information', *American Economic Review*, 75: 850–55.
Bodenhorn, H. (2003) 'Short-term Loans and Long-term Relationships: Relationship Lending in Early America', *Journal of Money, Credit and Banking*, 35: 485–505.
Boot, A. and Thakor, A. (1994) 'Moral Hazard and Secured Lending in an Infinitely Repeated Credit Market Game', *International Economic Review*, 35: 899–920.
Boot, A., Thakor, A. and Udell, G. F. (1991) 'Secured Lending and Default Risk: Equilibrium Analysis, Policy Implications and Empirical Results', *Economic Journal*, 101: 458–72.
Chan, Y. and Kanatas, G. (1985) 'Asymmetric Valuations and the Role of Collateral in Loan Agreements', *Journal of Money Credit and Banking*, 17: 84–95.
Chan, Y. and Thakor, A. (1987) 'Collateral and Competitive Equilibria with Moral Hazard and Private Information', *Journal of Finance*, 42: 345–64.

Degryse, H. and van Cayseele, P. (2000) 'Relationship Lending within a Bank-based System: Evidence from European Small Business Data', *Journal of Financial Intermediation*, 9: 90–109.

Dennis, S., Nandy, D. and Sharpe, G. (2000) 'The Determinants of Contract Terms in Bank Revolving Credit Agreements', *Journal of Financial and Quantitative Analysis*, 35: 87–110.

Diamond, D. W. (1989) 'Reputation Acquisition in Debt Markets', *Journal of Political Economy*, 97: 828–62.

Diamond, D. W. (1991a) 'Debt Maturity Structure and Liquidity Risk', *Quarterly Journal of Economics*, 106: 709–37.

Diamond, D. W. (1991b) 'Monitoring and Reputation: The Choice between Bank Loans and Privately Placed Debt', *Journal of Political Economy*, 99: 689–721.

Diamond, D. W. (1993) 'Seniority and Maturity of Debt Contracts', *Journal of Financial Economics*, 53: 341–68.

Elsas, R. and Krahnen, J. P. (2000) 'Collateral, Default Risk and Relationship Lending: An Empirical Study on Financial Contracting', Centre for Economic Policy Research, Discussion Paper 2540, CEPR, London.

Fitch Ratings (2002) 'The Vietnam Banking System', *Fitch Ratings Report*, July.

Flannery, M. (1986) 'Asymmetric Information and Risky Debt Maturity Choice', *Journal of Finance* 41: 19–37.

Freixas, X. and Rochet, J. C. (1997) *Microeconomics of Banking* (Cambridge, Mass.: MIT Press).

Gonas, J. S., Highfield, M. J. and Mullineaux, D. J. (2002) 'The Determinants of Secured Loans', Working paper, Belmont University, Louisiana Tech University and University of Kentucky, USA.

Gottesman, A. A. and Roberts, G. S. (2004) 'Maturity and Corporate Loan Pricing', *Financial Review*, 39: 55–77.

Greenbaum, S. I., Kanatas, G. and Venezia, I. (1989) 'Equilibrium Loan Price under the Bank–Client Relationship', *Journal of Banking and Finance*, 13: 221–35.

Grossman, S. J. and Hart, O. D. (1986) 'The Costs and Benefits of Ownership: A Theory of Vertical and Lateral Integration', *Journal of Political Economy*, 94: 691–719.

Guedes, J. and Opler, T. (1996) 'The Determinants of the Maturity of Corporate Debt Issues', *Journal of Finance*, 51: 1809–33.

Harhoff, D. and Korting, T. (1998) 'Lending Relationships in Germany: Empirical Evidence from Survey Data', *Journal of Banking and Finance*, 22: 1317–53.

Hart, O. D. and Moore, J. (1990) 'Property Rights and the Nature of the Firm', *Journal of Political Economy*, 98: 1119–58.

IMF (2000) 'Vietnam: Statistical Appendix and Background Notes', *IMF Country Report* 00/116 (Washington, DC: IMF).

IMF (2002) 'Vietnam: Selected Issues and Statistical Appendix', *IMF Country Report* 02/5 (Washington, DC: IMF).

IMF (2003) 'Vietnam: Statistical Appendix', *IMF Country Report* 03/382 (Washington, DC: IMF).

McCarty, A. (2001) *Microfinance in Vietnam: A Survey of Schemes and Issues* (Hanoi: Department for International Development (DFID)).

Merton, R. C. (1974) 'On the Pricing of Corporate Debt: The Risk Structure of Interest Rates', *Journal of Finance*, 29: 449–70.

Midle, H. and Riley, J. G. (1988) 'Signalling in Credit Markets', *Quarterly Journal of Economics*, February, 101–29.

Myers, S. (1977) 'On the Pricing of Corporate Debt: The Risk Structure of Interest Rates', *Journal of Finance*, 29: 449–70.

Nelson, F. and Olson, L. (1978) 'Specification and Estimation of a Simultaneous-equation Model with Limited Dependent Variables', *International Economic Review*, 19: 695–709.

Ninh, L. K. (2003) 'Investment in Rice Mills in Vietnam: The Role of Financial Market Imperfections and Uncertainty', PhD dissertation, University of Groningen, The Netherlands.

Petersen, M. A. and Rajan, R. G. (1995) 'The Effects of Credit Market Competition on the Lending Relationship', *Quarterly Journal of Economics*, 110: 406–43.

Pozzolo, A. F. (2002) 'Secured Lending and Borrowers' Riskiness', Working paper, Research Department, Bank of Italy.

Repetto, A., Rodriguez, S. and Valdés, R. O. (2002) 'Bank Lending and Relationship Banking: Evidence from Chilean Firms', Working paper, Superintendency of Banks and Financial Institutions and Central Bank of Chile, University of Chile.

Sharpe, S. A. (1990) 'Asymmetric Information, Bank Lending and Implicit Contracts: A Stylized Model of Customer Relationships', *Journal of Finance*, 45: 1069–87.

Smith, C. and Warner, J. (1979) 'On Financial Contracting: An Analysis of Bond Covenants', *Journal of Financial Economics*, 7: 117–61.

Soo-Nam, O. (1999) *Financial Deepening in the Banking Sector – Viet Nam* (Manila: Asian Development Bank).

Strahan, P. E. (1999) 'Borrower Risk and the Price and Nonprice Terms of Bank Loans', Staff Report 90, Federal Reserve Bank of New York.

Vietnam Investment Review, 21 August 2003. Available at: www.vir.com.vn.

World Bank (2002) *Banking Sector Review (Vietnam)* (Washington, DC: World Bank), June 2002.

World Bank (2003) *Vietnam Development Report 2003* (Washington, DC: World Bank).

Appendix A

Table 10.A1 Descriptive statistics of the exogenous variables

	liquidr	debta	inventc	profitbt	areceive	turno	taxa	amat	fsize	lsize	numberlc	loanc	debte	dummyus
Mean	11.142	0.565	0.308	0.054	0.141	2.507	0.005	4.365	16.880	13.511	8.875	0.308	1.771	0.454
Median	1.421	0.564	0.337	0.023	0.076	1.431	0.003	2.341	16.879	13.373	7.000	0.231	1.291	0.000
Maximum	235.341	0.930	1.541	0.436	1.345	15.522	0.038	34.816	24.823	19.050	28.000	0.999	13.324	1.000
Minimum	0.572	0.014	0.025	-0.053	0.000	0.274	0.000	0.001	9.499	9.979	1.000	0.004	0.014	0.000
Std dev.	45.671	0.173	0.183	0.087	0.200	3.184	0.007	5.422	2.182	1.148	6.845	0.225	1.534	0.500
Jarque–Bera	3153.184	11.141	970.348	1242.259	1182.408	971.133	430.015	456.080	180.492	107.270	35.051	103.173	3197.177	25.341
Observations	152	152	152	152	152	152	152	152	152	152	152	152	152	152

Source: Calculated from the loan sample by the authors.

Table 10.A2 Correlation matrix of the exogenous variables

	liquidr	debta	inventc	profitbt	areceive	turno	taxa	amat	fsize	lsize	numberlc	loanc	debte	dummyus
liquidr	1.00													
debta	−0.33	1.00												
inventc	0.21	0.06	1.00											
profitbt	−0.08	−0.34	0.02	1.00										
areceive	−0.05	0.02	0.13	0.15	1.00									
turno	−0.12	−0.11	−0.53	−0.07	−0.25	1.00								
taxa	−0.14	−0.04	−0.12	0.05	0.09	0.05	1.00							
amat	0.47	−0.23	0.01	−0.26	−0.21	−0.21	−0.16	1.00						
fsize	−0.03	0.05	−0.01	−0.06	−0.54	−0.11	−0.11	0.07	1.00					
lsize	−0.02	−0.06	0.05	0.06	0.11	−0.21	−0.05	0.08	0.43	1.00				
numberlc	−0.10	0.17	0.18	−0.13	−0.17	−0.14	−0.30	0.07	0.26	−0.07	1.00			
loanc	0.16	−0.48	0.05	0.22	0.51	0.04	−0.05	0.19	−0.71	−0.12	0.07	1.00		
debte	−0.19	0.78	0.11	−0.25	0.01	−0.10	−0.07	−0.06	−0.02	−0.08	−0.02	−0.35	1.00	
dummyus	0.22	−0.10	0.03	0.24	−0.26	−0.11	−0.13	0.03	0.25	0.01	0.12	−0.08	−0.15	1.00

Source: Calculated from the loan sample by the authors.

Appendix B

First step estimation results

Table 10.B1 First-step reduced-form estimates of the endogenous contract terms

	collat	*lmat*	*loanr*
C	112.048	−137.306	14.120
	(0.042)	(0.029)	(0.000)
liquidr	2.252	−0.017	0.001
	(0.102)	(0.519)	(0.441)
debta	−46.079	18.833	−2.163
	(0.006)	(0.403)	(0.003)
inventc	−12.641	15.485	0.232
	(0.172)	(0.105)	(0.218)
profitbt	168.469	−8.056	−0.355
	(0.032)	(0.608)	(0.255)
areceive	−9.787	−0.759	−0.043
	(0.144)	(0.957)	(0.902)
turno	−0.959	0.105	−0.012
	(0.099)	(0.821)	(0.395)
taxa	480.635	450.458	4.754
	(0.052)	(0.032)	(0.299)
amat	−0.738	0.649	0.003
	(0.018)	(0.091)	(0.793)
fsize	−3.824	3.691	−0.212
	(0.147)	(0.263)	(0.002)
lsize	−1.356	4.646	0.037
	(0.014)	(0.053)	(0.330)
numberlc	0.490	0.326	0.039
	(0.005)	(0.584)	(0.001)
loanc	−31.453	31.971	−2.143
	(0.068)	(0.259)	(0.005)
debte	7.009	0.609	0.105
	(0.002)	(0.573)	(0.005)
dummyus	−6.634	−13.069	0.566
	(0.015)	(0.000)	(0.000)
R^2		0.373	0.423
Adjusted R^2		0.309	0.365
McFadden R^2	0.630		
S.E. of regression	0.205	17.006	0.422
Sum squared resid.	5.759	39621.610	24.429
Log likelihood	−20.447	−638.486	−76.741
Mean dependent var.	0.882	15.704	10.006
S.D. dependent var.	0.324	20.453	0.530
Restr. log likelihood	−55.293		
LR statistic (14 df)	69.690		
Probability (LR stat)	0.000		

Note: Figures below the coefficients are P-values. The McFadden R^2 is defined as $R^2 = 1 - \mathrm{Logl}_{UR}/\mathrm{logl}_R$, where Logl_{UR} is the unrestricted Log likelihood and Logl_R is the restricted Log likelihood (it is the maximum of the likelihood function when maximized with the restriction that all slope coefficients are 0). The number of observations in all regressions is 152. The first equation is estimated with logit; the other two with OLS.

Table 10.B2 Cross-tabulation of actual and predicted outcomes for the logit model (reduced-form estimates)

		collat (predicted)		
		0	1	Total
collat (actual)	0	14	4	18
	1	6	128	134
	Total	20	132	152

Table 10.B3 Structural equation results without endogeneity effects

	collat	*lmat*	*Loanr*
collat		14.69927	0.042616
		(0.0004)	(0.6982)
lmat	0.16723		0.007703
	(0.0746)		(0.0051)
loanr	−0.80602	4.432324	
	(0.4229)	(0.16)	
C	101.9003	−179.995	14.63845
	(0.0613)	(0.0028)	(0)
liquidr	0.385248	0.11445	0.000848
	(0.5093)	(0.0001)	(0.1162)
debta	−52.559	5.287651	1.41811
	(0.0033)	(0.582)	(0.0061)
inventc	1.03562	21.95047	0.181012
	(0.8274)	(0.0452)	(0.2854)
profitbt	116.3808	−29.7695	−0.24389
	(0.0064)	(0.0269)	(0.3705)
areceive	−2.34279	22.99581	−0.11013
	(0.7406)	(0.0753)	(0.6649)
turno	−0.02336	0.965765	−0.01293
	(0.9323)	(0.058)	(0.2223)
taxa		352.8301	
		0.115	
amat		1.477678	
		0.0004	
fsize	−3.36099	2.063679	−0.2179
	(0.1059)	0.083	(0.0004)
lsize	−0.8682	6.127414	−0.01474
	0.0731	0.0075	(0.7115)
numberlc	0.32269		0.028288
	(0.0356)		(0.0014)

(Continued)

264

Table 10.B3 Continued

	collat	lmat	Loanr
loanc	−35.593		−2.13126
	(0.0522)		(0.0009)
debte	6.750035		
	(0.0098)		
dummyus			0.6975
			(0.000)
R^2		0.334786	0.323042
Adjusted R^2		0.277358	0.264599
McFadden R^2	0.587444		
S.E. of regression	0.214043	17.53993	0.410342
Sum squared resid.	6.322374	42763.24	23.23648
Log likelihood	−22.8113	−644.285	−72.9387
Mean dependent var.	0.881579	15.70395	10.00638
S.D. dependent var.	0.324174	20.45342	0.52973
Restr. log likelihood	−55.2926		
LR statistic (13 df)	64.96259		
Probability (LR stat)	6.70E-09		

Notes: Figures below the coefficients are P-values. The McFadden R^2 is defined as $R^2 = 1 - \text{Logl}_{UR}/\text{logl}_R$, where Logl_{UR} is the unrestricted Log likelihood, and Logl_R is the restricted Log likelihood (it is the maximum of the likelihood function when maximized with the restriction that all slope coefficients are 0). The number of observations in all regressions is 152.

Index